OFF THE BEATEN PATH®
MONTANA →

Help Us Keep This Guide Up to Date

We would love to hear from you concerning your experiences with this guide and how you feel it could be improved and kept up to date. Please send your comments and suggestions to:

editorial@GlobePequot.com

Thanks for your input, and happy travels!

…ATEN PATH® SERIES

EIGHTH EDITION

OFF THE BEATEN PATH®
MONTANA ➡

A GUIDE TO UNIQUE PLACES

MICHAEL McCOY

gpp®
travel

Guilford, Connecticut

All the information in this guidebook is subject to change. We recommend that you call ahead to obtain current information before traveling.

To buy books in quantity for corporate use
or incentives, call **(800) 962-0973**
or e-mail **premiums@GlobePequot.com.**

Editor: Amy Lyons
Project Editor: Lynn Zelem
Layout: Joanna Beyer
Text design: Linda R. Loiewski
Maps: Equator Graphics © Morris Book Publishing, LLC.

ISSN 1539-7033
ISBN 978-0-7627-5731-2

Printed in the United States of America
10 9 8 7 6 5 4 3 2 1

About the Author

Michael McCoy, a former eighteen-year resident of Big Sky Country, lives in Teton Valley, Idaho, where on a clear day he can still see Montana. His outdoor and travel writing has appeared in *Snow Country, Men's Journal, Bicycling, Montana,* and other national and regional publications, and he serves as editor of *Jackson Hole magazine* and field editor of *Adventure Cyclist* magazine. McCoy's Globe Pequot books include *The Wild West* and *Journey to the Northern Rockies,* and he edited *Classic Cowboy Stories* for the Lyons Press. He has also written for the National Geographic Book Division. His Web site is www.emptyhighways.com.

Dedication

For Boone, a remarkable town,
and all of its boys and girls . . .
young and old, there and gone

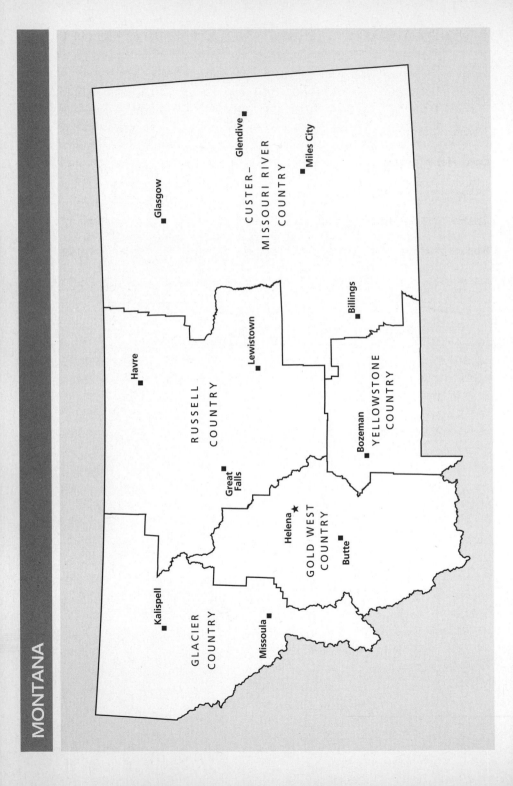

MONTANA

Glendive

Miles City

CUSTER–
MISSOURI RIVER
COUNTRY

Glasgow

Billings

Lewistown

Havre

RUSSELL
COUNTRY

YELLOWSTONE
COUNTRY

Bozeman

Great
Falls

Helena

GOLD WEST
COUNTRY

Butte

Kalispell

GLACIER
COUNTRY

Missoula

Contents

Introduction

My wife and I lived for several years in Troy, a timber town squeezed into a tight, tree-filled valley so far west in Montana that from there you can almost spit into Idaho, and so far north that half its residents speak with a Canadian accent. Having already resided in Montana for several years, I knew, theoretically, that it was big. But it wasn't until living in its extreme northwest corner that I came to appreciate just how big.

Early on a July morning in 1981, Nancy and I packed our Mazda sedan with more gear than it was meant to hold and took off to visit family in the Midwest. After driving for fifteen hours and covering more than 800 long, hot miles, we were disappointed at nightfall to find ourselves still in Montana. We were relieved, however, and honestly surprised to learn that we were more than halfway to where we were going in central Iowa.

Yes, Montana is spacious. Within its land area of 145,556 square miles, you could fit Maine, New Hampshire, Vermont, Delaware, Rhode Island, New York, and Pennsylvania and have room to spare. Here's the clincher: Fewer people live in Montana than in Rhode Island alone. While the typical Rhode Island square mile holds more than 1,000 people, an average of a little more than 6 occupy that space in Montana.

Montana is big, and it's a melting pot. During the short, 160-year history of white settlement, the state has been a magnet for the restless and intrepid, the displaced and persecuted—those willing or forced to take a chance with their lives. The result is an eclectic mix of people who settled in the state's mountains and valleys and on its windswept, arid plains. The Hi-Line Scandinavians. The many Germans, including the communal Hutterites of the north-central plains. The Butte Irish, the Butte Chinese, the Butte Polish, the Butte almost-anything-you-can-name. And, of course, those who came first, the American Indians, a glance at whose family trees will prove everyone else newcomers by a large measure.

So here in the immensity of Montana we have a wide cast of characters populating a land vibrant and beautiful, a country also cursed (or blessed, depending on your perspective) with a climate of extremes. These factors coalesce to create an atmosphere ripe for the fashioning of unorthodox ways to make ends meet. As a result, a fascinating mix of attractions—some strange, some wonderful, some strange and wonderful—awaits the traveler in Montana.

The setting for countless western novels and movies, Montana has been subjected to endless romanticizing and dealt more than its share of nicknames: the Bonanza State, Big Sky Country, the Treasure State, and—overused and overstated—the Last Best Place. Of all the descriptive phrases I've heard, far and away my favorite is *Montana: High, Wide, and Handsome,* the title of the 1943 book by Joseph Kinsey Howard. Unpretentious, honest, and unerringly accurate, it fits Montana like a well-worn pair of cowboy boots.

Speaking of which, as you might expect, you'll still find plenty of working cowboys, miners, and loggers in Montana, and you can still experience no-holds-barred Wild West celebrations (try Butte on St. Patrick's Day or the World Famous Bucking Horse Sale in Miles City). But you also can find gourmet restaurants employing Paris-trained chefs and surroundings that whisper rather than scream. You can bed down at night in a dude-ranch bunkhouse or under a fluffy comforter at a bed-and-breakfast inn as elegant as any found in New England or California's wine country. You might dine on buffalo-hump roast one night and Greek cuisine the next. You're bound to tour spectacular and highly touted Yellowstone and Glacier National Parks, but the lands beyond the park boundaries—some subdued and others of national park quality themselves—may catch you off guard.

The House committee charged with splitting the Montana Territory from the Idaho Territory in 1864 was leaning toward designating the Continental Divide as the boundary between the two. A group led by Sidney Edgerton, chief justice of the Idaho Territory, however, persuaded the committee to include in the Montana portion those lands west of the Divide and east of the Bitterroot Range. Consequently, cities including Missoula, Butte, and Kalispell today are in Montana rather than Idaho; likewise all of Glacier National Park ended up in Montana, rather than the majority of it residing in Idaho. Edgerton may not have won new friends among the Idaho delegation, but he did win the subsequent governorship of the newly created and larger-for-his-efforts Montana Territory.

Sidney Edgerton and fate were responsible for the boundaries Montana claimed when it finally became a state in 1889, and this book dishes out a sample of what's contained within them 121 years later. My goal with this book, now in print for some seventeen years, has always been to showcase a spicy mixture of the state's diverse attractions while emphasizing lesser-known places of both the natural and human-made varieties. Where well-known destinations, such as Glacier National Park, are included, I've highlighted features overlooked by the majority of visitors.

If an attraction in this broad and wide state seems too far removed and isolated to bother traveling to, know this: As you stray off the beaten path to visit some of my favorite places in Montana, you're bound to find others just as interesting and worthy of mention. Attempting to include them all would have been a Herculean task, and the data collected would fill a dozen volumes of this size.

To complement this guide, carry a state road map for getting an overall picture of where you are, and where you're headed. To verify that the hours of operation listed are still in effect, call ahead to attractions you absolutely do not want to miss.

With regard to restaurants, I've employed a three-tiered scale for the prices of entrees: inexpensive, less than $10; moderate, $10 to $20; and expensive, more than $20. For motels, bed-and-breakfasts, and hotels, I've used a similar ranking system: inexpensive, less than $50; moderate, $50 to $90; and expensive, more than $90.

The state promotion bureau has done a logical job of dividing Montana into six travel regions, and I've borrowed them for the book's chapters. However, I've covered the two easternmost regions—Custer Country and Missouri River Country—in a single chapter. Although the two "countries" comprise a staggeringly vast expanse of terrain, it's a wide-open, largely empty region, where services and attractions are relatively few and far between.

In closing, permit me to share a little background. I came into the world in this part of the country—Wyoming, actually—but when I was still an infant, my folks packed up and moved the family to Iowa, and there I sprouted, alongside the corn, soybeans, and piglets.

After napping through high school in Boone, a great little farming and railroad town originally known as "Montana," believe it or not, I returned to my birthright region in 1970 to attend college. Here I found myself confronted, confounded, and a little scared by the electrifying heights of the northern Rocky Mountain ranges—where mighty rivers come to life, conceived in winter and born in spring—and the impossible spaces of the plains between. Both were so different from my familiar surroundings that they shook me, unexpectedly, from an adolescent stupor. For the first time in nineteen years, I was truly awake, and awakened, to the power of landscape and the possibilities provided by strange faces and new ways of thinking. And I've rarely slept since.

If you're a resident of Montana or a return visitor, here's hoping this volume will lead you to some new favorite places. If it's your first time to the state that is high, wide, and ever so handsome, welcome! May the endless stretch of prairie, the magic of the mountains, and the smile of Montana's friendly citizens energize you as they did, and do, me.

About Montana

The following is a list of information and resources an off-the-beaten-path traveler like yourself might find useful.

- **Major newspapers:** *Missoulian, Helena Independent Record, Butte Standard, Billings Gazette, Great Falls Tribune*

- **Capital:** Helena (pronounced HEL-uh-nuh)
- **Cities and counties:** Montana is divided into 56 counties, with 126 incorporated cities and towns and two consolidated city-county governments.
- **Population:** 967,440
- **Schools:** Nearly 900 public schools serve 142,000 students. The State University System of Higher Education consists of the University of Montana in Missoula, the University of Montana Western in Dillon, Montana State University–Bozeman, Montana State University–Billings, Montana State University–Northern (in Havre), and the College of Mineral Science and Technology in Butte. The state also boasts three community colleges and three private colleges.

- **Average Annual Daily High and Low Temperatures**

	January		July	
	High	Low	High	Low
Billings	32.0	13.3	87.0	58.4
Bozeman	30.2	7.8	75.7	40.5
Butte	28.4	4.2	80.1	45.1
Great Falls	30.9	12.3	83.6	54.9
Missoula	29.8	14.0	84.8	50.4

- **Average annual precipitation:** Ranges from 12.16 inches on the north-central plains to 16.14 inches in the northwest valleys. The high mountains often receive much more than this (as much as 100 inches per year in parts of the northwest mountains).
- **Famous people from Montana:** Film stars Gary Cooper and Myrna Loy, newsman Chet Huntley, Chief Plenty Coups, stunt artist Evel Knievel, filmmaker David Lynch, longtime U.S. Senate majority leader and ambassador to Japan Mike Mansfield, Tour de France bicycle racer Levi Leipheimer, and Jeanette Rankin, the first woman to serve in the U.S. House of Representatives
- **Geographic center:** Fergus, 11 miles west of Lewistown

RECOMMENDED READING FOR CHILDREN:

- *Amazing Animals of Montana: Incredible True Stories,* Gayle C. Shirley, Globe Pequot Press, 2005. (ages nine to twelve, nonfiction)
- *B is for Big Sky Country: A Montana Alphabet,* Sneed B. Collard III and Joanna Yardley, Gale Group, 2003. (kindergarten to third grade, nonfiction)

- *Montana in Words and Pictures,* Dennis Fradin, Children's Press, 1981. (second grade, nonfiction)
- *Montana,* Allan Carpenter, Children's Press, 1979. (fourth grade, nonfiction)
- *One Summer in Montana,* Dayton O. Hyde, Atheneum, 1985. (sixth grade, fiction)
- *Torosaurus and Other Dinosaurs of the Badlands Digs in Montana,* Dougal Dixon, Picture Window Books, 2008. (ages four to eight, nonfiction)

RECOMMENDED READING FOR ADULTS:

- *The Big Sky,* A. B. Guthrie Jr., Houghton-Mifflin, 1947.
- *Out West: American Journey Along the Lewis and Clark Trail,* Dayton Duncan, Penguin Books, 1987.
- *A River Runs Through It and Other Stories,* Norman Maclean, University of Chicago Press, 1976.
- *Tough Trip Through Paradise,* Andrew Garcia, Houghton-Mifflin, 1967.

STATE SYMBOLS:

- **State animal:** Grizzly bear
- **State bird:** Western meadowlark
- **State flower:** Bitterroot
- **State tree:** Ponderosa pine
- **State fish:** Cutthroat trout
- **State fossil:** Anatosaurus
- *(Maiasaura peeblesorum)*
- **State song:** "Montana Melody"

A SAMPLING OF RADIO STATIONS:

- **KBLG,** 910 kHz, Billings
- **KBOZ,** 1090 kHz, Bozeman
- **KMMS-FM,** 95.1 MHz, Bozeman
- **KBOW,** 500 kHz, Butte
- **KMON,** 560 kHz, Great Falls
- **KOFI,** 1180 kHz, Kalispell
- **KGRZ,** 1450 kHz, Missoula
- **KUFM-FM,** 89.1 MHz, Missoula (National Public Radio)

tourist information

Travel Montana offers free vacation guides and accommodations listings.

Address: 1424 Ninth Avenue, P.O. Box 200533, Helena, MT 59620-0533

Telephone: (800) 847-4868

Web site: www.visitmt.com

AREA CODE:

The area code for the entire state of Montana is 406.

GLACIER COUNTRY →

Boasting the terrific city of Missoula, world-famous Glacier National Park, and the skiing-golfing-boating mecca of Flathead Valley, it is no surprise that Glacier Country is Montana's preeminent tourism region. An area of stunning natural beauty, it is graced with forested mountains and lush valleys teeming with fish-filled lakes and streams.

Although you can jump in and join the narrative at any point, the best place to begin is in the timbered vastness of the Yaak River Valley, nestled in the extreme northwest corner of Montana. From there forest roads wind their way to Eureka, from which point Highway 37 leads to Libby and US 2. You'll then follow Highway 56 as it snakes through the memorable Bull River Valley, a tangle of wild terrain that would not appear out of place in Alaska, to the valley of the Clark Fork River and Highway 200. After going through Thompson Falls and Paradise, you'll travel to the Mission Valley and along the shores of massive Flathead Lake. From there it is on to Kalispell and Whitefish, jumping-off point for Glacier National Park and the Blackfeet Indian Reservation. Finally, Highway 83 takes you through the forested, lake-adorned Seeley-Swan Valley to a juncture with Highway 200, which leads west to

CANADA
UNITED STATES

Yaak
Lake
Koocanusa
Eureka
Mount
Cleveland

GRIZZLY COUNTRY

Cut Bank

Kootenai R.
Whitefish
Browning

Libby

R O C K Y   M T S

Kalispell

KOOTENAI
TIMBERLANDS

Flathead
Lake

South Fork
Flathead R.

Polson

Clark Fork R.

MONTANA
IDAHO

LEWIS AND CLARK TRAIL

Missoula

N

Hamilton

0   40 mi
0   40 km

Missoula. From Montana's unofficial capital of art and recreation, and undisputed bastion of liberalism, US 93 leads south up the Bitterroot Valley to Lost Trail Pass, from which point you'll descend into Gold West Country.

Kootenai Timberlands

The remote Yaak River Valley, occupying the northwest notch of Montana, is home to the settlement of **Yaak,** a tiny island of enterprise set amid a rolling sea of timber. Road warriors who enjoy visiting places seen by relatively few travelers should not miss venturing into the Yaak River country. Not many places remaining in the contiguous forty-eight states can claim to be more off the beaten path than this isolated corner of the Big Sky State.

If you do find your way to the town of Yaak, you can't miss the **Dirty Shame Saloon,** a funky bar and eatery with a decor to match the kicked-back and independent character of the majority of local residents. Yaak is situated along Highway 508, 30 miles northeast of US 2 (beginning 3½ miles southeast of the point where US 2 crosses the Montana-Idaho state line). The enterprise also boasts a half dozen rustic hillside cabins that go for just $25 a day ($35 a day on weekends). The Dirty Shame's phone number is 295-5439 and its Web site is www.dirtyshamesaloon.com.

AUTHOR'S FAVORITES

A Carousel for Missoula
Missoula
(406) 549-8382

Clearwater Canoe Trail
Seeley Lake
(406) 677-2233

Dirty Shame Saloon
Yaak
(406) 295-5439

Garden Wall Inn
Whitefish
(888) 530-1700

Hornet Peak Fire Lookout
Polebridge
(406) 387-3800

Lee Metcalf National Wildlife Refuge
Stevensville
(406) 777-5552

Montana Valley Bookstore
Alberton
(406) 722-4950

Rockin' Rudy's (music store and more)
Missoula
(406) 542-0077

St. Ignatius Mission
St. Ignatius
(406) 745-2768

Wildhorse Island State Park
Big Arm
(406) 752-5501

The Yaak River drains a large portion of the Purcell Mountains, a range teeming with ancient coniferous forests and not-so-ancient clear-cuts. "The Yaak," as the surrounding countryside is typically referred to, is a backwoodsy backwater that has attracted an eclectic mix of human residents, including back-to-the-land Mother Earth types, artists and writers, tree fellers, tree huggers, and plain old hermits. As diverse as the homesteaders are, though, all share this trait: They enjoy getting away from it all and being left alone. Either that or they don't last long in the isolated Yaak River country.

While "up the Yaak," as the locals say, consider also following Pete Creek to Hawkins Lakes and the **Northwest Peaks Scenic Area,** a spectacular setting of rocky crags, sparkling lakes, and sky-scratching peaks reaching more than 7,700 feet above sea level. The area, roughly 19,000 acres in size, is like a miniature and little-visited version of Glacier National Park, and it's ideal for hiking, picnicking, and car camping. Getting there is a journey in itself, for from the already remote outpost of Yaak, it is 3 miles west on Highway 508, then 22 miles north and west on FR 338 (12 miles paved and 10 dirt). Call the Three Rivers Ranger District at 295-4693 for maps and information.

Also worth the trip is **West Fork Falls,** gracing the West Fork of the Yaak River. The falls are located at the end of a short trail that begins in a parking area near the 39-mile marker on the Yaak River Road. The falls and the deep, amazingly clear pool they feed can be viewed from a wooden observation deck, built courtesy of the Kootenai National Forest.

In the town of Eureka, just east of the Yaak area, is the **Tobacco Valley Historical Village,** featuring structures dating from the 1880s through the 1920s. The Peltier log home (Eureka's first residence) and the Rexford train depot are located here, as are a vintage hand-hewn log ranger cabin, a one-room school, the old Fewkes Store—with works by local artists on sale—and several other buildings, all connected by a stout boardwalk. The museum houses artifacts and interpretive displays illustrating the Kootenai Indians' movement through the region and the Eureka area's logging heritage. There's no charge to visit the historical village, open daily from 1 to 5 p.m. Memorial Day through Labor Day at South Main Street. Call 297-7654. (The U.S. portion of the **Great Divide Mountain Bike Route** runs past the village, and starts not far north of town; see the sidebar on page 67 for more on this popular trail.)

One mile west of US 93 on the Fortine Creek Road, 12 miles south of Eureka, is the **Ant Flat Natural Resource Education Center and Historic Site.** Location of the first Forest Service administrative activities in the area, Ant Flat features several historic buildings, picnic grounds, and a mile-long nature trail. The first portion of the trail is wheelchair accessible, ending at a boardwalk and observation deck that extend out over a vibrant wetland. It's a great spot for bird-watching . . . and mosquito-slapping! Contact Murphy Lake Ranger Station at 882-4451 or www.fs.fed.us/r1/kootenai for more information on the site, which is listed in the National Register of Historic Places and open in summer only.

Libby Logger Days, the premier summerfest in *Lincoln County,* celebrates the heritage of Lincoln County's most important industry. Professional and amateur loggers alike test their skills—or lack thereof—as woodsmen and woodswomen in competitions such as the double-buck saw and the Bull of the Woods boxing challenge. Non-loggers needn't feel left out, for also on tap are a parade, foot and bicycle races, water fights, a rafting competition, a carnival, and more. Logger Days are held in late June. Call the Libby Area Chamber of Commerce at 293-4167 to request further information. On the Web you can find information at www.libbychamber.org.

montanatrivia

The Nature Conservancy's Dancing Prairie Preserve, located outside Eureka, is one of the Mountain West's few remaining leks, or dancing and mating grounds, of the formerly abundant Columbian sharp-tailed grouse. The birds are unable to thrive in grasslands that have been altered by the plow or grazed by cattle.

Libby townsfolk have suffered tremendously in recent years, with the discovery that many of the people associated with the venerable vermiculite-mining industry were exposed to and poisoned by asbestos. But this is a town filled with survivors; Libby has a legacy of dealing with adversity, facing as it has the on-again, off-again nature of the timber industry. Don't hurry through town; take some time to mosey around the side streets and have a look. One treasure you may come across is the *Libby Cafe,* at 411 Mineral Ave.

Reading the Wild Yaak

If you'd like to delve more deeply into the Yaak River country without leaving home, a good place to begin is with the volume entitled *The Roadless Yaak: Reflections and Observations about One of Our Last Great Wild Places* (The Lyons Press, 2003). According to the back cover copy, "The million-acre Yaak Valley is home to only 150 people but untold numbers of elk, deer, grizzly bears, cougars, and other critters, big and small. An astonishing 175,000 acres remain roadless in this remote area near the Canadian border." Edited by the prolific writer and Yaak resident Rick Bass, the anthology contains essays by such Montana literary luminaries as William Kittredge and Annick Smith, along with stories by a host of lesser-known writers.

(293-3523). The down-to-earth eatery has long been known for its muffins, cinnamon rolls, huckleberry swirls, and other luscious treats. In fact, you can try out the enterprise's goodies even if you can't make it to Libby, by ordering from its Web site, www.montanamuffins.com.

Between Troy and Libby, just below US 2, the broad Kootenai River flows through clefts and over cliffs, resulting in a stunning stretch of foaming white water known as *Kootenai Falls.* The protected site is sacred to the Confederated Salish and Kootenai tribes, who have joined with the state and county to build a park adjacent to the falls. The park includes picnic grounds and a mile-long hiking trail to the falls, which splashed across the big screen in the 1994 production *The River Wild,* starring Meryl Streep and Kevin Bacon in a particularly dastardly role.

montanatrivia

The lowest elevation in Montana, at 1,820 feet above sea level, is where the Kootenai River flows into Idaho northwest of Troy.

A pair of monumental fires raged through the forests of northwest Montana and northern Idaho in 1890 and 1910, taking with them a large share of the old-growth timber. But for a fortuitous location, the giant cedars at the *Ross Creek Scenic Area* would have gone up in smoke, too. A visit to the enchanting grove, situated above the scenic Bull River Valley and in one of the wettest spots in Montana, might make you wonder for a moment if you've unknowingly been whisked to a Northwest coastal rain forest. The mile-long interpretive trail through the shade of the robust, tall trees—some more than 175 feet high and 500 years old—is perfect for an easy hike on a hot summer's day or for a mystical cross-country skiing experience come winter. The trail is wheelchair accessible.

From Troy, the Ross Creek Scenic Area is 3 miles east on US 2, 16 miles south on Highway 56, and then 3 miles up FR 398. Call Kootenai National Forest headquarters at 293-6211 for information.

Also barely surviving the 1910 fire was the *Bull River Guard Station,* now in the National Register of Historic Places. The high and jagged peaks of the Cabinet Mountains Wilderness form a stirring backdrop for the two-story log structure, which rests in a tranquil meadow above the East Fork of the Bull River.

The station was built in 1908 by district ranger Granville "Granny" Gordon and served for years as his headquarters and family home. Before going to work for the Forest Service, Granville served as a guide for *"Buffalo Bill" Cody,* and his wife, Pauline, had been Cody's pastry maker. The spirited couple's dances and home cooking made the ranger station and its grounds a popular and sometimes rompin', stompin' stop for those living in or traveling through the Bull River country. Today, you can make your own brand of fun there, as the Forest Service rents out the Bull River Guard Station for $55 per night. It sleeps up to eight, has no indoor plumbing (there's an outdoor toilet), and boarders must haul in their own bedding, cooking and eating utensils, and drinking water.

To get there, go 9 miles south on Highway 56 from the turnoff to the Ross Creek Scenic Area; at the 8-mile marker turn east onto FR 407. Proceed for 1½ miles, then go right onto gravel at the fork on FR 2278, and in another ½ mile you'll arrive at the ranger station. For more information call the Trout Creek Ranger Station at 827-3533 or visit www .fs.fed.us/r1/kootenai.

En route from the historic guard station to the small community of Trout Creek, between mileposts 8 and 7, you'll pass the left-hand turn into the ***Bighorn Lodge B&B,*** a little bit of civilized surrounded by a sea of wild. Canoeing, mountain biking, horseback riding, and fishing are among the many outdoor pursuits readily at hand from the lodge, which can host up to twenty guests in its five lodge rooms and two-room River House cabin. Nightly rates range from $125 to $350. For information or reservations call 847-4676 or go to www .bighornlodgemontana.com.

Trout Creek calls itself the Huckleberry Capital of Montana (and has even been proclaimed so by the state legislature), and the community has been underscoring the nickname early each August for almost thirty years by hosting its annual ***Huckleberry Festival.*** Closely related to the blueberry, the fruit has never been successfully domesticated, but in a good year millions, some as big as marbles, ponderously hang from their greenery high in the mountains of northwest Montana.

bullriver guardstation

One of Granny and Pauline Gordon's three daughters, Blanche Gordon Claxton, recalled that during the conflagration of 1910 the family stationed buckets of water filled with soaking gunnysacks on the porch of their Bull River Guard Station. Mrs. Gordon advised the girls that if the fire advanced toward the house, they should wrap the gunnysacks around their bodies and run for their lives to the river.

The station endured, and through the ensuing years it was used off and on as a residence for teachers, rangers, and forest work crews. Eventually it fell into disrepair, and in 1989 volunteers from the Cabinet Wilderness Historical Society joined with the Forest Service to renovate the old building—fighting continuously, it was written, "incessant rain storms, blistering heat, enraged pack rats, and annoyed bats." The station now sits atop a sound foundation and sports a new roof, windowpanes, and porches.

Fun runs, huckleberry-pancake breakfasts, a parade, the Huckleberry Hounds Dog Agility Club demonstration, horseshoe-tossing competitions, a Young Miss Huckleberry Pageant, and other events round out the huckleberry happenings. Call 827-3301 for additional information.

montanatrivia

David Thompson, a native of England, explored northwest Montana beginning in 1808. In 1797, on behalf of the North West Company, Thompson visited the Mandan villages in future North Dakota—seven years before Lewis and Clark arrived there. Among the explorer's Montana namesakes are the town of Thompson Falls and the nearby Thompson River.

In *Thompson Falls* the unusual *Old Jail Museum* houses relics from the town's past, including the jail itself, which operated from about 1908 until 1980. A quick peek inside one of the claustrophobic cells will make you thankful you never ran afoul of the law in Thompson Falls during those years. The facility also includes revolving and permanent displays, such as an exhibit detailing the involvement of local men and women in World War II. The museum, located just south of Main Street behind the present-day sheriff's office, is open daily Mother's Day through Labor Day, from noon to 4 p.m., and is free of charge to enter. Call 827-4002 for more information.

Twenty-five miles southeast of Thompson Falls on Highway 200 is the village of *Plains,* home to the *Old Log Schoolhouse* and its collection of locally created crafts and artwork for sale. The solid old Wild Horse Plains schoolhouse was completed in the mid-1880s (until 1884 Plains was called "Horse Plains") and used for its intended purpose until about 1898. It subsequently served various other functions for many years thereafter. In 1976 it was moved from its original site to town.

Four miles farther southeast along Highway 200 is the community of *Paradise,* whose founders obviously found to be quite a special place. Maybe the naturally hot waters that now fill the pools at *Quinn's Hot Springs Resort* had something to do with their choice in town names. From Paradise, the resort is 3 miles southeast on Highway 200, then 2 miles southwest on Highway 135. Year-round the large pool is maintained at or near 96 degrees and the smaller Jacuzzi pool at a toasty 105 degrees. For $8, adults can soak away any worries they might still have after spending a few days touring northwest Montana. The cost for kids is $6.

montanatrivia

Among the lowest and perennially one of the warmest spots in Montana, Thompson Falls recorded an Arizona-like temperature of 109 degrees on July 12, 1953.

The resort also includes the Glacier Lodge (whose fifteen rooms go for between $125 and $160 per night), twenty-two Canyon Cabins ($155 to $205 per night), the duplex Riverside Suites ($450 for a minimum two-night stay), a dance hall, and moderately priced breakfast, lunch, and dinner seven days a week in the Harwood House restaurant. For more information and reservations call 826-3150 or visit http://quinnshotsprings.com. The resort's address is 190 Highway 135.

Grizzly Country

Lake County is named after massive Flathead Lake—at 27 miles long, 8 to 15 miles wide, and with 124 miles of shoreline, the largest body of fresh water west of the Mississippi. The lake, in turn, was named for the **Flathead Indians,** whose reservation, home to the Confederated Salish and Kootenai tribes, takes in most of Lake County. The reservation also covers a sizable portion of Sanders County, as well as smaller parts of Missoula and Flathead Counties.

Both humans and nature have the capacity to create wondrous works of beauty. These potentials coalesce at the St. Ignatius Mission, where the stunning **Mission Mountains** form the backdrop for the house of worship that

Good Medicine

Big Medicine was a bison born on the National Bison Range outside Moiese, Montana, in 1933. Although white in color, **Big Medicine** was not a true albino, for his eyes were light blue (not pink), his hooves were tan rather than white, and his topknot was of dark-brown hair. In his prime Big Medicine weighed just a few pounds under a ton, stood 6 feet high at the hump, and measured nearly 12 feet long from the tip of his tail to his nose. He became one of the monarchs of the National Bison Range, fathering many offspring—including Little Medicine, a true albino bison born deaf and blind in 1937. Little Medicine was transported to the National Zoological Gardens in Washington, D.C., where he survived for twelve years.

White bison are an exceedingly rare phenomenon, and to Plains Indians such as the Blackfeet, they are believed to carry potent good medicine tied to the power of the sun. Such was the case with Big Medicine, who was highly revered by the Native Americans. On his death in 1959, his hide was sent for tanning to the renowned Jonas Brothers in Denver, then shipped to Browning, Montana, where the late sculptor-taxidermist Bob Scriver molded a mannequin on which he mounted Big Medicine's hide. On July 13, 1961, Governor Donald G. Nutter dedicated the Big Medicine mount at the Montana Historical Society's museum in Helena, where hundreds of thousands of travelers have since paid him visits.

gave the range its name. The **St. Ignatius Mission,** originally established by Father Pierre DeSmet along the Pend d'Oreille River in Washington State, was moved to the Mission Valley in 1854 at the request of the Flathead Indians. The resplendent church you walk through today was built in 1891 under the direction of Jesuit missionaries by Native American workers, using local materials to fire bricks on the spot. Inside, the walls and ceilings are adorned with dramatic murals depicting the biblical history of humankind. Brother Joseph Carignano, a mission cook with no formal art training, created the masterpieces in his spare time.

The St. Ignatius Mission, open free of charge daily in summer from 9 a.m. to 7 p.m. and in winter from 9 a.m. to 5 p.m., is immediately off US 93 in **St. Ignatius,** a town also known locally as "Mission." Call 745-2768 for information.

Next, stop in at the **Four Winds Indian Trading Post,** located 3 miles north of St. Ignatius on US 93. It's open daily in summer—from Memorial Day to Labor Day—from 9 a.m. to 7 p.m., and from noon to 5 p.m. Mon through Sat the remainder of the year. Several pre-statehood log structures have been moved to the site over the years, lending the post an authentic feel. The original log store, constructed in 1870 by Duncan McDonald, was relocated from nearby Ravalli to its current place of residence by Preston Miller more than thirty years ago. Since then, the proprietors have developed a museum of artifacts, including some from the fur-trading era. In other buildings you'll discover a fantastic selection of American Indian material goods, old and new—tools, quillwork, traditional dress, weapons, tobacco twists, medicine pouches, and much more. Some of Four Winds' inventory is so uncommon that it has appeared in the movies: The owners have supplied artifacts to the producers of *Dances With Wolves, Far and Away, Son of the Morning Star,* and other films. Call 745-4336 or e-mail 4winds@blackfoot.net for more information on this unusual enterprise that's been in business for more than three decades.

Approximately 5 miles north of Four Winds, immediately opposite the Ninepipe National Wildlife Refuge, you'll encounter a beautiful museum overflowing with Native American artifacts, historical items relating to Anglo exploration and settlement of the Mission Valley, western art, and wildlife mounts. The **Ninepipes Museum of Early Montana,** which opened in 1998, is a dream fulfilled for the Cheff family, longtime residents and ranchers of the area. Admission is $4 for adults, $3 for students, and $2 for children ages six to twelve (kids younger than that are admitted free of charge). There's also an associated restaurant and motel next door. You can learn more by calling 644-3435 or visiting www.ninepipes.org.

The People's Center, located south of **Polson** in **Pablo,** celebrates the unique cultural heritages of the Native Americans who call the Flathead Indian Reservation home—the Salish, Kootenai, and Pend d'Oreille peoples. Visit here and, as they say, you'll gain an altogether new perspective on the phrase "Made in Montana." More than a simple museum filled with displays and artwork, The People's Center offers dynamic opportunities to become intimately acquainted with the life-ways of the tribes through classes, demonstrations, and interpretive tours of the reservation. The center is open Mon through Sat from 9 a.m. to 5 p.m., June 1 through Sept 30, and Mon through Fri from 9 a.m. to 5 p.m. the rest of the year. Admission is free for tribal members; the fee for the general public is $5 for adults and $3 for teens and seniors. The People's Center is located at 53253 US 93 West. Call 883-5344 or visit the Web site www.peoplescenter.org for additional information.

A mile south of Polson on US 93 is the *Miracle of America Museum,* an eclectic collection of memorabilia and artifacts ranging from the ordinary to the preposterous. More than 100,000 objects are displayed; among them, early-day farm implements, World War I and World War II poster art and troop-transport vehicles, vintage motorcycles and musical instruments, and a horse-drawn hearse from the 1880s. You can see one of Teddy Roosevelt's saddles, along with a plethora of Montana-related sheet music framed and mounted; classics—both recognizable and little-known—like "Beneath Mon-

montanatrivia

Ninepipe National Wildlife Refuge outside Charlo contains active rookeries of double-crested cormorants and great blue herons, and is also home to the Flathead Valley's only nesting western grebe colony. At Pablo National Wildlife Refuge, 12 miles north of Ninepipe, a small number of common loons are seen almost every year during the nesting season, but the existence of nests has not been confirmed.

tana Skies," "Come on Down to Billings Town," "Mission Mountain Moon," "Montana Anna," and "Cassie, That Virginia City Lassie." Also residing at the museum is the land-stranded *Paul Bunyan,* a 65-foot logging tow listed in the International Register of Historic Large Vessels. For years the *Paul Bunyan* transported felled logs across Flathead Lake to the mills. The Miracle of America Museum, founded in 1981 and still run by Gil and Joanne Mangles, is open daily from 8 a.m. to 8 p.m. during the summer months; the rest of the year it's open Mon through Sat from 8 a.m. to 5 p.m. and Sun from 1:30 to 5 p.m. Expect to pay a $5 admission fee ($2 for kids three to twelve). For more information call 883-6804 or visit www.miracleofamericamuseum.org. You'll find the museum at 36094 Memory Lane in Polson.

MAJOR ATTRACTIONS WORTH SEEING

Conrad Mansion
Kalispell

Daly Mansion
Hamilton

Glacier National Park

National Bison Range
Moiese

While in town, stop by ***Richwine's Burgerville,*** a Polson institution since the 1950s. The meat for the burgers—reputed to be the best in Montana—is ground on-site in a meat room behind the restaurant. Try a Royal Burger (a single, double, or triple cheeseburger), their most popular item, named after Royal Morrison, the Polson football coach who founded Burgerville in the early 1950s before moving on to coach in Missoula.

Burgerville (883-2620) ordinarily opens sometime in Feb and closes again in the late fall. It's hard to miss: Just watch for the orange windmill and the neon cow wearing a police uniform.

Is there an establishment anywhere, other than ***Three Dog Down,*** with a shingle on the door reading, SORRY: WE'RE OPEN? Owner "Bronco Bob" Ricketts has parlayed his zany sense of humor, sharp acumen for marketing, and strong belief in customer service into one of the most popular businesses in Montana.

Ricketts, a music-business dropout who sang with the Cincinnati Opera and the Lyric Opera of Chicago, is still an entertainer. It's not uncommon to see him strolling about the store, accordion in hands, singing off-the-wall tunes in a rich tenor. Customers can also sing—and for discounts. A sign near the cash register reads, sing your national anthem. The quality of the singing determines the discount, which can range from $1 to $10. Countless renditions of "The Star Spangled Banner," as well as the anthems of countries far beyond America, have been heard resounding through the display rooms at Three Dog Down.

At Three Dog Down you'll find comforters, jackets, pillows, and other down products at prices well below those you might find elsewhere. The business is located, as the ad goes, "a bridge and a bump north of Polson on 93," and it's open seven days a week (9 a.m. to 7 p.m. in summer; 9 a.m. to 6 p.m. weekdays and 10 a.m. to 6 p.m. weekends the rest of the year). You can call (800) DOG–DOWN (364-3696) or visit www.threedogdown.com for more information.

Also in Polson is the lavish ***Best Western KwaTaqNuk Resort.*** Unveiled in 1992 and renovated in 2009, KwaTaqNuk represents a landmark effort by the Confederated Salish and Kootenai tribes to enhance their role in the region's burgeoning tourist trade. The large resort, staffed primarily by tribe members, features a full-service marina, a 112-room hotel, restaurants, indoor and outdoor pools, and a centerpiece gallery brimming with a collection of fine western and American Indian art and photography.

KwaTaqNuk, which translates to "where the water leaves the lake," is situated on the shores of Flathead Lake. Call 883-3636 or (800) 882-6363 or find it on the Web at www.kwataqnuk.com for more information.

The 2,164-acre mountain of timbered ridges and slopeside meadows rising high above the waters of Big Arm Bay is *Wild Horse Island State Park,* the largest island in massive Flathead Lake. On the island, purchased by the state in 1978, one can still spot an abandoned resort hotel and old homestead around the shoreline, and, in fact, fifty-six private lots remain. The island is home to a growing bighorn sheep population as well as bald eagles, numerous songbirds, and, fittingly, several wild horses captured and relocated here through the Bureau of Land Management's adopt-a-horse program. (The Salish and Kootenai Indians reportedly used the island in times past to keep their horses safe from enemy tribes.)

Open for day use only, Wild Horse Island is one state park not likely to become overcrowded soon because the only way to get there is by watercraft. Call Pointer Scenic Cruises (837-5617) to arrange transportation to the island; alternatively, captain-it-yourselfers can rent a boat at Sunny Shores Marina (849-5622). KwaTakNuk Resort's 148-passenger lake cruiser *Shadow* (883-3636) also makes daily trips to the island in the warm months. For more information on Wild Horse Island, call the Montana Department of Fish, Wildlife, and Parks in Kalispell at 752-5501.

The *Mission Mountain Winery,* situated just outside *Dayton,* produces award-winning wines, a feat not expected at these northern reaches. It seems the climate and soils of the Dayton area are ideal for growing the grapes used in making products like Mission Mountain's pinot noir and certain other wines. As relatively mild as the weather is here in Montana's "banana belt," however, the growing season is a couple of weeks too short for most grape varieties, so the majority of their fruits are imported from the Rattlesnake Hills of Washington State. (They do grow grapes in Montana for such wines as their pinot noir and pinot gris.) Producing some 6,500 cases per year, the family-owned Mission Mountain Winery is open for tours and

montanatrivia

January means minimum temperatures in the state range from a high of 21.1 degrees in Thompson Falls, situated in northwest Montana, to 4.5 degrees in Westby, in the far northeast.

TOP ANNUAL EVENTS

OSCR Cross-Country Ski Race
Seeley Lake; late Jan
(406) 677-2880

Foresters' Ball
Missoula; early Feb
(406) 243-4636

Winter Carnival
Whitefish; early Feb
(406) 862-3501

Montana Storytelling Roundup
Cut Bank; late Apr
(406) 873-2295

International Wildlife Film Festival
Missoula; May
(406) 728-9380

Bigfork Whitewater Festival
Bigfork; late May
(406) 837-5888

Chief Victor Days
Victor; mid-June
(406) 642-3997

Libby Logger Days
Libby; late June
(406) 293-4167

North American Indian Days
Browning; early July
(406) 338-2344

Standing Arrow Pow Wow
Elmo; late July
(406) 849-5541

Daly Days
Hamilton (Daly Mansion); late July
(406)363-6004

Yaak Wilderness Festival
Yaak; late July
(406) 295-9736

Cycle Montana
(route of weeklong ride changes yearly)
June
(406) 721-1776

**Rocky Mountain Accordion
Celebration**
Philipsburg; early Aug
(406) 859-3812

Huckleberry Festival
Trout Creek; early Aug
(406) 827-3301

Western Montana Fair & Rodeo
Missoula; mid-Aug
(406) 721-3247

Northwest Montana Fair
Kalispell; late Aug
(406) 758-5810

First Night Missoula
Missoula; New Year's Eve
(406) 549-4755

tasting from 10 a.m. to 5 p.m., May 1 through Oct 31. Call 849-5524 for information or visit their Web site, www.missionmountainwinery.com.

After choosing your wine, drive north on US 93 for 5 miles to *M & S Meats,* renowned for its selection of buffalo meats, sausages, and jerky—all said to be lower in fat and cholesterol, and higher in protein, than their beef counterparts. Honey-cured hams are another favorite. The store, established in

1945, is open 8 a.m. to 7 p.m. in summer, and 7:30 a.m. to 5:30 p.m. the rest of the year. There you can also pick up a loaf of French bread, then head out for an unforgettable picnic along the shore of sparkling Flathead Lake. Contact them at 844-3414 or (800) 454-3414 or at www.msmeats.com.

Continuing north along the west shore of Flathead Lake, you'll pass through Lakeside and Somers en route to *Bigfork.* Plan on devoting at least a day and an evening to gadding about this tastefully decked-out tourist town located at the northeast end of Flathead Lake. Here you can attend a performance at the *Bigfork Summer Playhouse,* which in 2009 celebrated its fiftieth season of presenting Broadway-style shows. The "theater by the bay," as it's known, operates from late May until Labor Day, during which time plays are staged Mon through Sat, with the occasional Sunday matinee. The playhouse is at 526 Electric Ave., and the box office number is 837-4886. You can check out the show schedule at www.bigforksummerplay house.com.

Eva Gates Homemade Preserves have been cooked down and put up in the Bigfork area since 1949, a year when—so the story goes—the Gateses' strawberry patch produced more than the family could eat on its own. So man of the house George designed a label and started selling to neighbors pint jars filled with the delectables cooked up by Eva on her wood-burning range.

montanatrivia

Some 11,000 plant species thrive—or at least survive—in Glacier National Park, approximately 100 of them trees and shrubs.

Today the preserves and wild huckleberry and chokecherry syrups are still a family tradition, concocted by Eva's granddaughter, Gretchen Gates, along with other relatives. The Gateses have maintained their products' consistency by adhering to the "why fix it if it ain't broke?" philosophy: Just as when Eva was at the kitchen helm, the girls prepare, cook, bottle, and label every jar by hand, in five-pint batches, using no additives or preservatives.

The shop is downtown at 451 Electric Ave. Visitors are welcome seven days a week and evenings from mid-June through Aug, and from 9 a.m. to 5 p.m. the remainder of the year. Call (800) 682-4283 or visit www.evagates.com to order a jar of Montana flavor for your breakfast table.

Immediately south of Bigfork on Highway 35, watch for the unassuming sign marking the entrance to the not-so-unassuming *Averill's Flathead Lake Lodge and Dude Ranch.* If you have a few spare days on your hands—and a spare $3,206 (per adult) in your pocket—consider a week at this first-class lodge and dude ranch. Even if a lack of time or money precludes a layover, drive out and have a look, for a grander scene is hard to envision. It belongs in a 1930s Cary Grant–Katharine Hepburn movie.

The enterprise includes more than 2,000 acres of mountain timberland and meadow. At the core of the ranch are two log lodges and several smaller cabins, a large corral and rodeo grounds, several acres of lawn, a swimming pool, tennis courts, and a long stretch of sandy Flathead Lake beach.

The Averills, who opened the ranch in 1945 as a getaway for folks from the world over, are intent on keeping their dudes busy: Fishing, swimming (pool or lake), tennis, golf, barbecues, trail rides, sailing, water-skiing, mountain biking, river-raft trips, horse games and rodeo training, breakfast rides, and volleyball are but a few of the diversions at hand. Some guests even help with the chores. Others, somehow, find time to just lie around, resting.

The lodge operates on the American plan (all meals and recreational options included), and a full week's worth of guests arrive and depart simultaneously. For additional information call 837-4391 or log on to www.averills .com.

For digs that are a bit more reasonably priced, consider overnighting at the *Candlewycke Inn Bed and Breakfast,* situated 3 miles from downtown Bigfork at 311 Aero Lane. The open log lodge, featuring five guest rooms, sits on ten secluded acres of woods near the foot of the spectacular Swan Range. Decks, walking paths, horseshoe pits, and other amenities invite outdoor living, while there's plenty to keep you occupied indoors as well. Nightly rates are $125 to $165, depending on the time of year (a two-night minimum stay may apply during the high season). For information call (888) 617-8805 or visit www.candlewyckeinn.com.

Also not far from Bigfork is the *Coyote Roadhouse Inn,* owned and operated by master chef and successful restaurateur Gary Hastings. Considered one of Montana's finest restaurants—in fact, *Travel & Leisure* magazine once called it the state's very best—the establishment specializes in gourmet Mayan, southwestern, Tuscan, and Cajun delectables. Call 837-4250 or visit www .coyoteroadhouse.com for requisite reservations or to learn about overnighting options in the Coyote Riverhouse Cabins.

The *Jewel Basin Hiking Area,* located 10 miles north of Bigfork, resides at the northern end of the sweeping Swan Range. The 15,000-acre preserve is designated by the Forest Service as a hikers-only area—no pack stock, motorized vehicles, or bicycles permitted. The hiking area offers good fishing in many of its twenty-eight lakes, and includes 35 miles of trails, many suitable for neophyte hikers and kids.

To find the trailhead, travel 2 miles north from Bigfork on Highway 35 and turn right onto Highway 83. In about 2½ miles, turn left onto Echo Lake

Road, and after another 2½ miles, follow the Noisy Creek Road east to the parking area (a high-clearance vehicle is recommended for the last couple of miles). For more information call the Flathead National Forest at 758–5200 or visit www.fs.fed.us/r1/flathead.

Continue north from the Bigfork area toward the wide spot in the road called *Creston.* Lovers of gardening and flowers may be rendered speechless at the *Gatiss Gardens,* just south of Creston along Highway 35. The resident families—until a few years ago the Gatisses, and now the Sibleruds—have spent thousands of hours working the four-acre grounds. Hundreds drive by the spot gaping in disbelief, wondering how anyone could grow such extraordinary gardens, and not knowing that they're open to the public.

A mile-long, self-guided trail winds through the profusion of color provided largely by a vast assortment of perennials. The gardens are open daily in the summer, 9 a.m. to dusk, and there's also a small gift shop on the premises. The guest register and trailhead are adjacent to the free parking area, a hundred yards west of the houses, just off Broeder Loop Road. For more information call 755-2418.

Immediately across the road from Gatiss Gardens is Fish Hatchery Road. Follow it to the north for a mile and you'll come to the *Creston Fish and Wildlife Center,* the rearing grounds for thousands of FLMs (Future Lunkers of Montana). One of the hatchery's primary roles is that of providing trout for fishery management activities on the seven Indian reservations in the state. You can take a walk around the grounds and watch swarms of rainbow and cutthroat trout breeding stock and their offspring swimming about in raceways. Spawning, a fascinating procedure to watch, takes place between Jan and Mar, with maximum fish populations generally attained in Apr. No dummies, numerous fish-eating birds also live in the vicinity and will be spotted by the observant: belted kingfishers, ospreys, and great blue herons, to name three. There's also a picnic ground adjacent to the hatchery, open daily from 8 a.m. to 4 p.m. For more information call 758-6868 or visit http://creston.fws.gov. The address is 780 Creston Hatchery Rd., *Kalispell.*

montanatrivia

The discovery of a fragment of woodland caribou antler in the Whitefish Range in the early 1990s provided evidence that the animals still occasionally wander from Canada into northwest Montana.

Eight miles north of *Whitefish,* a pretty little resort town located 14 miles north of Kalispell, is the *Whitefish Mountain Resort,* one of Montana's most popular ski areas. During the warm months you can ride the Big Mountain Express lift to the summit ($5 one way; $10 round trip). En route, keep an eye

Let It Snow

Any skier worth his or her boots, bindings, and boards knows that Montana boasts a quartet of destination ski resorts: the Whitefish Mountain Resort, Big Sky, Moonlight Basin, and Red Lodge Mountain. Less known is that the state features more than a dozen other ski resorts. These tend to be hills frequented by locals, although some of them, such as Bridger Bowl north of Bozeman and Montana Snowbowl outside Missoula, claim statistics that are anything but small-town. Here's a summary of where you can go downhill schussing or shredding under the big sky, and what to expect when you get there:

Bear Paw Ski Bowl, Havre;
(406) 265-8404　　　　　Vertical Drop: 900'　　　　Average Snowfall: 140"

Whitefish Mountain Resort, Whitefish;
(406) 862-2900　　　　　Vertical Drop: 2,353'　　　Average Snowfall: 300"

Big Sky, Big Sky;
(406) 995-5750　　　　　Vertical Drop: 4,350'　　　Average Snowfall: 400"

Blacktail Mountain, Lakeside;
(406) 844-0999　　　　　Vertical Drop: 1,440'　　　Average Snowfall: 250"

Bridger Bowl, Bozeman;
(406) 586-1518　　　　　Vertical Drop: 2,600'　　　Average Snowfall: 350"

Discovery Basin, Anaconda;
(406) 563-2184　　　　　Vertical Drop: 1,670'　　　Average Snowfall: 210"

Great Divide, Marysville;
(406) 449-3746　　　　　Vertical Drop: 1,560'　　　Average Snowfall: 180"

Lookout Pass, Wallace, Idaho;
(208) 744-1301　　　　　Vertical Drop: 1,150'　　　Average Snowfall: 400"

Lost Trail, Conner;
(406) 821-3211　　　　　Vertical Drop: 1,800'　　　Average Snowfall: 300"

Maverick Mountain, Polaris;
(406) 834-3454　　　　　Vertical Drop: 2,020'　　　Average Snowfall: 180"

Montana Snowbowl, Missoula;
(406) 549-9777　　　　　Vertical Drop: 2,600'　　　Average Snowfall: 300"

Moonlight Basin, Big Sky;
(406) 993-6000　　　　　Vertical Drop: 4,150'　　　Average Snowfall: 400"

Red Lodge Mountain, Red Lodge;
(406) 446-2610　　　　　Vertical Drop: 2,400'　　　Average Snowfall: 250"

Showdown Ski Area, Neihart;
(406) 236-5522　　　　　Vertical Drop: 1,400'　　　Average Snowfall: 245"

Teton Pass, Choteau;
(406) 466-2209　　　　　Vertical Drop: 1,010'　　　Average Snowfall: 300"

Turner Mountain, Libby;
(406) 293-2468　　　　　Vertical Drop: 2,110'　　　Average Snowfall: 250"

To learn more about any of these areas, visit http://skimt.com. The Winter Montana Web site features snow reports (updated daily), information on groomed cross-country trails, details on snowmobile rentals and trails, and a lot more.

out for wildlife—bears, moose, deer, mountain lions, coyotes, and any number of smaller animals can be seen on the slopes at one time or another.

At the basement level of the Summit House Restaurant, you'll find the **Summit Nature Center.** The Flathead National Forest joined Winter Sports Inc. to develop this illuminating, hands-on interpretive center, where kids of all ages can run their hands through a coyote or wolf pelt, inspect a variety of western Montana's owls (they're stuffed), or borrow a pair of binoculars to get a close-up view of the ice-clad peaks of Glacier National Park, looming to the east.

Knowledgeable Forest Service personnel or volunteers are on hand to answer questions and aid visitors to better understand and appreciate the natural history of Glacier Country. At scheduled times staffers present lectures on topics such as endangered species, wetlands and fisheries, and the bears of Montana. The center is open daily from Father's Day to Labor Day, 10 a.m. to 5 p.m.

After enjoying the nature center and savoring the 360-degree view earned at the summit, some visitors forgo the gondola and opt to hike back to the base area, through timber stands and "gardens" of wildflowers, on the 5.6-mile **Danny On Memorial Trail.** (A much smaller number of visitors hike up the challenging but well-graded trail to reach the summit, an elevation gain of more than 2,000 feet.) The Whitefish Mountain Resort also maintains an extensive network of mountain-biking trails, and full-suspension mountain bikes can be rented on-site.

The trail was dedicated to the memory of a man who touched the lives of hundreds of Flathead Valley residents and visitors. Danny On was a Forest Service silviculturist, acclaimed nature photographer, and ardent skier who died here in 1979, skiing on the slopes that he loved. On was known for taking novices under his wing and showing them the ropes, whether they be the ropes of downhill skiing, natural history, or photography. For further information on the Whitefish Mountain Resort, visit www.skiwhitefish.com or call 862-2900. (Inquire also about the unique Walk in the Treetops, a harness-and-safety-line-aided stroll for those age ten and older.)

Back down below, along the Whitefish Lake Road at a point 1 mile north of the Big Mountain junction, you'll see a left-hand turn onto a gravel road that leads down to the parking area for **Les Mason Park.** From the parking area a short trail leads to a brush-embraced

montana**trivia**

The area surrounding the Trail of the Cedars in Glacier National Park is an "inland-maritime micro-climate." Translation: an inland forest that is similar to a coastal rain forest.

beach. This quiet lakeside spot can be deserted even when sunbathers are lying nose-to-toes at the very popular City Beach. Les Mason Park is supported by donations.

Unlike many alpine ski resorts, Whitefish was a town long before it became a destination for schussers. At the renovated 1927 **Burlington Northern Depot,** the Stumptown Historical Society maintains a museum exploring the old days, with exhibits on the area's Native Americans, early logging practices, the Great Northern Railroad, and more. An exquisitely restored 1940s Pullman car guards the museum, situated at the north end of Central Avenue. The hours of operation vary, so call 862-0067 in advance of visiting.

The **Garden Wall Inn,** located at 504 Spokane Ave., is Whitefish's original bed-and-breakfast inn. Several others have sprung up, but the Garden Wall, whose name derives from a well-known feature in nearby **Glacier National Park,** remains one of the best choices. Five antiques-appointed rooms provide intimate and comfortable quarters just 2 blocks from downtown. Afternoon/evening sherry in front of the fireplace is one Garden Wall tradition; another is an incredible, multicourse breakfast. Skiing is spoken here—both cross-country and alpine—and owners (and avid skiers) Rhonda and Mike Fitzgerald and Chris Schustrom have collected an impressive and entertaining library of skiing-related books. Rooms start at $155 and range up to $255 for a two-bedroom suite; for additional information call 862-3440 or (888) 530-1700, or visit www.garden wallinn.com.

If you prefer your breakfasts on the lighter side, or if the Garden Wall's no vacancy sign is hanging, try the light and airy **Good Medicine Lodge,** located at 537 Wisconsin Ave., on the way to the Big Mountain. The nine-bedroom lodge (with six spacious rooms and three suites) features a western ambience of dark-stained cedar beams, banisters, and loft railings, highlighted with Native American–inspired textiles and accessories. All rooms have private bath, telephone, and air-conditioning, and most feature balconies with mountain views. There's also a television/videotape machine with a great movie selection in the smaller of the inn's two sitting rooms. Rates for double occupancy range from $150 to $250 in summer and $99 to $190 in winter. Call for reservations at (800) 860-5488 or visit www.goodmedicine lodge.com.

Leading north from Columbia Falls is Highway 486, a secondary road paralleling the west shore of the wild and scenic North Fork of the Flathead River. The road soon turns into FR 210 and becomes gravel before leading to the town of *Polebridge,* 35 miles north of Columbia Falls. Check out the historic *Polebridge Mercantile* (888-5105; try the cinnamon rolls!) and the funky *Northern Lights Saloon and Cafe* (888-5669), where you're bound to hear more than one bear story, or

other north-country tall tale, from a local. (Much like the Yaak, we're talking way off the beaten path here, so it's a good idea to pick up a detailed map for navigational purposes. Stop by the Glacier View Ranger Station in Columbia Falls and ask for the visitor map of the North Half of the Flathead National Forest. And don't leave Columbia Falls without provisions and a full tank of gas.)

Another 10 miles north of Polebridge along FR 210 is the Ford Work Center. To visit the *Hornet Peak Fire Lookout*—the last D-1 Standard fire-lookout tower remaining in its original location—from Ford proceed 3½ miles up FR 318, and then go 5 miles on FR 9805. The forest roads are generally passenger-car friendly. From the obvious turnout, it's a steep mile-plus hike to the historic lookout tower, but the effort spent is not wasted: The lookout is attractive and intriguing, and from atop Hornet Mountain you'll admire one of the best views in northwest Montana. From the peak, elevation 6,744 feet, you can see far to the east into Glacier National Park and pick out many of its jagged, high peaks.

The lookout was constructed in 1922, largely with native, on-site materials. Forest Service employees cut timber with crosscut saws, squared the logs and fit the corners with broadaxes, and split roofing shingles with froes. More recently members of the North Fork Preservation Association have contributed hundreds of hours of free labor to restore the old structure to near-new condition. For more information call the Hungry Horse–Glacier View Ranger Station at 387-3800.

Once back in Polebridge, consider driving the narrow and winding 14-mile road that leads to sparkling *Kintla Lake.* The long body of water fills one of the deep, glacier-carved clefts striating the relatively little-visited western reaches of *Glacier National Park.* The view from the lakeshore campground is nothing short of stunning. (Alternatively, the rustic road makes for a terrific out-and-back mountain-bike ride of 28 miles.)

US 2 between Columbia Falls and West Glacier is one of those free-enterprise-gone-berserk stretches of road that seem to spring up near the entrances to our national parks. It features the sort of attractions parents may shun but kids inevitably love: waterslides, go-kart tracks, mazes, caged bears, T-shirt and souvenir shops, chainsaw-art galleries. . . You'll encounter all of these and much more.

One of the most curiously named towns in Montana is **Hungry Horse** (it relates to a couple of freight horses that wandered away from camp and nearly starved during the winter of 1900–01), which is situated along this section of US 2 and includes its share of the tacky and wacky. Among its more subdued yet impressive attractions is the **Hungry Horse Dam Visitor Center.**

Hungry Horse Dam impounds the lower stretches of the South Fork of the Flathead, a river that runs wild for mile after mile through the Bob Marshall Wilderness before being tamed and flattened into an immense reservoir by the eleventh largest concrete dam in the United States. The visitor center, operated by the Bureau of Reclamation, explains the history and functions of the dam and also contains displays on the Flathead National Forest and area natural history. The visitor center is open Memorial Day through Labor Day, 9:30 a.m. to 6 p.m. every day, with guided tours offered on the hour between 8 a.m. and 3 p.m. The dam and visitor center are 4 miles southeast of town. Call 387-5241 for information.

There's a great new/old find in West Glacier, near the west entrance of **Glacier National Park:** the **Belton Chalet,** built a century ago in 1910 as the first of James J. Hill's Swiss-style Great Northern Railroad hotels. This Rip Van Winkle of a lodge slept for half a century; newly renovated and listed as a National Historic Landmark, in the summer of 2000 it again began receiving guests. The chalet's thirty period rooms (no televisions or phones) go for $155 to $180, while an adjacent cottage sleeping up to six costs $325 per night. There's also a restaurant, taproom, and spa on the premises. Call Belton Chalet, which is located next to the Belton Station Amtrak depot, at 888-5000, or check out their Web site at www.beltonchalet.com.

The Great Northern Railroad's isolated line over Marias Pass is subject to heavy snows and strong winds in the winter, and the task of keeping the tracks open is a mighty one. The **Izaak Walton Inn** in Essex is another inn with ties to the area's railroading past. It was built in the late 1930s to house the men servicing the line, and their numbers grew rapidly as winter strengthened its

montanatrivia

The Chief Mountain Hot Shots from Montana's Blackfeet Indian Reservation are among the most respected wildfire fighters in the United States.

Winning an Oscar

My first cross-country ski marathon was a dilly. Known as OSCR—pronounced "Oscar" and standing for *Ovando to Seeley Citizens Race*—the February 1985 race was slated to start at the Whitetail Ranch near Ovando and end 50 kilometers, or 31 miles, later in the town of Seeley Lake.

The temperature at the supposed start time of 9 a.m. was an Arctic-like 27 degrees below zero. Nervous conversations rattled like tinkling ice in the frozen morning air. Still, we wannabe racers knew in our hearts that the event would be canceled and that inside a couple of hours we'd be back in the warm comfort of our homes.

But after an hour the temperature had warmed all the way to minus 20 degrees, and suddenly the race director fired the starting gun. We were off, thirty-one strong, our skis gliding across the cold, humidity-free snow about as readily as rubber-soled gym shoes slide across a basketball court covered in sandpaper. Everyone, even the eventual winner, would be out at least four hours, so keeping noses and digits from freezing was of more concern than the finishing order. The warmest temperature reported along the course that day was minus 14 degrees. Still, it was a brilliant day, filled with deep-blue sky, snow-smothered mountain slopes, and bright winter sunshine.

As I reached the last of three aid stations, each of which was manned by two or three volunteers from the Seeley Lake snowmobile club, I blurted, "How much farther?" I remember being pleased to find that my mouth still moved. "Ten kilometers," said one of the men. "No—10 miles!" contended the other. They couldn't reach an agreement, so they offered me a blast of warmth from their bottle of Jack Daniels as consolation. I thanked them but declined and skied off, not knowing whether I had 6 miles or 10 miles of bitter, frozen Montana wilderness still to contend with.

---

icy north-country grip. Still, the inn was built larger than needed for even the largest of crews, for Essex once was slated to become the central entrance into Glacier National Park—an idea eventually erased from the drawing board.

Even lacking a nearby park entrance, the Izaak Walton has become a popular tourist stop. Its railroading legacy continues: Essex is a flag stop on Amtrak's Empire Builder line, and passengers can load or unload literally at the Izaak Walton's front door. Railroading memorabilia hang from the walls, and groups of up to four can opt to spend the night in one of four refurbished historic cabooses, replete with modern plumbing and cooking facilities.

The inn is a popular summer spot for hikers, mountain bikers, and fly fishers, who cast in the spirit of the celebrated angler after whom the inn is named. The Izaak Walton Inn's long winters and well-groomed trails also make it one of the most popular spots for cross-country skiing in Montana. Lodge rooms go for $117 to $255, and cabooses for $690 for three nights, the minimum stay. There's also a pair of family cabins that rent for $230 per night. For reservations and more information, call 888-5700 or tap into www .izaakwaltoninn.com.

Browning is the social, economic, and administrative headquarters for those Blackfeet Indians living south of the international border. Here you'll find the **Museum of the Plains Indian,** home to a comprehensive collection of Blackfeet artifacts. The museum also showcases arts and crafts—not only the Blackfeet's, but also those of the Crow, Northern Cheyenne, Sioux, and other Plains tribes, all traditional enemies of the Blackfeet. A highlight in the permanent display area is an exhibit of traditional costumes, while "Winds of Change," a multimedia show narrated by the late Vincent Price and produced by Montana State University, illuminates the continuing evolution of Indian cultures.

The Man Who Talks Not

Tucked away in a small structure on the main street of *East Glacier* is the *John L. Clarke Western Art Gallery and Memorial Museum.* Clarke, whose Blackfeet name was Cutapuis, "The Man Who Talks Not," was a Blackfeet Indian born in Highwood in 1881. Epidemics of smallpox and scarlet fever swept through the area in the early 1880s, killing five of Clarke's brothers and leaving him, at age two and a half, deaf and unable to speak.

After his father moved what remained of the family to Midvale, near the present site of East Glacier, Clarke was sent away at age thirteen to a school for deaf children. There he learned wood carving, and his obvious talent for the skill led to a budding career in art. His first big break came in 1917, when the Academy of Fine Arts in Philadelphia began regularly exhibiting his work. Then, a year later at age thirty-seven, he met and married Mamie Peters Simon, an astute businesswoman who became Clarke's promoter, interpreter, and secretary-manager. With their combined talents, Clarke soon became known as one of the world's best portrayers of western wildlife.

Clarke's specialty was detailed cottonwood carvings of bears, mountain goats, and other wildlife thriving in his home territory. After he died in 1970, his friend J. W. Tschache, an avid collector of Clarke's works, said about a carving of a big grizzly bear freeing itself from a trap that "the real significance of this work is that J. L. Clarke created it when he was approaching ninety years old, when his eyes were so clouded with cataracts that he could barely see. He created this sculpture almost entirely by feel."

In addition to his intricate wildlife carvings, Clarke also modeled in clay, painted in watercolors and oils, and sketched in charcoal and crayon. At the memorial museum in East Glacier—which his adopted daughter, Joyce Clark Turvey, started in 1977 and is open daily through the summer—limited editions of Clarke's works are for sale, along with the creations of numerous other western artists.

In the changing-exhibits area, the works of modern-day sculptors, carvers, painters, and other artists and craftspeople are highlighted. The sales shop, offering a wide variety of contemporary products, is operated by the Indian-owned Northern Plains Indian Crafts Association.

The museum, founded in 1941, is administered by the Indian Arts and Crafts Board, operating under the Department of the Interior. The Museum of the Plains Indian, located at the junction of US 2 and US 89 just west of town, is open daily June through Sept from 9 a.m. to 4:45 p.m. and, during the rest of the year, Mon through Fri from 10 a.m. to 4:30 p.m. Admission is free in winter and $4 for adults and $1 for children six to twelve in summer. For more information call 338-2230.

North American Indian Days is held each July in Browning at the Blackfeet Tribal Fairgrounds, next to the Museum of the Plains Indian and near the new Glacier Peaks Casino. The four-day celebration brings together Indians from throughout the United States and Canada, as well as non-Indian visitors, for dancing, games, sporting events, and more. For details call 338-7406 or check out www.blackfeetcountry.com.

Twenty-five-passenger coach tours along the legendary Going-to-the-Sun Road in *Glacier National Park*, guided by Native Americans from the Browning area, are available through *Glacier National Park Sun Tours.* On these informative outings you'll have the opportunity to listen to the Blackfeet Indians' interpretation of the sacred landscape of Glacier National Park, a philosophy markedly different from the often impersonal, scientific outlook common among those of European descent. Arrangements can also be made to be picked up in either East Glacier or St. Mary. Sun Tours is an authorized concessioner of the National Park Service. The season runs June 1 through Sept 30; call 226-9220 or (800) 786-9220 for more information.

Lewis and Clark Trail

As you motor along Highway 83 in the sleepy Seeley-Swan Valley, that's the *Bob Marshall Wilderness* straddling the *Continental Divide* to the east. "The Bob," named in honor of a pioneer in the American wilderness movement, joins with the Great Bear and Scapegoat Wilderness Areas to form one of the largest wilderness complexes in the lower forty-eight states. More than 1½ million acres of protected forest are accessible only by trails—nearly 2,000 miles of them.

Approximately 7 miles south of the turn to picturesque Holland Lake Lodge, watch for FR 4370 going northeast. After roughly 5 miles the gravel road bends southward, leading in 2½ more miles to the ½-mile-long foot trail that will take you to sparkling and little-visited **Clearwater Lake.** A better place for a summer's picnic and cooling dip is tough to envision. Don't be surprised if you encounter a party or two of loaded-down mountain bikers while prowling these backroads: FR 4370 is part of the 2,708-mile Great Divide Mountain Bike Route, a project of the Missoula-based Adventure Cycling Association.

When Lolo National Forest recreation planners were looking for a peaceful stretch of river that novice and solo paddlers could manage without getting in over their heads, they couldn't have done better than the **Clearwater Canoe Trail.** The river trail, beginning 5 miles north of the town of Seeley Lake off Highway 83, peacefully meanders to the south for 4 miles before reaching the open and often more turbulent waters of Seeley Lake.

The canoe trail is one of the best bird-watching locales in western Montana. Large raptors, such as bald eagles and ospreys, can be seen fishing for dinner, the sounds of warblers and other songbirds are abundant in the spring, and common loons nest along the shores of Seeley Lake not far from the river trail's inlet.

The Clearwater Canoe Trail enjoys protection under the Wild and Scenic Rivers Act. For information and maps call the Seeley Lake Ranger District at 677-2233.

For overnight accommodations in the area, consider **The Lodges on Seeley Lake,** consisting of more than a dozen cabins along a third of a mile of shoreline—and all beginning with the letter *L* (Lilypad, Lumberjack, and Lindbergh, for example). Nightly rates range from around $139 to $228, depending on the cabin's size and amenities. For information call (800) 900-9016 or visit www.lodgesonseeleylake.com.

Alternatively, at the **Double Arrow Lodge,** traditional western fare— spelled beef and trout—is found at its best. The Double Arrow offers food and lodging all year long, golf in summer, and groomed cross-country ski trails and horse-drawn sleigh rides in winter. The log lodge, with its massive rock fireplace, was built in 1929 by international financier and Dutch cavalry officer Jan Boissevain. Following his tour of America after World War I, Boissevain labeled the American West a "wasteland." But he radically changed his thinking after accepting an invitation from Allen Toole, son of Anaconda Company executive John H. Toole, to stay at his family's cabin in the Seeley-Swan Valley. Boissevain was captivated by the area's beauty, and he set out with partner Colonel George Weisel to build a private retreat where he could share his newfound love of the West with others.

It's interesting to note that the Double Arrow brand came to Montana, by way of Holland, from Montana. Boissevain first saw the brand on a horse given to him by his father; that particular horse had come to Holland from the Spears brothers' Double Arrow Ranch in Drummond, Montana.

Meals at the Double Arrow range from moderate to expensive in price. The resort also offers lodge rooms and log cabins for overnighting, with rates ranging from $100 for a standard cabin to $450 for the three-bedroom Cougar Cottage. You'll also find an abundance of recreational opportunities at hand, including an eighteen-hole golf course. Call 677-2777 or visit the Web site at www.doublearrowresort.com for reservations and information.

montanatrivia

The Montana Native Plant Society, headquartered in Missoula, boasts over 600 members in a half dozen chapters around the state.

Garnet Ghost Town, one of Montana's best-preserved pioneer settlements, celebrated its one hundredth birthday on the fourth of July weekend in 1995. Although placer gold miners had been active in the Garnet Range as early as the 1860s, it wasn't until the mid-1890s, when thousands of miners were suddenly unemployed as a result of the repeal of the Sherman Silver Purchase Act, that activity in the Garnet area shifted into high gear. In 1895 Dr. Armistead Mitchell built an ore-crushing mill at the head of First Chance Gulch, around which grew a town—first called Mitchell, but by 1897 known as Garnet, named after the semiprecious, ruby-colored stones found in the nearby hills.

By 1898, when a rich vein was struck at the Nancy Hanks mine, nearly 1,000 people called Garnet home. It consisted of numerous cabins, a doctor's office, an assay building, a union hall (boasting what was regarded as one of the best dance floors in Montana), thirteen saloons, two barbershops, four stores, four hotels, and more. Many miners brought families with them to Garnet, so, not surprisingly, the social life here was more civilized than in some of the other, more bachelor-abundant Montana gold camps.

As in most boomtowns, buildings were built quickly and bereft of sound foundations. Most have collapsed, although several of the 1800s buildings remain intact more than a century after being constructed. The Bureau of Land Management is working with the nonprofit Garnet Preservation Association

Floating the Clearwater Canoe Trail

After turning west off Highway 83 at a point 4 miles north of the community of Seeley Lake, Nancy and I began bumping down the track that leads to the put-in for the *Clearwater Canoe Trail.* A mile back we'd stopped in at the Seeley Lake Ranger Station, where a knowledgeable ranger had guaranteed us that this river "trail" is suitable for any level of canoeist. In fact, he told us, the Forest Service designated it for precisely that quality: The agency wanted to promote a stretch of river that nearly anyone can safely and enjoyably navigate. Unlike many streams in the region, the channel on this stretch of the Clearwater River is deep enough that beavers haven't managed to close it off by constructing dams, and logjams don't commonly block the river's flow the way they do on many area streams.

We were very pleased to hear from an official that the Clearwater Canoe Trail is negotiable by neophytes, because that's certainly what we were. At the parking area, ¾ of a mile from the highway, we wrestled the bright red canoe, generously lent to us by a friend in Missoula, off the top of the Jeep. Then we gently set it down close to the launching point while we retrieved lunch, binoculars, spare clothing, and other necessities from the car. After we donned our life jackets, Nancy crawled into the bow and I pushed us adrift, jumping into the stern just before the water deepened dramatically.

We paddled from the brackish backwaters put-in area into the main channel. Even there the water was so placid that we could hardly detect a current. Our efforts at synchronized paddling fell far short of Olympic perfection; in fact, it took a while before we stopped spinning down the river like a top turning counterclockwise circles. I decided to try simply using the paddle as a rudder to steer and keep us in the channel, while Nancy paddled. It worked. Our canoe sliced smoothly through the mirror surface of the water, cutting a "V" that ultimately spread the width of the stream behind us.

Finally the river widened and we gained sufficient distance from the embracing willows that we could see our surroundings. It was a flawless fall day: probably 65 degrees and not a cloud in the sky, its blue brilliance rivaled and simultaneously complemented by the rich colors of early October. Amid blanketing stands of Douglas fir towered thick-trunked western larch trees, their needles burned gold by the season. Occasionally a breeze blew some loose and they drifted earthward, sparkling in the sun's rays like gold dust. Far to our east loomed the Swan Range, one of several mountain ranges contributing to a 1½-million-acre wilderness complex that includes the Scapegoat, Bob Marshall, and Great Bear Wilderness Areas. Add to these the nearly one million acres of Glacier National Park, which is separated from the Great Bear only by a road corridor, and you've got a wildlands continuum larger than Yellowstone National Park.

The treeless tops of the Swan Range's highest peaks were dusted with white. We guessed that the snow had fallen the day before, while we were enduring hours of rain in the valley. To the west, and much closer than the Swans, hung the bulky peaks of the Mission Mountains Wilderness. I spotted an osprey high overhead in a dead snag some 50 feet off the river, apparently surveying all that was happening in her domain. Unfortunately, our intrusion spooked her; we could actually hear the large bird's wings cutting through the crisp fall air as she flapped into flight.

It seemed that each bend in the madly meandering stream was followed by a turn. We began wondering if there was a straight stretch on the entire river trail. A flock of coots scooted away, flying just above water level, as we rounded one bend. Then, there they were, waiting for us at the next, where they repeated their short flight to perceived safety. In some places the river twisted through willow thickets so high and tight that they blocked out the sun and surrounding mountains, causing us to lose all sense of direction. It didn't matter, though, because there was really no way to become truly lost. With the mountains obscured, the marsh environment made it easy to imagine that we were in Minnesota rather than Montana.

After about an hour on the water, we heard a strange "wobbly" noise. We rounded a left-hand bend and encountered the source of the sound: a common loon, bobbing along close to the starboard bank. (For you fellow landlubbers, that's the right side—as Nancy, who grew up in a Seattle seafaring family, informed me.) According to the canoe-trail brochure we'd obtained at the ranger station, the bird is anything but common here in the Northern Rockies. The brochure also informed us that in the spring, songbirds like thrushes, finches, and warblers are common along these waters. A host of other critters hang out in, on, and around the canoe trail, too: Part- and full-time residents include fish such as perch and landlocked kokanee salmon (whose fall spawning helps explain the presence of ospreys), painted turtles, muskrats, moose, and white-tailed deer. Even the occasional elk and mountain lion have been spotted by alert paddlers.

Shortly we pulled up to a clearing and stepped onto dry land. It was a heavenly spot for a picnic. Peanut-butter sandwiches, potato chips, and orange pop had never tasted so good. I lay down on the grass face up, while Nancy tried her hand at tempting a trout by casting a fly. Ah, autumn in the Rockies: intense sunshine, very few bugs, and the hearty scent of decaying leaves rich in the air. Absolute peace and quiet.

We pushed off again, and all too soon the Clearwater emptied into Seeley Lake, taking us along for the ride. In contrast to the intimacy enjoyed on the canoe trail, we suddenly felt overly exposed. Mellow waters yielded to a surface shattered by a gusty breeze. The final ½ mile to the take-out at the ranger station was our first real test at making forward progress. But we did get there, where we pulled the canoe up onto the sprawling lawn.

Underscoring just how wildly the 4-mile canoe trail twists and turns, we found the hiking trail that parallels the river and led us back to our car to be only 1 mile long. Though merely a few hundred feet from the river, it penetrated an altogether different world, a forest of old-growth spruce, larch, and pine, where the geese and ducks of the waterway were replaced by goshawks and owls. On that fall day the crackling forest seemed as desiccated as the canoe trail was waterlogged.

Exactly four hours after setting afloat we reclaimed our car. Our only wish was that the outing had taken twice that long.

—Adapted from *Journey to the Northern Rockies* by Michael McCoy to save and stabilize the remaining structures, including the impressive, three-story J. K. Wells Hotel, built in the winter of 1897 on a wooden-post foundation.

You'll also find several newer buildings. Two 1930s-vintage cabins are available for rent during the winter, one of them for $30 and the other $40 per night, making the ghost town a popular destination for cross-country skiers and snowmobilers. Another fun time to come is during the preservation association's annual fund-raiser, the Hard Times Dinner and Dance, held sometime during the summer (the date changes).

montanatrivia

Fifteen owl species live in or occasionally visit Montana: the snowy, eastern screech, western screech, northern pygmy, northern saw-whet, long-eared, short-eared, great gray, burrowing, flammulated, barred, boreal, northern hawk-owl, the rarely seen barn owl, and the most common of all, the great horned owl.

To get to Garnet, which some old-timers claim is a ghost town actually inhabited by specters, from near the 22-mile marker on Highway 200 east of Potomac, turn onto the well-signed Garnet Range Road and travel approximately 11 miles. The road is closed to wheeled vehicles between Jan 1 and Apr 30, when it turns into an over-snow route for snowmobilers and skiers. For information call the Bureau of Land Management at 329-3914, or visit www.garnetghosttown.net.

Missoula, best known for the University of Montana, is considered by many to be the state's cultural center and most progressive city (although many residents of Billings, Bozeman, and other towns are quick to disagree). Missoula's attractions range from quaint to sophisticated to off the wall.

Several national organizations are headquartered in Missoula, including the Boone and Crockett Club, the Adventure Cycling Association, the Outdoor Writers Association of America, and the **Rocky Mountain Elk Foundation,** a group dedicated to enhancing and increasing elk habitat throughout the West. The foundation's Elk Country Visitor Center, located in the organization's spectacular new digs at 5705 Grant Creek Rd., provides a glimpse of the ways of the wild wapiti and also features collections of wildlife art and outstanding taxidermy, including mounted grizzly bears and mountain goats. From May 27 through Dec 22, the center is open weekdays 8 a.m. to 6 p.m. and Sat and Sun from 9 a.m. to 6 p.m. Dec 23 through May 26, it's open 8 a.m. to 5 p.m. Mon through Fri and 10 a.m. to 5 p.m. on Sat (closed Sun). For information call 523-4500 or visit www.rmef.org.

The **USDA Forest Service Smokejumpers Visitor Center** is adjacent to Johnson-Bell Airport, 7 miles west of town. The facility is the largest active smokejumper base and training center in the United States.

Rocky Mountain Oysters

The **Rock Creek Testicle Festival,** held annually in late Sept at the Rock Creek Lodge (22 miles east of Missoula), has been described as the "last best party in the last best place." The raucous event's highlight—outshining the dancing, cowpie tossing, and constant beer swilling—is the munching of Rocky Mountain oysters, a euphemistic label for the testicles of bulls, calves, sheep, and/or lambs. They're known by other nicknames, too, including "cowboy caviar," "calf fries," and "Montana tendergroins." Nearly 10,000 pilgrims have come to the festival to sample the butterflied, beer-marinated, breaded, and deep-fried testicles, whose flavor ranges— depending on who's eating them and on the age of the animal when neutered—from a taste described as similar to chicken, to that of liver, to that of bungee cords sauteed in cod-liver oil.

For another out-of-the-ordinary culinary experience—this one available twenty-four hours a day any day of the week—the epicurious can head for downtown Missoula to **The Oxford Saloon** and try the house specialty of brains and eggs, aka "He Needs 'Em." Sampling them once is considered a rite of passage to becoming a Missoulian; to try them more than once, well . . . maybe it means you've been in Missoula too long. The Oxford, a popular drinking and live-poker game establishment, is located at 337 North Higgins Ave. Arguably it's also the best place in Missoula to view a parade of the city's astoundingly diverse array of humanity.

Here the visitor will come to appreciate the "ups and downs" encountered by the Forest Service's elite corps of air-delivered firefighters. Murals, videos, and displays detail the seventy-year history of these men and women who risk their lives by parachuting from planes into remote wildfires. Also, guided tours are available of the parachute loft and training facilities, daily from Memorial Day through Labor Day. The center is open from 8:30 a.m. to 5 p.m. during the same dates; call 329-4934 for information on special group tours and tours during the off-season.

The prices are reasonable and the coffee strong at **The Shack** (aka **Cafe 222**), which claims—not without some justification—to serve the best breakfasts in Montana. They're so good, in fact, that you can get them for lunch or dinner, as well as at the more conventional time of day. Considering the upscale surroundings, you may wonder what the term shack has to do with anything, but until the mid-1980s the restaurant truly did occupy hovel-like quarters. The name and great food remain the same—only the place has changed. The Shack (549-9903; www.theshackcafe.com) is located downtown at 222 West Main St., Missoula.

Those who enjoy lusting over high-quality guitars should not miss visiting the **Stringed Instrument Division,** located at 500 North Higgins Ave. The

montanatrivia

enterprise sells new and vintage guitars from owner and master luthier Peter Barberio, as well as from makers such as Guild, Dobro, and Bozeman-based Gibson (along with banjoes, fiddles, and other stringed instruments). Call 549-1502 or visit www.netguitar.com to find out more about the shop, open Mon through Fri from 10 a.m. to 2 p.m. or by appointment.

The golden age of logging, the day-to-day affairs of a young Missoula, and much more are recalled at the ***Historical Museum at Fort Missoula.*** The museum features more than 25,000 objects and thirteen historical structures—including a relocated fire-lookout tower—on a thirty-two-acre parcel of grassy land adjacent to the Bitterroot River.

Fort Missoula was constructed in 1877 in response to the demands of a growing citizenry that wanted protection from Indians and other perceived frontier threats. One of the most compelling events in the fort's history occurred in 1897, when Lt. James Moss and his 25th Infantry, made up entirely of black soldiers, mounted a bicycle expedition from Fort Missoula to St. Louis, Missouri. The corps pedaled their chain-driven, single-speed bicycles for 1,900 miles over dirt tracks and muddy roads, making St. Louis in a respectable forty-five days. The army never did warm up to Moss's idea of utilizing the bicycle for large-scale troop transportation, but the 25th Infantry's feat was remarkable all the same. (Perhaps Moss is enjoying the last laugh, for today Missoula is heralded as one of the major cycling cities in America and is home to the nation's largest bicycling organization, the Adventure Cycling Association.)

To find the Historical Museum at Fort Missoula, go west on South Avenue past Reserve, then watch for the sign on your left. The museum is open daily Memorial Day weekend through Labor Day weekend, from 10 a.m. to 5 p.m. Mon through Sat and from noon to 5 p.m. on Sun. During the rest of the year, it's open Tues through Sun from noon to 5 p.m. Admission is $3 for adults, $2 for seniors, and $1 for students. For more information call 728-3476 or visit the museum's Web site, www.fortmissoulamuseum.org.

Out to Lunch is one of two exceedingly popular celebrations taking place regularly throughout the summer in downtown Missoula. The food-and-music bash runs from 11 a.m. to 2 p.m. at Caras Park, sitting alongside the Clark Fork River, every Wednesday from June through Aug.

Out to Lunch began in 1986, when crowds averaging one or two hundred ventured out for the lunchtime live tunes; now the event draws upward of 4,000 to listen to top regional bands and sample the goods of dozens of food vendors. Out to Lunch has become the midweek social event in Missoula, and its enviable success has spawned similar lunch-fests in Hamilton, Butte, Helena, and other communities.

After enjoying the tastes and tunes of Out to Lunch, saunter across the Caras Park grounds to have a look at the trotting, cantering, and bucking

On a Carousel

The Missoulian at the forefront of the creation of the marvelous **Carousel for Missoula** was Chuck Kaparich, who as a child played on the carousel at Butte's Columbia Gardens, a now-defunct amusement park that shone like a diamond in the rough copper-mining town.

It began innocently enough when, several years back, Kaparich and his wife happened across the turn-of-the-twentieth-century carousel at Riverfront Park in Spokane, Washington. Kaparich, a lifelong woodworker, was simultaneously transported back to his childhood and smitten by the beauty of the carved wooden horses. It occurred to him that an antique carousel horse might look good in the front room of his home. Soon, however, that relatively modest thought sprouted into a vision that captured the collective imagination of Missoula's citizens and rapidly blossomed into one of the most unifying movements ever to hit a Montana town. "I will deliver to you a carousel and sign it over to the city as a gift," Kaparich proclaimed to the Missoula Redevelopment Agency in the summer of 1991. "In return, I would like the city to give it a good home."

In its fine home at Caras Park, the carousel stands out as a captivating work of art, yet some of its brightest beauty is found in the dozens of stories telling of its creation. Hundreds of hands-on volunteers were involved, and thousands of others donated money to the effort. Grade-school classes held a "Pennies for Ponies" competition to see who could raise the most money. By the end of 1994, the not-for-profit A Carousel for Missoula Foundation had raised three-quarters of a million dollars.

Now, visitors can mount one of the carousel's thirty-eight ponies—each of which took volunteers under Kaparich's tutelage several hundred hours to carve—and spin around, at up to 11 miles per hour, to musical accompaniment provided by America's largest military band organ. (The foundation purchased the 400-pipe music machine for $65,000.) Leading all the horses, whose tails are fashioned from actual horsehair, is the stately, patriotically bedecked "Columbia Belle," named in honor of the Columbia Gardens in Butte, which Chuck Kaparich so enjoyed as a boy and which burned to the ground in 1973.

A Carousel for Missoula celebrates the beauty of horses and wood, the history and spirit of a city, and the difference one man can make . . . with an army of a thousand volunteers at his side.

horses that grace *A Carousel for Missoula.* The carousel operates daily from 11 a.m. to 7 p.m., Memorial Day through Labor Day, and 11 a.m. to 5:30 p.m. the rest of the year. Adjacent to the carousel is *Dragon Hollow,* a fantastic play area that was constructed in just nine days, thanks to several thousand volunteers.

montanatrivia

Marcus Daly, who made his fortune in Butte copper, established Hamilton in 1890 and built his 24,000-square-foot mansion outside of town in 1897. It boasts more than forty rooms, including twenty-four bedrooms and fifteen bathrooms.

The community's other popular gathering is the *Missoula Farmers' Market.* Boasting humble origins like Out to Lunch—it began in 1972 with only seven sellers—in thirty years the market has blossomed and fruited into a biweekly extravaganza, with more than one hundred booths and thousands of shoppers each Saturday morning. A large share of the sellers are Hmong, a Laotian mountain people, several hundred of whom settled in Missoula after the Vietnam War. Theirs are known consistently to be among the tastiest and most beautifully displayed vegetables.

Sensory overload is a real danger: You'll behold seasonal bouquets of cut flowers and colorful displays of yellow, red, green, and orange vegetables; you'll smell newly cut herbs and fresh-baked breads; and you'll hear live music and the chatter of friends meeting friends. The Saturday market runs from 8:30 a.m. to noon, and the smaller Tuesday version begins at 5:45 p.m. To find the market, go north through downtown on Higgins Street until you can't go any farther. Now, if only you can find a parking space.

At *Lolo*, a formerly small, distinct town that has burgeoned into a bedroom community of Missoula, be sure to swing in at *Travelers' Rest State Park.* Opened in 2002—just in time for the 2003–2006 National Lewis & Clark Bicentennial Commemoration—the small park is situated immediately south of the main junction in town, west off US 93 a short distance up Mormon Creek Road. Developed under a partnership involving the Travelers' Rest Preservation and Heritage Association and the Montana Department of Fish, Wildlife and Parks, Travelers' Rest State Park preserves the Native American campsite that Lewis and Clark availed themselves of and referred to as "Traveller's Rest." Here the Corps of Discovery stayed the nights of Sept 9 and 10, 1805, resting

montanatrivia

On the walls of Charlie B's, a popular watering hole in downtown Missoula, hang portraits of a cast of local characters caught on film over the span of many years by the late cowboy-turned-photographer Lee Nye.

up before their grueling journey through the Bitterroot Range. The men laid over here again for two days in early summer 1806, before splitting into two groups to explore new routes back to the Missouri–Yellowstone confluence at the Montana–North Dakota border. Today, the fifteen-acre park is an island of calm in a sea of development, making it a particularly poignant harbor of history, recalling a day when the spot was surrounded by vast wilderness. From Memorial Day through Labor Day, the park is open daily from 8 a.m.

On the Trail of Sam

The late Sam Braxton was best known in Missoula as the proprietor of a long-running family bicycle shop, where he custom-built some of the best touring bicycles made during the 1970s and '80s. Sam and his employees at the shop, where the apt slogan was "An Oasis for the Cyclotourist," were responsible for getting countless broken-down bicycle tourists back on the road and out of Missoula, a crossroads of bicycle touring activity.

Sam—a railroad man on the Northern Pacific and Burlington Northern, with the bike shop as a "sideline"—was also very active in his earlier days as a mountaineer and trail-builder. His name lives on in the *Sam Braxton National Recreation Trail,* a 3.4-mile path winding through old-growth stands of western larch and ponderosa pine in the Pattee Canyon National Recreation Area. With its rolling-to-quite-steep terrain, moderate elevation gain (from 4,100 to 4,450 feet above sea level), and beautiful shaded setting, the trail is a popular getaway for Missoula hikers, runners, and mountain bikers. If you manage to find your way there, look closely for evidence of old homesteads now largely reclaimed by nature. You can also spot a wide array of wildlife.

It's probably no exaggeration to say I logged at least 500 miles on the Sam Braxton Trail during the years I lived in Missoula in the late 1970s, the 1980s, and early '90s. However, a certain crisp, clear October morning in 1990 stands in my mind above all the other times I ran or biked the trail. On this day I was on foot, and over the course of my half-hour jog, I encountered (I'm not making this up): a great horned owl swooping low overhead, a five-point bull elk that let me get within 40 feet before bolting, a cow moose, and a full-grown black bear waddling through the pines and brush maybe 50 yards above me. I was beginning to wonder if the Forest Service had turned the southeast corner of the Pattee Canyon National Recreation Area into a zoo without announcing it. And then, out of the woods to my right, came a mule deer doe, blasting across the trail with a coyote on her tail.

The Sam Braxton Trail begins near the top of the Pattee Creek–Deer Creek divide, just 5 miles above Missoula from the junction of Southeast Higgins Avenue and Pattee Canyon Road. The trail is signed, but numerous old skid trails can lead to confusion, so it's best to acquire a Pattee Canyon brochure before heading out. Call the Missoula Ranger District at 329-3814 or visit their offices at Building 24-A, Fort Missoula.

Child's Play

The nationally renowned *Missoula Children's Theatre* owes its existence in Montana's Garden City to car problems. In the summer of 1970, Jim Caron was at loose ends in his life. While en route from Chicago to a friend's wedding in Oregon, his Volkswagen van broke down in western Montana, and the closest service station was in Missoula. While waiting there for repairs to be made, Jim ran across a poster announcing that auditions were being held for a local production of *Man of La Mancha*. For kicks, he decided to try out, and landed a part in the play. One thing led to another, and Jim ended up helping to found the Missoula Children's Theatre.

to 8 p.m.; the rest of the year it's open Mon through Fri 9 a.m. to 4 p.m. and weekends noon to 4 p.m. Nonresidents of Montana are charged a $2 entry fee. Special programs by interpreters are available by making arrangements in advance. For additional information call 273-4253 or visit the Web site, www.travelersrest.org.

Nearby, and free to visit by appointment only, is the Holt Heritage Museum, 6800 US 12 West in Lolo. On display is Bill Holt's incredible collection of celebrity cowboy boots—approximately 300 pairs, once worn by the likes of Gene Autry, Johnny Cash, Reba McEntire, Roy Rogers, Dan "Hoss" Cartwright" Blocker, Patsy Cline, President Ronald Reagan . . . the list goes on. Also exhibited is a vast array of other western artifacts. To learn more, call 273-6743 or visit www.holtheritagemuseum.com.

From the town of Lolo, go 26 miles southwest on US 12 to find **Lolo Hot Springs Resort,** where the Lewis and Clark party camped and enjoyed hot baths in a natural pool. Amenities not found when the explorers visited include a bar and restaurant, RV campground, rental cabins (they go for between $60 and $120 per night), and clean concrete pools open year-round. Call 273-2290 or visit www.lolohotsprings.com to learn more.

Lolo Hot Springs is an especially popular spot for snowmobilers, snowshoers, and cross-country skiers, who flock by the hundreds between November and April to play on the snowy trails at the **Lolo Pass Winter Sports Area.** The visitor center at the pass—a joint effort by the Clearwater National Forest and the states of Montana and Idaho—opened in 2003 to coincide with the 2003–2006 bicentennial of the Lewis & Clark expedition. In addition to serving as a warming hut for winter-sports enthusiasts, the center is a rest stop for travelers following the **Lewis and Clark National Historic Trail** through the US 12 corridor. Exhibits inside focus on the Corps of Discovery's epic journey through the Bitterroot Mountains, which was probably the most grueling leg of their entire trip from St. Louis to the Pacific Ocean. In winter you'll find Forest Service interpretive staff on hand from 9:30 a.m. to 5 p.m. (mountain time; the center sits on the Idaho side of the state line within the Pacific time zone) Fri, Sat, Sun, and Mon. Call the Powell Ranger District at (208) 942-3113 for more information on Lolo Pass, where a $5 parking permit is required in winter if you'll be staying longer than a half hour.

Early in the twentieth century, vast stands of timber in northern Idaho and northwest Montana were destroyed by a series of huge wildfires—including the infamous fire of 1910, which took more than three million acres and eighty-two lives. The year 1929 brought another particularly dry summer, and the available firefighting resources rapidly dwindled. Inadequately trained emergency crews and stock were sent out, resulting in inefficient efforts.

This gave regional forester Evan Kelley the impetus to create a centralized depot at Ninemile to serve as a training and dispatching center for mules and work crews. Wanting it to be a showplace and not just another rustic, backwoods ranger station, Kelley built the depot to resemble a well-manicured Kentucky horse farm, with Cape Cod–style buildings sporting green-shake roofs, erected by the Civilian Conservation Corps.

For the next two decades the depot served as a major hub of backcountry activities. Two factors combined to bring the center's role as a remount depot to an end: the introduction of aerial firefighting (one of the first Forest Service smokejumper centers was established near Ninemile) and the post–World War II demand for lumber to build new houses. The latter resulted in an ever-growing network of roads, making access to the backcountry easier and mules no longer vital. The remount depot closed in 1953.

In 1962 the buildings and grounds became the ***Ninemile Remount Depot and Ranger Station.*** More recently the Forest Service established the Ninemile Wildlands Training Center at Ninemile, where they conduct clinics in

Tour of Discovery

The states along the **Lewis and Clark National Historic Trail** geared up big time for the 2003–2006 bicentennial commemoration of the expedition. Montana—where the explorers traveled more than 8,000 miles and which claims dozens of related sites you can visit—is no exception. Although the bicentennial itself is now history, the lore and the many attractions remain. For information on building a vacation with the Corps of Discovery as its focus, tap into http://lewisandclark.state.mt.us. Or, you can call Travel Montana at (800) 847-4868 and request the brochure that details Lewis and Clark sites accessible by car.

Riding the Missing Rails

At the far western end of Montana's long stretch of I-90 awaits a special treat for bicycling enthusiasts: the **Route of the Hiawatha,** a rail-trail shared by Montana and Idaho that follows the route of the historic **Milwaukee Road** electrified railway through the northern Bitterroot Range. Although the trail traverses extremely steep, heavily forested mountain slopes, it manages to maintain a gentle grade through the use of numerous trestles and tunnels—most notably, the nearly 2-mile St. Paul Pass (or "Taft") Tunnel, which burrows beneath the Montana–Idaho state line.

In the early 1990s, a decade before the tunnel officially reopened for public use, I had the opportunity to bicycle through it with a pair of companions, Julie Huck from the Missoula-based Adventure Cycling Association and Andy Kulla of the Lolo National Forest. It was literally the darkest experience of my life: By the time we reached the middle of the tunnel, nearly a mile from either end, the blackness was absolute. Moreover, our feet were soaked, as we had to splash blindly through cold puddles, the result of water leaking in from above and pooling on the compacted dirt surface.

To track down the Montana trailhead of the old railway grade, considered by those in the know as perhaps the most beautiful rail-trail in all of America, take exit 5 on I-90 and head south on FR 506, aka the Rainy Creek Road. In about 2 miles you'll come to the East Portal of the St. Paul Pass Tunnel. If you prefer not to experience the somewhat claustrophobic tunnel, you can still join up with the Route of the Hiawatha in Idaho by continuing another 2 or 3 miles on FR 506. After surmounting and then descending Roland Pass, you'll arrive at the Roland Trailhead.

Although there's plenty of good riding available, the trail is still under development; eventually 31 miles will be included in Montana. The 15-mile segment currently open in Idaho includes ten tunnels and seven high steel trestles. You can get updates on the trail's status and learn about trail passes and shuttles by calling the Lookout Pass Ski Area, where bike rentals are available in summer, at (208) 744-1301 or by finding them on the Internet at www.skilookout.com/hiawatha. You can also obtain information from the Idaho Panhandle National Forest at (208) 245-4517. Among the rules and regulations: Lights and helmets are required.

packing, backcountry skills, and the use of primitive tools. Such "lost skills" are again becoming important, especially for crews working in the wilderness areas where motorized vehicles and power tools are prohibited.

The station also is home to the Forest Service mule pack train, which can be seen in parades and celebrations throughout the West (they marched in the 1991 Tournament of Roses Parade and also have appeared on the *Today* show). No one can say these irresistible critters are all show and no go, however, for they'll be found packing workers into the wilds or packing garbage out just as often as they're seen prancing in parades.

The Ninemile Remount Depot and Ranger Station is 24 miles west of Missoula, exit 82 off I-90, on Remount Road. The visitor center, open since 1989, details the intriguing history of the outpost. The center is open weekdays throughout the year, from 8 a.m. to 4:30 p.m. The entire, intriguing remount depot—classic weathervanes and all—is listed in the National Register of Historic Places. For information call the Ninemile Ranger District of the Lolo National Forest at 626-5201.

If you've run short on reading material, head to tiny Alberton, located a few miles west of the Ninemile exit along I-90. Here, in a 1910 building on Railroad Street, the **Montana Valley Bookstore** stocks some 100,000 used books for sale.

Store owner-operator Keren Wales is understandingly comfortable in the bookselling business, for she's been working in bookstores since age eight. Her father opened the Alberton store in 1978, with 30,000 volumes on the shelves, another 50,000 in storage awaiting pricing, and 15,000 en route from the "East Coast branch." (Her family also owned the Gwynedd Valley Bookstore outside Philadelphia.) Wales, who like all independent booksellers must compete with remainder bookstores, megachains, and Internet outlets, has found her special niche in stocking plenty of western novels, out-of-print and tough-to-find books, poetry—six shelves full of it—and even a few rare books.

A question regularly asked of Wales by customers is, "Do you really have 100,000 used books?" Her stock answer: "Let me know when you're done counting." (Actually, she says, today it's closer to 150,000.) The Montana Valley Bookstore opens for browsing and book-counting 365 days a year from 8 a.m. to 7 p.m. Call 722-4950 or tap into www.montanavalleybookstore.com for more information.

Ravalli County is rich in history, wildlife, scenery, and opportunities to soak in naturally heated waters. At **Stevensville,** Montana's oldest town and original capital, you can see the **St. Mary's Mission,** established by Father Pierre DeSmet in 1841, only thirty-six years after the Lewis and Clark expedition first passed through the Bitterroot Valley.

The arrival of the Jesuits, or "black robes" as the American Indians called them, marked the opening of the western frontier to white settlement. Ironically, although their arrival ultimately

montanatrivia

A human's best defense against grizzly bears—other than taking preventative measures that include making lots of loud noise when hiking in bear country—is to carry a canister of pressurized pepper spray, widely available at Montana sporting-goods stores.

Trail of the Great Beer

The *Trail of the Great Bear* is a well-promoted tourist route linking the Rocky Mountains of Montana and Alberta, Canada. With a great deal of help from the Glacier Country regional tourism commission, I discovered a route entirely within northwest Montana that I fondly refer to as the "Trail of the Great Beer."

Like many areas of the country, western Montana has experienced a boom in microbreweries. These can make a nice addition to, or even the focus of, a journey through the region; sort of like cowboy country's version of a California wine-country tour. Just be sure you have a designated driver along! The breweries differ vastly in scope, in the taste of their products, and in the names they employ to brand their brews: from the understated (Bayern Amber) to the outrageous (Moose Drool). At the more laid-back end of the microbrewing spectrum is Lang Creek Brewery, operating out of an old aircraft hangar in rural Marion—making it, according to *New Brewer Magazine,* the most remote brewery in the United States. At the other end is Bayern Brewing of Missoula, the big baby of master brewer Jürgen Knoller. Jürgen, who studied and apprenticed long and hard in his native Germany to learn to make beer the old country way, adheres to the venerable German Law of Purity of 1516. (I once heard Jürgen say this about the American custom of serving green beer on St. Patrick's Day: "Over my dead body would I allow anyone to put green dye in my beer.") As disparate as their operations are, though, all of these brewers seem to be very much alike in some basic ways: outspoken, gregarious, fiercely independent, and proud of their beers.

Here's a list of the breweries our tour group visited, along with the vital facts:

Great Northern Brewing Company
2 Central Ave.
downtown Whitefish
(406) 863-1000
www.greatnorthernbrewing.com

Lang Creek Brewery
655 Lang Creek Rd.
west of Marion
(406) 858-2200
www.langcreekbrewery.com

Big Sky Brewing Company
5417 Trumpeter Way
Missoula
(406) 549-2777
www.bigskybrew.com

Kettlehouse Brewing Co.
602 Myrtle St.
Missoula
(406) 728-1660
www.kettlehouse.com

Bayern Brewing, Inc.
1507 Montana St.
Missoula
(406) 721-1482
www.bayernbrewery.com

Bitter Root Brewing
101 Marcus St.
Hamilton
(406) 363-7468
www.bitterrootbrewing.com

signaled the undoing of many native cultural traditions, the missionaries came west at the urging of Indians. It is told that Shining Shirt, a prophet and medicine man, predicted the coming of the black robes even before Lewis and Clark arrived. Shining Shirt learned through visions that the men with long black robes would give the Indians a new strength.

In 1831 a delegation of four braves traveled to St. Louis in an attempt to persuade priests to come back west with them. The first recruiting trip was unsuccessful, as were at least two subsequent ones. Finally, a group of Indians that traveled east in 1839 and met with Father DeSmet in Council Bluffs, Iowa, convinced him to come west. Soon afterward DeSmet was guided to the Bitterroot Valley, where he supervised construction of the St. Mary's Mission and was joined by Father Anthony Ravalli.

Today at the site, located at the west end of Fourth Street, you can see the mission building, as well as Father Ravalli's log house, the cabin of Chief Victor, and an old Indian cemetery. Admission is $3 ($1 for students), and tours are conducted Tues through Sat from 10 a.m. to 4 p.m. between Apr 15 and Oct 15. Call 777-5734 or visit www.saintmarysmission.org for further information.

montanatrivia

The Bitterroot Valley is one of many namesakes of Montana's official state flower, the bitterroot. The first Anglo to collect the beautiful flower was Capt. Meriwether Lewis, which he did in 1806 in the Bitterroot Valley. Botanist Frederick Pursh later named it *Lewisia rediviva,* in honor of the explorer.

Stevensville is also your base for the **Watchable Wildlife Triangle,** which includes the Lee Metcalf National Wildlife Refuge, the **Willoughby Environmental Education Area,** and the Charles Waters Nature Trail. Designated by the USDA Forest Service and U.S. Fish and Wildlife Service, the triangle presents the opportunity to view an impressive array of animals native to numerous habitats, all inside a 30-mile drive. You'll visit streamsides, old-growth forest, sagebrush benchlands, forested bottomlands, meadows, and wetlands. For maps and additional information, call 777-5552.

The somewhat hard-to-find **Deer Crossing Bed & Breakfast** is situated on a twenty-five-acre spread of pines and pasture at 396 Hayes Creek Rd., outside the bustling community of **Hamilton**. To find it, from south of town turn west onto Camas Creek Loop, go ¾ mile, and then turn left onto Hayes Creek Road and continue until you see the inn. A pair of private rooms and two suites are available, along with two cabins, one of them a converted old bunkhouse dating to when the place was homesteaded. In the main house the Charlie Russell Suite is a favorite, with its sitting area, soaking tub, western-eclectic

montanatrivia

Mountain View Orchards, situated in the foothills of the Sapphire Range northeast of Corvallis, produces some 10,000 bushels of apples each year. About half are McIntosh, while the rest are Fuji, Red Delicious, and other varieties.

decor, and expansive cathedral ceiling. Rates begin at $100 and top out at $149, based on the room or cabin selected, on single or double occupancy, and on the time of year. Your hosts will provide a breakfast you'll long remember, served in the light-filled Sun Room. Call the Deer Crossing at 363-2232 for reservations or visit www.deercrossingmontana.com.

The ***Historic Darby Ranger Station,*** located along the highway at the north end of the Old West–flavored settlement of ***Darby*** on the way to Lost Trail Pass, focuses on the Forest Service's wildlife management practices during the Great Depression and World War II eras. The museum, housed in a station built by the Civilian Conservation Corps in the late 1930s, is open to visitors Mon through Sat from Memorial Day through Thanksgiving, 9 a.m. to 4:30 p.m. Call 821-3913 for more information.

Places to Stay in Glacier Country

TROY-LIBBY-EUREKA

Huckleberry House B&B
1004 Main St.
Libby
(406) 293-9720

Ksanka Motor Inn
Jct. US 93
and Highway 37
Eureka
(406) 297-3127
Moderate

Libby Super 8
448 US 2, West Libby
(800) 800-8000
Moderate

Swanson Lodge
1076 Swanson Lodge Rd.
Troy
(888) 305-4555
Expensive

POLSON

**Best Western
KwaTaqNuk Resort**
US 93
(800) 882-6363
Expensive

**Hawthorne House
Bed & Breakfast**
304 Third Ave. East
(800) 290-1345
Moderate

Port Polson Inn
US 93
(800) 654-0682
Moderate

NORTHERN
FLATHEAD LAKE

Bridge Street Cottages
309 Bridge St.
Bigfork
(888) 264-4974
Expensive

Marina Cay Resort
180 Vista Lane
Bigfork
(800) 433-6516
Expensive

Timbers Motel
8540 Hwy. 35 South
Bigfork
(406) 837-6200
Moderate

Woods Bay Resort
26481 E. Shore Route (SR 35)
near Bigfork
(406) 837-3333
Moderate

KALISPELL-WHITEFISH

Garden Wall Inn
504 Spokane Ave.
Whitefish
(888) 530-1700
Expensive

Good Medicine Lodge
537 Wisconsin Ave.
Whitefish
(800) 860-5488
Expensive

Grouse Mountain Lodge
2 Fairway Dr.
Whitefish
(800) 321-8822
Expensive

Kalispell Grand Hotel
100 Main St.
Kalispell
(800) 858-7422
Expensive

The Outlaw Hotel
1701 US 93, South
Kalispell
(406) 755-6100
Moderate

Red Lion Hotel
20 North Main St.
at Kalispell Center
(406) 751-5050
Expensive

Whitefish Super 8
800 Spokane Ave.
Whitefish
(800) 800-8000
Moderate

ST. MARY-EAST GLACIER

Mountain Pine Motel
P.O. Box 260
East Glacier 59434
(406) 226-4403
Moderate

Red Eagle Motel
near the east entrance to
Glacier National Park
St. Mary
(406) 732-4453
Expensive

The Resort at Glacier
St. Mary
(406) 732-4431
Expensive

SEELEY-SWAN VALLEY

Holland Lake Lodge
between Swan Lake
and Seeley Lake
1947 Holland Lake Rd.
Swan Valley
(877) 925-6343
Expensive

**The Lodges on
Seeley Lake**
Boy Scout Rd.
P.O. Box 568
Seeley Lake 59868
(800) 900-9016
Expensive

Montana Pines Motel
Highway 83 North
outside Seeley Lake
(406) 677-2778
Moderate

The Tamaracks Resort
Seeley Lake
3481 Hwy. 83 North
Seeley Lake 59868
(800) 477-7216
Expensive

MISSOULA

Creekside Inn
630 E. Broadway St.
(406) 549-2387
Moderate

**Holiday Inn Downtown at
the Park**
200 S. Pattee St.
(888) 465-4329
Expensive

Ponderosa Lodge
800 E. Broadway St.
(406) 543-3102
Moderate

BITTERROOT VALLEY

**Best Western Hamilton
Inn**
409 S. First St.
Hamilton
(800) 426-4586
Moderate

**Deer Crossing Bed
& Breakfast**
396 Hayes Creek Rd.
Hamilton
(800) 763-2232
Expensive

Super 8 Hamilton
1325 N. First St.
Hamilton
(406) 363-2940
Moderate

Hamilton Town House Inn
1113 N. First St.
Hamilton
(406) 363-6600
Moderate

Places to Eat in Glacier Country

TROY-LIBBY

4-B's
in Libby at
442 US 2 West
(406) 293-8751
Inexpensive

Libby Cafe
411 Mineral Ave.
(406) 293-3523
Inexpensive

M-K Steak House
in Libby at
9948 US 2 South
(406) 293-5686
Moderate

Red Dog Saloon & Pizza
outside Libby at
6788 Pipe Creek Rd.
(406) 293-8347
Moderate

Silver Spur
in Troy at
120 US 2 North
(406) 295-2033
Moderate

POLSON

**Best Western
KwaTaqNuk Resort**
US 93
(406) 883-3636
Expensive

4-B's
south of town at
Jct. US 93 and SR 35
(406) 883-6180
Inexpensive

Regatta Pizza
59240 US 93
(406) 883-5459
Moderate

NORTHERN FLATHEAD LAKE

Bigfork Inn
604 Electric Ave.
Bigfork
(406) 837-6680
Expensive

Ciao Mambo
234 E. Second St.
Whitefish
(406) 863-9600
Moderate

Garden Bar & Grill
451 Electric Ave.
Bigfork
(406) 837-9914
Inexpensive

Showthyme (gourmet)
downtown Bigfork
(406) 837-0707
Expensive

Swan River Inn
360 Grand Ave.
Bigfork
(406) 837-2328
Expensive

KALISPELL/WHITEFISH

Buffalo Cafe
514 Third St. East
Whitefish
(406) 862-2833
Moderate

Cafe Kandahar
located above town at
the Whitefish Mountain
Resort
Whitefish
(406) 862-6247
Expensive

Cafe Max
121 Main St.
Kalispell
(406) 755-7687
Moderate

Hellroaring Saloon
(Mexican)
located in the Chalet
at the Whitefish Mountain
Resort
Whitefish
(406) 862-6364
Moderate

Tupelo Grille (Cajun)
17 Central Ave.
Whitefish
(406) 862-6136
Moderate

**Whitefish Lake Golf Club
Restaurant** (fine dining)
at the Whitefish Lake
Golf Course on US 93
North
(406) 862-5285
Expensive

ST. MARY-EAST GLACIER

**Great Northern Dining
Room**
Glacier Park Lodge
in East Glacier
(406) 892-2525
Expensive

Park Café
3147 US 89
St. Mary
(406) 732-4482
Moderate

SEELEY-SWAN VALLEY

Elkhorn Cafe
1 mile north of Seeley Lake
(406) 677-2181
Inexpensive

The Filling Station
Seeley Lake
(406) 677-2080
Inexpensive

**Lindey's Prime
Steak House**
Seeley Lake
(406) 677-9229
Expensive

MISSOULA

Bagels on Broadway
223 W. Broadway St.
(406) 728-8900
Inexpensive

The Bridge Bistro
600 S. Higgins Ave.
(406) 542-0002
Expensive

Hob Nob Cafe
531 S. Higgins Ave.
(406) 541-4622
Moderate

Iron Horse Brew Pub
501 N. Higgins Ave.
(406) 728-8866
Moderate

The Keep Restaurant
(fine dining)
102 Ben Hogan Dr.
(406) 728-5132
Expensive

**MacKenzie River
Pizza Co.**
137 W. Front St.
(406) 721-0077
Moderate

The Shack
222 W. Main St.
(406) 549-9903
Moderate

BITTERROOT VALLEY

Bitter Root Brewery
101 Marcus St.
Hamilton
(406) 363-7468
Moderate

Cantina la Cocina
US 93
Victor
(406) 642-3192
Moderate

**The Hamilton
A Public House**
104 Main St.
Victor
(406) 642-6644
Moderate

Skalkaho Steak House
Mile Marker 7, Skalkaho
Highway
Hamilton
(406) 363-3522
Moderate

GOLD WEST COUNTRY →

Perhaps more than any other region of the state, Gold West Country embodies the Montana of the imagination, reflecting the image of Big Sky Country held by thousands of folks who have visited or have yet to visit. It is a broad expanse of majestic mountains, basins filled with haystacks and Herefords, crumbling old mining camps, and big, blue sky. As you travel through some areas—such as the remote country penetrated by the Big Sheep Creek Back Country Byway—you may be convinced that you've been transported back in time fifty or a hundred years.

From Lost Trail Pass the narrative leads you past the Big Hole Battlefield National Monument, a major regional attraction, then through a string of one-horse cow towns including Wisdom, Wise River, and Jackson. From the Big Hole Valley, it is on to the ghost town of Bannack, then to the very-much-alive town of Dillon. After following a dirt road through the Red Rock Lakes National Wildlife Refuge, you'll travel through a small corner of Idaho and back into Montana via the Madison River Valley. From Ennis it's on to Virginia City, from which point Highways 287, 41, and 69 wind north to Boulder, where a left turn onto I-15 leads to Butte. From Butte a loop around I-90 and Highway 1 will take you through Anaconda,

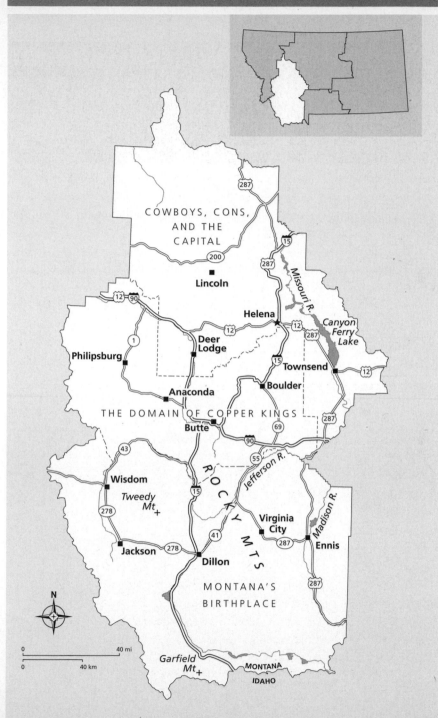

COWBOYS, CONS,
AND THE
CAPITAL

Lincoln

Helena

Philipsburg

Deer
Lodge

Anaconda

Townsend

Boulder

THE DOMAIN OF COPPER KINGS

Butte

Wisdom

Tweedy
Mt

R O C K Y   M T S

Virginia
City

Jefferson R.

Madison R.

Ennis

Jackson

Dillon

MONTANA'S
BIRTHPLACE

Garfield
Mt

MONTANA

IDAHO

Missouri R.

Canyon
Ferry
Lake

N

0   40 mi
0   40 km

Philipsburg, Drummond, and Deer Lodge. Finally, there's historic Helena and several smaller towns lying to the north and west of the capital city.

Montana's Birthplace

The *Continental Divide* serves as the western and northern boundaries for the vast sweep of meadow and mountain country known as *Beaverhead County.* It's obvious that a lot of people have tried to make a living here at one time or another, for in Beaverhead County (and all of southwest Montana) ghost towns are abundant. This is where the 1860s gold rush started, first as a trickle, then as a flood. The rigorous weather and rough terrain have precluded dense settlement, however, and Beaverhead remains among the most sparsely populated counties in the state.

If you've come to enjoy the winter wonders of southwest Montana, consider contacting the Beaverhead National Forest to inquire about overnighting at rustic *Hogan Cabin.* Skiers reach the 1920s-era cabin via one of two trails, while snowmobilers follow a separate route. The cabin sleeps four in relative comfort and comes equipped with firewood and a stove, beds, and cooking utensils. Campers haul in their own sleeping bags and food.

AUTHOR'S FAVORITES

Bannack State Park
Bannack
(406) 834-3413

Big Sheep Creek Back Country Byway
Dell
(406) 494-5059

The Bungalow
Wolf Creek
(406) 235-4276

Jackson Hot Springs
Jackson
(406) 834-3151

Lost Creek State Park
Anaconda
(406) 542-5500

Montana's Museum
Helena
(406) 444-2694

Old Works Golf Course
Anaconda
(406) 563-5989

Red Rock Lakes National Wildlife Refuge
Lakeview
(406) 276-3536

World Museum of Mining and Hell Roarin' Gulch
Butte
(406) 723-7211

Yesterday's Calf-A
Dell
(406) 276-3308

Taking the High Road

The *Pioneer Mountains National Scenic Byway,* paved for most of its 46 miles, runs between the east and west sub-ranges of the Pioneer Mountains. The byway begins at an elevation of 5,600 feet above sea level at Wise River and climbs to 7,782 feet before dropping again into the valley of Grasshopper Creek.

As you will see, the two components of the Pioneers appear dramatically different from one another. Some seventy million years ago, the western mountains subsided about ½ mile in relation to the eastern range, along the fault running through the valley separating them. The higher and more rugged East Pioneers have therefore endured far more erosion, exposing the underlying granites. By comparison, the West Pioneers are rolling, subdued mountains, blanketed in dark timber.

Much of the terrain penetrated by the byway, although surrounded by the imposing Pioneers, is surprisingly flat. In Harrison and Moose Parks you'll see thousands of rocks and boulders littering the ground, ranging in size from tiny to huge. The rocks, called glacial erratics, are composed of the same rock as the high East Pioneer Mountains. The erratics broke off thousands of years ago and were transported to the open meadows by glaciers and mudflows.

Hogan Cabin ($25 a night) is available by reservation only between Dec 1 and Mar 31. During the summer it becomes a working Forest Service outpost, but the drive up Trail Creek Road to the cabin still comes highly recommended for the sensational display of wildflowers that often fills the surrounding Trail Creek Meadows. Call the Wisdom Ranger District at (406) 689-3243 for information.

Continue east into the Big Hole River Valley, also known as "the land of 10,000 haystacks." The basin's rich soil is ideal for growing high-quality hay, which Montana ranchers often export in large quantities to other regions of the country. Throughout the Big Hole you'll see numerous "beaver slide" haystackers standing about the valley like so many tilted monuments. First developed in the Big Hole, and patented in 1910 as the Sunny Slope Slide Hay Stacker, this clever contraption allowed ranchers to stack hay much higher than previously was possible, utilizing horses to run the belts that hauled hay to the top of the inclined slide before depositing it on the stack. Many beaver slides are still in use, although in most cases motors have replaced horse power.

In the town of ***Wisdom,*** it's hard to miss ***Conover's Trading Post*** (689-3272). Country music typically blares into the streets from loudspeakers mounted on the garishly painted building, which features a likeness of an Indian maiden reclining above the entrance. What all you'll find available for sale inside is anybody's guess. (If your sense of humor leans toward the weird, don't miss having a peek at the "rearwolf" taxidermy mount.)

From Wisdom continue following Highway 43 and the Big Hole River. In 39 miles you'll arrive at the blink-and-miss-it town of *Wise River.* Here you'll find the northern terminus of the *Pioneer Mountains National Scenic Byway,* which wends its way south through the grand backcountry separating the East and West Pioneer Mountains. The ribbon of blacktop skirts a selection of exceptionally pleasant Forest Service campgrounds with names like *Lodgepole Campground, Willow Campground,* and *Little Joe Campground.* Any one of these comes highly recommended if you're outfitted for camping.

Approximately 29 miles from Wise River, the Pioneer Mountains National Scenic Byway passes *Crystal Park,* where the Butte Mineral & Gem Club maintains mining claims. In partnership with the Forest Service, the club keeps the claims open to the public, which is permitted to dig crystals, using hand tools only. A first-rate picnic area featuring hard-surfaced sites, picnic tables, and fire grates sits adjacent to the digging grounds. For a map of the area and a list of rules and regulations, call the Beaverhead–Deerlodge National Forest at 683-3900.

Just south of Crystal Park, the road goes steeply downhill for 4 miles; at the bottom, you'll encounter the first of two nearby, natural hot-water fun spots, *Elkhorn Hot Springs.* The *Anaconda Standard* in 1921 reported, "It is possible that within the next two years Montana will have another national park, to be known as the Elkhorn national park...which will contain scenery second to none of the national parks now in existence."

The prediction proved overzealous. Still, though the accommodations found at the resort range from rather rustic to extremely rustic, Elkhorn does occupy a beautiful spot. At its timbered setting in the Grasshopper Valley, you can soak in a pair of outdoor hot pools or a cedar-lined indoor wet sauna, and order a meal in the lresort's restaurant. The pools and restaurant, open seven days a week all year, are particularly inviting after a day of downhill skiing

MAJOR ATTRACTIONS WORTH SEEING

Big Hole National Battlefield
Wisdom

Grant-Kohrs Ranch National Historic Site
Deer Lodge

Lewis and Clark Caverns State Park
between Cardwell and Three Forks

Virginia City

at nearby Maverick Mountain. The resort also rents snowmobiles and cross-country ski gear in the winter. The B&B-style rooms in the lodge start at $40 per night, while the ten rustic cabins start at $60 for two people. Call 834-3434 or visit www.elkhornhotsprings.com for information and reservations.

Turn right (west) on reaching Highway 278, and in 15 miles you'll arrive at the town of Jackson, home to *Jackson Hot Springs.* The resort made the national news in the wake of the August 1992 Hurricane Andrew, when the proprietors rounded up volunteers to help fill thousands of gallon jugs with the pure water bubbling from the ground here. The drinking water then was shipped on trucks to Florida to aid in recovery efforts.

The area's other hot-water spot, Jackson Hot Springs Lodge, sports a large bar and an oak dance floor of gymnasium proportions. The full-service restaurant with moderately priced meals and the outdoor, 30-foot-by-75-foot hot pool round out the scene. Year-round you can overnight in lodge rooms or cabins, which go for between $32 and $85 a night. It costs $5 just to use the pool at the resort, which also features an RV park and tent sites. For more information call 834-3151 or go to www.jacksonhotsprings.com/jackacc.htm.

On July 28, 1862, John White and a group of fellow Coloradans discovered placer-gold deposits in the waters of Grasshopper Creek. The "White's Bar" discovery was the first recorded mining claim in the region, and it triggered a gold rush. People flocked to the area in droves, and the town of *Bannack,* today a well-preserved ghost town, sprang up almost overnight.

Within a year, some 3,000 persons lived in Bannack. Most were prospectors, but arriving also were the tradespeople who inevitably followed to offer those who struck it rich somewhere to spend their money. Saloons, bakeries, doctors' offices, a brewery, barbershops, general stores, blacksmith shops, a bowling alley, and more quickly graced the streets of the burgeoning town.

The population boom was short-lived, though, and within two years most had moved on to "golder" pastures, at Virginia City and elsewhere along Alder Gulch. But a stable population of miners and service providers remained, and Bannack began to mature. When in 1864 the Montana Territory was split and created from the year-old Idaho Territory, Abraham Lincoln appointed Sidney Edgerton as governor. He, in turn, named Bannack the capital, and the first Territorial Legislature convened here on December 12, 1864.

Bannack's reign as capital also was short-lived: Along with the hundreds of prospectors, the territorial capital moved to Virginia City in 1865. But the town endured until the 1940s, by which time most mine-milling activity had ceased, and Bannack was virtually deserted.

More than fifty structures remain at Bannack, many in excellent condition, and the fascinating walking tour of the town can easily steal half a day. Among

The Plummer Gang

The life of one Henry Plummer shed some notoriety on Bannack in the early 1860s. The territorial court determined that Bannack and Virginia City, 70 miles apart, needed only one sheriff, and Plummer managed to get himself elected to the post. During his eight-month tenure—the purpose of which allegedly was to protect the public—Plummer and his gang of road agents terrorized those traveling the road connecting the two settlements. It's estimated that they killed no fewer than 102 individuals, while relieving countless others of their heavy burdens of gold.

Late in 1863 frontier justice prevailed when the Vigilantes Committee formed; they hanged or banished all known members of Plummer's crew. Plummer was hanged early in 1864 from the gallows he himself had erected only a year earlier. Today a replica of the gallows stands above Bannack at the approximate site of the hanging.

the highlights are the Graves House, built in the mid-1860s as the first frame house in the Montana Territory; the Masonic Temple, the first floor of which served for years as the Bannack school; and the Meade Hotel, originally the Beaverhead County courthouse.

Bannack Days, held during the third weekend in July, celebrates the past with buffalo barbecues, horse-and-buggy rides, a muzzle-loader shooting competition, old-time crafts and music, a "Henry Plummer hanging," and more. *Bannack State Park,* located 4 miles south off SR 278 from midway between Jackson and Dillon, is open year-round, except for Dec 24 and 25. Winter hours are 8 a.m. to 5 p.m. Summer hours (May to early Oct) for the grounds are 8 a.m. to 9 p.m. The visitor center is open seven days a week during the summer months from 10 a.m. to 6 p.m. For more information on the ghost town, Bannack Days, and the state park campground, call 834-3413 or visit www.bannack.org.

In the county seat of *Dillon,* enjoy the historic walk through town and visit the *Beaverhead County Museum,* since 1947 one of Montana's finest small-town museums. Housed in a historic log building downtown on Montana Street, among its many displays are Indian artifacts and exhibits on the area's natural history and rich record of mining and ranching. Recently added to the complex are the renovated 1909 brick depot of the Utah and Northern Railroad (now the Union Pacific) and a pioneer's log cabin. Additional gems include the likes of Beaverhead County's first flush-toilet outhouse. Year-round the museum is open Mon through Fri from 8 a.m. to 5 p.m., and in summer only on Sat from 9 a.m. to 5 p.m. Admission is free, but as at nearly any small-town museum, donations are gladly accepted. Call 683-5027 for more information.

You might be surprised also to find in Dillon the **Patagonia Outlet** store. Lovers of the rugged outdoor apparel make the pilgrimage here from all over western Montana and beyond to find deals on their favorite clothes. The outlet is located at 34 North Idaho St., and the phone number is 683-2580. Hours are Mon through Sat 10 a.m. to 6 p.m. and Sun 11 a.m. to 5 p.m.; it's closed only on Thanksgiving, Christmas, New Year's Day, and Easter Sunday. (Hint: On special weekends, such as those around Labor Day, President's Day, and Memorial Day, the outlet runs blow-out sales.)

Words can't do justice to **Yesterday's Calf-A,** located in **Dell**, just off I-15 at exit 23. Stop in for some home cookin' and you'll see for yourself why it's one of Montana's most unusual eateries . . . and why people come from literally hundreds of miles away to sample the homemade pies.

The old school Calf-A is housed in *was* a school from 1903 until 1963, with an average enrollment of twenty kids, and then opened as a restaurant in 1978. Its walls, shelves, and bare pine floor are blanketed with memorabilia: fur-bearing trout, piles of old *Life* magazines, vintage rifles, an old piano with yellowed sheet music, rocks and fossils, a bedpan banjo, well-worn school desks, pull-down maps, spurs, kerosene lanterns, a ceramic water cooler, and a whole lot more.

The past flows through the entryway and spills into the yard, where you'll find a veritable museum of life on the western frontier. It's worth stopping to browse around the grounds even if the restaurant is closed (which is unlikely). Crosscut saws, farm equipment, elk antlers, wagon wheels, bison skulls, windmills, and dozens of other items are scattered about.

The cowboy coffee-pot is always on at Calf-A, where you'll sit on press-back chairs at a large oak table and, likely as not, join a local stock grower and his family or an over-the-road trucker as you dine. The restaurant opens daily at 7 a.m. year-round for breakfast, lunch, and dinner. Prices are inexpensive to moderate. Call 276-3308 if you need to know more.

montanatrivia

An individual sagebrush plant, a species ubiquitous in Montana, can live as long as 200 years.

If you're a fan of truly wide-open spaces, consider tackling the rough-and-tumble **Big Sheep Creek Back Country Byway.** Beginning near **Dell,** the rugged road is one of several Back Country Byways designated throughout the West by the Bureau of Land Management. These tend to be unpaved and rougher than the Forest Service–designated National Scenic Byways also common throughout the West (such as the Pioneer Mountains National Scenic Byway described earlier). To find the road, from Dell pass under I-15 and take the first left. For information on road conditions, which can change daily, call the Butte District Office of the Bureau of Land Management at 494-5059.

The near ghost town of **Monida** sits beside I-15 at exit 0, immediately north of the **Continental Divide** and the state of Idaho. (Mon-Ida—get it?) Although never a metropolis by anyone's measure, the town did boast 125 residents in the mid-1920s, when it served as one of the most active stock-shipping railheads in the state. The railroad has long since pulled out, the U.S. Post Office closed shop in 1970, and the last business in Monida was boarded up more than a decade ago. Only a handful of residents remain.

During its heyday the town also served another several hundred people who ranched in the Centennial Valley to the east. Today, the starkly beautiful valley is almost deserted; old-timers will tell you that's because of the **Red Rock Lakes National Wildlife Refuge,** which removed some of the most

Big Sheep Creek

The **Big Sheep Creek Back Country Byway** loops through a sweep of some of the emptiest country in the West. This area is not only way off the beaten path, much of it is devoid of paths altogether. It makes a great day (or longer) trip if your vehicle and spirit of adventure are up to the challenge.

The byway leaves I-15 at **Dell,** rejoining pavement 60 miles to the northwest, where a turn east leads back to I-15. Or, by turning left rather than right at the junction with pavement, you can follow paved, gravel, and rough dirt roads up and over 7,373-foot Lemhi Pass, where the Lewis and Clark expedition first crested the Continental Divide.

Anglers in particular will find the bubbling waters of Big Sheep Creek inviting, while history buffs will relish tracing portions of the 1860s wagon supply road that joined the Bannack mining camp with the Union Pacific railhead in Corinne, Utah. Prong-horns, mule deer, and eagles are common to the environs, and bighorn sheep can often be spotted at dusk in the tight portions of the Big Sheep Creek canyon. Unde-veloped camping sites abound, particularly along the first 20 miles of the route. After leaving the relatively narrow canyon of Big Sheep Creek, the road shoots through a broad swath of open country bordered on the west by the barren Beaverhead Moun-tains, whose ridgeline forms the Continental Divide and the Montana-Idaho state line. In some locations you'll drive through grassy meadows where, if you listen carefully, you may be treated to the delightful melody of a western meadowlark or two.

You'll find the Big Sheep Creek Back Country Byway to be rough and muddy in places—possibly even impassable—so a high-clearance vehicle is advised. Also be sure you're equipped with a spare tire and tire-changing tools, a full tank of gas, a good map, and an adequate supply of food and water.

Quiet by Nature

Awakening at Upper Lake Campground in *Red Rock Lakes National Wildlife Refuge* in mid-June, we found, is a bit like greeting the day on Montana's version of a Tarzan movie set, considering all the noise the local critters make.

It started when it was still dark and starry with the resonant hoot of a great gray owl and two choruses of coyotes yipping, yammering, and squealing back and forth. From our tent it sounded like a demonstration of stereo speakers: One bunch of coyotes was over there to the west; the other was clearly off in another direction, somewhere to the southeast in the foothills of the Centennial Range.

With the first hint of light in the eastern sky, the Canada geese began honking, followed by the deeper and louder honking of trumpeter swans. Then ducks—hundreds of them, maybe thousands—began chiming in with their variously timbred quacking. Finally, dozens of songbirds added their melodic two cents to the mix. It all coalesced into a cacophony that was terribly dissonant if we tried to separate the sounds but marvelously musical if we just took it in as a whole. I've never heard anything quite like it anywhere else.

Upper Lake Campground, on the shore of shallow Upper Red Rock Lake, is a primitive campground with few services other than a pair of outhouses, several tent sites, and a spring delivering cold, tasty water. Canoeing (after July 15 on Upper Lake and after mid-September on the lower lake), mountain biking, hiking, and wildlife-viewing opportunities are all right at hand, and the sunrises and sunsets are out of this world.

productive land in the area from use by ranchers when it was established in 1935.

At the refuge, the shallow waters of Upper and Lower Red Rock Lakes and Swan Lake and adjacent marshlands provide a home for a proliferation of birds and wildlife. The preserve is nestled between the spectacular Centennial Mountains on the south and the also-impressive Gravelly Range to the north.

The 40,000-acre refuge was created primarily to provide sanctuary for the trumpeter swan, which in the 1930s was in danger of extinction. The bird's population had dwindled to fewer than 100 in the tristate area by the end of the Great Depression, while only a few other remnant populations remained in Canada and Alaska. Happily, today in the Greater Yellowstone Ecosystem there are nearly 500 resident swans, and the influx of migratory birds from the north brings the number to several thousand in winter.

The refuge received additional protection in 1976, when three-quarters of it was designated a federal wilderness area, meaning that motorboats and other mechanized equipment are prohibited. Also, through the acquisition of private properties, the refuge has grown substantially larger since being created.

Moose are year-round residents, and deer, elk, and pronghorn are common in the snowless months. The bird life rivals that of nearly any place in the Rocky Mountain region: No fewer than 258 species can be seen at one time of the year or another, including bald eagles, avocets, long-billed curlews, great blue herons, sandhill cranes, white pelicans, tundra swans, and twenty-three species of ducks and geese. Migratory birds by the thousands appear during the spring and fall.

The impressive, snow-white trumpeters, which visitors are urged to view from no closer than 400 yards, are immense birds, measuring up to 4 feet from beak to toe and 8 feet from wing tip to wing tip, and weighing as much as thirty pounds. And they're hungry big birds with phenomenal metabolisms: It's common for an adult to eat up to twenty pounds of wet herbage in a day's time.

To experience this isolated piece of country occupying the extreme southwest corner of the state is well worth the trouble of getting there. The outpost of *Lakeview*—population ten—stands sentinel over the wetlands, and the refuge headquarters are found there. Lakeview is midway along the 60-mile gravel road connecting I-15 at Monida and Highway 87 west of West Yellowstone. The road is generally not passable by automobile until mid-May and is usually snowed in again by early Nov. For more information on Red Rock Lakes National Wildlife Refuge, call 276-3536 or go to www.fws.gov/redrocks.

TOP ANNUAL EVENTS

Race to the Sky Sled Dog Race
Helena and points beyond
mid-Feb
(406) 881-3647

St. Patrick's Day Festival
Butte; Mar 17
(406) 782-0742

Governor's Cup Road Runs
Helena; early June
(800) 447-7828

Gold Rush Fever Day
Virginia City; mid-June
(406) 843-5555

The National Folk Festival
Butte; early July
(406) 497-6464

Bannack Days
Bannack State Park; late July
(406) 834-3413

Madison County Fair and Rodeo
Twin Bridges; mid-Aug
(406) 684-5824

Dillon Jaycee Rodeo
Dillon; Labor Day weekend
(406) 577-1683

Madison Fly Fishing Festival
Ennis; early Sept
(406) 682-3148

Bald Eagle Migration
Helena; mid-Nov through
mid-Dec
(406) 475-3128

If you succumb to the Centennial Valley's charms as you breeze through and find that you'd like to return to share the special spot with your family and/or friends, you can do so in great comfort by renting *The Old Anderson Place* for a week or longer. The graciously renovated, century-old log homestead structure features three bedrooms and two full bathrooms, large living and dining areas, and a fully equipped kitchen and laundry. It accommodates up to six people. And there's a second restored home—the Smith House—also available to rent on the ranch, which sprawls across 10,000 acres adjacent to the Red Rock Lakes Wildlife Refuge. Rates vary by the season and start at $2,295 per week—a week full of privacy and bird- and wildlife-viewing opportunities like you may have never experienced. For additional details contact Montana Vacation Rentals in Bozeman at (800) 550-4589 or www.mountain-home.com.

From Red Rock Lakes, continue east on gravel over Red Rock Pass to Highway 87, where you'll want to turn north. In 12 miles, turn east onto US 287, and soon you'll arrive at the *Madison Canyon Earthquake Area.* Displays at the visitor center explain the geologic and

montanatrivia

Montana's eight species of lagomorphs include the pika, blacktailed jackrabbit, white-tailed jackrabbit, eastern cottontail, desert cottontail, mountain cottontail, pygmy rabbit, and snowshoe hare.

human stories of the fateful night of August 17, 1959, when at 11:37 p.m. a 7.5-magnitude earthquake rocked the area, causing a large portion of a mountain to slide. Twenty-eight of the 250 campers in the canyon below were killed, and the Madison River was dammed by rocks and debris (enough to fill the Rose Bowl ten times), forming *Earthquake Lake.*

Dead, skeletal trees rise above the lake's surface, and the gash on the mountainside and the rocks and rubble scattering the countryside below remain as testimony to the violence of the recent geologic past. The Madison Canyon Earthquake Area visitor center opens daily 8:30 a.m. to 6 p.m. Memorial Day through late Sept. For more information call 823-6961.

You'll know the minute you pull into *Ennis,* 42 miles north of the earthquake center, that it's a sporting town. In autumn huge elk racks, still attached to their recently deceased owners, sprout from pickup truck beds. In winter snowmobiles parked along Main Street await their owners, who are in drinking coffee to wake up and warm up. And in summer drift boats and rafts on trailers line the street, and storefronts connected by a boardwalk advertise fly-fishing gear, guided trips, and anglers' specials.

An unexpected find here is *The Continental Divide* gourmet dinner restaurant, established almost thirty years ago by chef Jay Bentley, who was first drawn to the area because of its world-class fly-fishing opportunities. The menu is described as "nouvelle eclectic," and any given dish might never be prepared twice in exactly the same way. The Continental Divide's Cajun-style seafood and 2-inch-thick marinated steaks are celebrated far and wide, but you're just as apt to find Thai or Vietnamese dishes on the menu. The restaurant, located at the east end of Main Street, usually opens around Mother's Day in May and closes in late Oct. For more information and requisite reservations, call 682-7600.

Tasty wildlife tidbits, which some refined diners may consider more gruesome than gourmet, can be sampled at the annual *Ennis Hunters Feed and Wild Game Cook-Off* in late Oct. The event, a kickoff to the hunting season, fills the crisp autumn air in Ennis with the aroma of simmering, frying, and baking bear, moose, cougar, pronghorn, elk, deer, and even rattlesnake. It happens along Main Street, where locals compete for prizes by fixing their favorite dishes containing wild ingredients. You can learn more by calling 682-4388.

The *Ennis National Fish Hatchery,* located in the Madison River Valley since 1933, rears milliions of rainbow trout eggs and some 350,000 fingerling rainbow trout in an average year in the consistently cold waters of Blaine Springs. One of eighty hatcheries in America operated by the U.S. Fish and Wildlife Service, this one is found 12 miles southwest of Ennis at the foot of the sensational Gravelly Range, making the drive worth the trip even if no trout waited at the end of the line.

But they do. Humans—through logging, mining, drawing down water for agricultural use, and too much sportfishing—have radically altered the fish habitat in Montana's waters. It's the job of the Ennis facility to stock trout where they're needed in many parts of the state, in order to bring the numbers closer to what might have existed had people not intervened. The manipulations that workers perform to bring the male and female trout together and to raise adults from eggs to fry to fish make a fascinating study.

Most trout leave for waters beyond when they're 5 to 8 inches long, via insulated tank trucks holding up to a ton of wiggling fish. But each year the hatchery also releases a number of 24-inch-plus lunkers that have played out their roles as breeding machines.

From Ennis go 2 miles west on Highway 287 toward *Virginia City,* and then turn south onto the Gravelly Range Road/Varney Road. Eight miles after leaving SR 287, bear right at the fork, following the sign to the hatchery, which is open 7:30 a.m. to 5 p.m. seven days a week. For more information call 682-4847 or visit www.fws.gov/ennis.

Perhaps your visit to the hatchery has you hankering to wet a line in wild waters and catch a wily trout. Back at the earlier-mentioned fork, turn to the east and you'll arrive at the door of the **9T9 Ranch Bed and Breakfast,** a small inn just a short stroll away from the Madison River. The guest floor of the 9T9 ranch house features a private living room (with TV, stereo, and telephone), two bedrooms that share a bath, and one bedroom with a private bath. Hosting a small number of guests at a time allows owner Judy Herrick to furnish each one with a personal dose of western hospitality, which is how she wants it.

Breakfast, served as early or late as you like, is a hearty affair that'll keep you going on the river for most of the day. You can fish the Madison, one of the world's premier blue-ribbon streams, for trophy rainbow and brown trout, wading the waters or using a boat or raft available from the 9T9. Overnights range from $75 to $125. For reservations or information (including details on the guide service), call the 9T9 Ranch at 682-7659, or visit www.9t9ranch.com.

As you travel north from **Virginia City,** pull into the wide spot in the road known as **Laurin** (pronounced *la-ray)* and have a look at the resplendent **St. Mary of the Assumption Catholic Church.** The sturdy chapel, built of locally quarried cut stone, is listed in the National Register of Historic Places. In concert with its bucolic surroundings, the church lends the small town an air of peace and dignity.

Contrast the tranquility at Laurin with what **Robber's Roost,** a few miles north, *might* have been like in an earlier day. Peter Daly built the important stage stop sometime in the 1860s, and according to some it was here that Henry Plummer's gang of road agents plotted their attacks on gold-bearing travelers. Others dispute this, claiming that the building wasn't constructed until 1867, three years after Plummer and his friends had met their maker. Regardless of who did or did not spend time in it, the two-story, square-hewn log building remains a picturesque and uncommon example of frontier architecture.

Avid anglers will want to swing into the **R. L. Winston Rod Company** in **Twin Bridges**, where the Rolls-Royce of fly-fishing rods is fashioned. The company started in 1929 in San Francisco and quickly became known for its tournament-winning bamboo rods. It moved to Montana in 1976, by which time fiberglass was the material used in making most rods. Today a boron-graphite composite is the substance of choice for Winston's state-of-the-art trout and saltwater rods, although they still produce bamboo rods for the traditionalist.

If you're thinking of shopping here, be sure your credit card's slate is fairly clean, for Winston's handcrafted rods begin at around $545 and go higher than $3,000 for the best bamboo models. Their newish facility, located at 500 S. Main St., is open between 8 a.m. and 4:30 p.m. weekdays, with tours beginning at 11 a.m. Call 684-5674 for more information. For a preview of their wares, visit their Web site at www.winstonrods.com.

The community of *Pony,* which almost became a ghost town, is perched on the inclined flank of the Tobacco Root Mountains. So steep is the approach to Pony, and so tight the little nook it occupies, that one resident penned this little ditty about the Northern Pacific branch line leading to it:

Pony, Pony the beautiful little town,
where the train backed in 'cause it couldn't turn around.

The town is the namesake of Tecumseh "Pony" Smith, who filed the first placer claim here in 1868. Within a few years, the placer technique had yielded to more serious mining methods, and at least four steam- or water-driven stamp mills were pounding gold from ore in the hills surrounding Pony. Several impressive buildings remain, including the two-story brick Morris bank building and the splendid community church, revealing the fact that this was no mere overnight camp. You can also locate the decaying remnants of the Morris & Ellings Gold Stamp Mill. Several late-Victorian houses are still used as residences, and new houses are popping up, as well. Pony is simply too pretty to quit. The town is located up a paved road, 6 miles west of Harrison, which is 15 miles southeast of I-90 from Cardwell.

In *Norris*, 10 miles south of Harrison on US 287, check out the *Old Norris Schoolhouse Cafe,* specializing in south-of-the-border fare. Last used as a school in 1960 (and first used in 1917), the brick restaurant features down-home—some might call it redneck—humor hanging on the walls. That aside, you'll be served surprisingly good Mexican food, ribs, or buffalo burgers as you relax at a slat-barrel table. The cafe, located at 6511 Hwy. 287, is open noon to 8 p.m. Wed through Sun (closed Jan and Feb). Call 685-3200 for more information.

montanatrivia

Montana's beavers and river otters give birth in April, the beavers safe in their lodges, and the otters secure in dens they've excavated into river and stream banks.

After filling up on educational food, head ¼ mile up Highway 84 to the *Norris Hot Springs,* a good spot for a soothing soak (at $5 per adult or $3 for kids under 12) in what the proprietors claim to be the "water of the gods." The low-key resort, which also includes a campground and small store, is open year-round (closed on Mon and Tues), with hours that change seasonally. Call 685-3303 or visit www.norrishotsprings .com for more information. (Although the author hasn't verified the claim, a

Norris local told him that imbibing soaker-campers definitely should sample a beer in the on-site No Loose Dogs Saloon.)

The Domain of Copper Kings

You might say "Weed control grew out of control" at the ***Tizer Botanic Gardens*** (866-933-8789) outside ***Jefferson City*** (between Boulder and Helena). It all began in 1998 as an effort by landowners Belva Lotzer and Dick Krott to control their problem with obnoxious weeds. However, what started out as a fairly modest garden containing flowers such as cosmos and poppies has bloomed into a botanic bonanza encompassing thousands of flowering plants, a greenhouse and garden shop, and themed gardens connected by footpaths. There's the spectacular Rose Garden, for example, and the Children's Garden, over which a half dozen blooming "upside-down trees" stand sentinel. The colorful spot has also evolved into a popular venue for weddings and other celebrations. It's open to visitors daily Apr through Sept from 10 a.m. to 6 p.m.; general admission is $4. The owner-proprietors maintain a Web site at www .tizergardens.com.

Where Hope Shines On

The proprietors of the *Free Enterprise Radon Health Mine,* 2 miles west of Boulder, boast of their unmedical approach to health. One component of this approach: America's only "ionizing inhalatorium," where those suffering from arthritis, asthma, allergies, lupus, and a dozen other ailments inhale concentrated radon gases purported to possess healing properties. Here Montana's first commercial uranium mine opened for business in 1949 under the supervision of Wade V. Lewis Jr., president of the Elkhorn Mining Company. In the ensuing years, thousands of pilgrims have traveled to Boulder to go underground in old mines to relax and breathe radon gas. The ionizing radiation, some say, is more effective than prescription drugs, and testimonials of miracle cures abound. (One theory is that radon stimulates the pituitary gland into producing greater quantities of health-enhancing hormones.)

Radon gas occurs naturally when radium, in the process of breaking down, oxidizes. It is, of course, the same gas that thousands of residents in the Rocky Mountains and other regions of the country have spent hundreds of dollars on, in attempts to rid their basements of what is generally considered a potentially dangerous substance.

If you're hurting, though, or curious, consider coming to have a look. Just be sure to read the fine print before descending! The Free Enterprise Health Mine opens daily throughout the year. The facility also maintains an RV park. Call 225-3383 or visit the Web site www.radonmine.com for more information.

A host of old mining camps lie rotting in the hills between Helena and Boulder, 30 miles south of the capital city. Foremost is impressive **Elkhorn,** mostly a ghost town, with its striking examples of frontier architecture, including the marvelous old two-story, Greek Revival Fraternity Hall. The building once hosted boxing matches, dances, theatrical performances, and other social affairs. As you'll see, the streets of Elkhorn were laid out in a steep meadow sloping down from the flanks of Crow and Elkhorn Peaks. An intriguing side trip, weather permitting, leads to the old cemetery. Head from the north side of town along the road as it winds east around a mountainside. In approximately ½ mile, go right at the intersection and continue for several hundred yards. You'll see the cemetery, where graves from the late 1800s are still marked, on the hill to the right.

But first things first: To find Elkhorn, go 6 miles south of Boulder on Highway 69, and then travel 12 miles north on the gravel Elkhorn Road. On the way there, along the main highway you'll pass **Boulder Hot Springs** (225-4339, www.boulderhotsprings.com), where the indoor and outdoor geothermal pools and plunges range in temperature from 96 to 106 degrees and rooms in a turn-of-the-twentieth-century hotel go for between $65 and $139. (The origins of the hot-springs resort itself date as far back as 1863.) For more information on Elkhorn, call the Montana Fish, Wildlife & Parks' Helena Area Resource Office at 449-8864, extension 154.

montanatrivia

The annual Evel Knievel Days in late July bring hundreds of Harley-Davidson enthusiasts and other visitors to Butte to revel in the spirit of the late, legendary motorcycle madman. A lucky few of them—on a calmer note, perhaps—get to hole up at the exquisite Toad Hall Manor, an 11,000-square-foot bed-and-breakfast inn featuring rooms named for characters from the classic children's book *The Wind in the Willows.*

How does one begin to describe **Butte**? The city sits atop the "Richest Hill on Earth" . . . or atop part of it, anyway, for since excavations began in 1955 much of the hill has been carried away and smelted for copper. Now a gaping hole in the earth that's rapidly filling with toxic water, the 7,000-foot-long, 5,600-foot-wide, and 1,800-foot-deep **Berkeley Pit** is one of the city's primary tourist attractions and the butt of more than one Butte joke. To find the Berkeley Pit observation stand, simply head north from I-90 on Continental Drive.

Butte residents are unwaveringly proud of their hometown, and given half a chance, many will expound on it *ad nauseum.* But when the newcomer first gazes on the source of this pride, he or she probably just won't get it, for to say that Butte is a little rough around the edges is a world-class understatement. The neophyte Butte visitor will probably wonder also at how row houses ever came to be situated amid the gracious Montana landscape in this city that feels like an eastern-seaboard worker's town. One might wonder, finally, why anyone would even go to Butte on purpose.

But if you take the time to have a closer look and visit with some of those who call it home, you'll begin to glean an inkling of what it is that makes Butte special. It is a one-of-a-kind place, and its citizens are likewise unique; they even speak in an idiom unique in Montana. Thankfully, not all

montanatrivia

Mark Twain, after lecturing at a Butte theater in summer 1885, entered these words in his journal: "Beautiful audience. Compact, intellectual and dressed in perfect taste. It surprised me to find this London-Parisian-New York audience out in the mines."

are as wild as hometown boys and motorcycle madmen *Evel Knievel,* who passed away in 2007, and his son Robbie Knievel. However, the father-son duo seem an appropriate pair of ambassadors for this unorthodox place. Butte's National Historic Landmark District is the second-largest in the country, bettered only by the historic district of a small southern burg called New Orleans.

In the late 1800s Butte became the world's leading copper producer, and by 1917 its population had mushroomed to over 100,000. The earliest skilled miners were of Cornish background, but word about the mineral wealth spread quickly, and soon workers and families from the world over headed to the new mining center. Those of Irish derivation became the largest group represented, hence Butte's modern St. Patrick's Day celebration, an all-out, spill-into-the-streets party. Others came from Italy, China, Finland, Croatia, Serbia, Lebanon, Mexico, Austria, Germany, and elsewhere.

The dangers of working underground and for sometimes ruthless mine owners led to Butte's becoming so solidly unionized that it earned a national reputation as the "Gibraltar of Unionism." At the 1906 organizational meeting of the Industrial Workers of the World in Chicago, the single largest delegation arrived from—where else?—Butte, Montana.

The best place to get a feel for how Butte became what it is, is at the *World Museum of Mining and Hell Roarin' Gulch.* By no means miss this attraction, but be warned: The place is big and captivating. You can easily while away a full day at the re-created town and adjacent mining museum, which occupy the forty-four-acre site of the old Orphan Girl silver and zinc mine. This "town" of 1899 was a labor of love and completed only through the donation of thousands of hours of volunteers' time.

The cobblestone streets of Hell Roarin' Gulch are lined with dozens of buildings; they, in turn, brim with the relics of days gone by. You can visit the Chinese laundry and herbal-healing store, assayer's office, funeral and embalming parlor, lawyer's office, sauerkraut factory, millinery shop, general store and soda fountain, school, church . . . Especially if you're a lover of antiques, you'll wonder at how the organizers ever got their hands on so much *great stuff.*

The two floors of the Orphan Girl's old hoist house, adjacent to Hell Roarin' Gulch, are dedicated to the World Museum of Mining. Included among the many displays is a collection of old photos of Butte, which offer a glimpse at the past and help the visitor understand just how big this town and its mining operations were (and just how bad the air pollution problem was). An on-site underground mine tour is also available.

To get to the World Museum of Mining and Hell Roarin' Gulch, go west to the end of Granite Street. The attraction is open 9 a.m. to 6 p.m. seven days a week from Apr 1 through Oct 31. It's closed Nov 1 through Mar 31. The entrance fee for those nineteen and older is $7, while kids twelve and younger (accompanied by an adult) are admitted for $2 and teens for $5. An additional fee is assessed for the optional underground-mine tour. Call 723-7211 or visit www.miningmuseum.org for more information.

The World Museum of Mining is one of many stops on the route of the *Butte Trolley,* a gas-powered replica of the electric trolley cars that once plied the hilly streets of Butte. Two-hour outings depart from the visitor center in Butte several times daily from June through Sept. Other stops along the way include the Berkeley Pit overlook, the Mineral Museum at Montana Tech, and the Mai Wah, a one-time noodle parlor containing displays on the Asian heritage of Butte. Call the chamber of commerce at 723-3177 for details.

As had been their custom in the old country, early Welsh and Cornish miners in Butte often carried the bomb-proof pasty (pronounced *PASS-tee*) in their lunch boxes and down into the mines. You needn't go underground to try one today, for the meat-and-potatoes pie has become a Butte institution, as grounded in tradition here as corned beef and cabbage washed down with green beer on St. Patrick's Day. Several restaurants serve pasties, including

Joe's Pasty Shop, at 1641 Grand Ave. (723-9071), an eatery that's small on space but big on flavor.

A few men, like Marcus Daly and William A. Clark, became fabulously wealthy from the mines at Butte and left behind a legacy of extravagant homes. Today you can visit—and sleep in, if you choose—Clark's home, now known as the **Copper King Mansion** bed-and-breakfast.

It took four years for nineteenth-century European craftsmen to build the home, which features white oak woodwork, hand-carved stairways, and mosaic floors. Its thirty-four rooms were completely restored in the 1960s and are open for tours daily, May 1 through Sept 30, from 9 a.m. to 4 p.m. and by appointment the rest of the year. It operates year-round as a bed-and-breakfast, with five rooms going for $65 to $115 a night. The mansion is located at 219 West Granite St. (Just east on Granite Street, rival copper king Daly built his Leonard Hotel, allegedly for the purpose of blocking Clark's expansive view.) Call 782-7580 or tap into www.thecopper kingmansion.com for lodging reservations and tour information.

William A. Clark's son, Charles, also built an impressive home in Butte in 1898-1899. Located at 321 W. Broadway St., the lavish structure now houses the **Clark Chateau Museum** and brings to mind a turreted king's castle amid a sea of serfs' dwellings. The Clark Chateau Museum features a gallery and museum, with period furnishings on loan from the University of Montana. It's open for tours daily May through Sept from noon to 5 p.m., and by appointment the rest of the year. Call the Butte Silver Bow Arts Foundation at 723-7600 or visit www.bsbarts.org for more information.

In the early 1980s, when the city's mining economy turned bad, Butte boosters began exploring ways to diversify. A few visionaries, perhaps reflecting on their childhood memories—neighborhood skating rinks are another Butte institution—proceeded to establish the **U.S. High Altitude Sports Center.** They were snickered at by many outsiders, and even by some insiders, who wondered, "Who would come to Butte in the winter to ice-skate?"

Naysayers ignored, the facility was finished in 1987, and in November the outdoor oval served as the venue for the only World Cup speed-skating event held in America that year. By the time 1992 rolled around, of all the

montanatrivia

In 2006 the Copper King Express began offering a 52-mile round-trip excursion train trip between Butte and Anaconda, by way of scenic Durant Canyon. The trains follow the route of the Butte, Anaconda and Pacific Railroad, incorporated in 1892. It's the first regular passenger service on the line in a half century. It makes regular runs from May to September and operates for special events at other times of the year. Learn more at www.copper kingexpress.com.

medal-winning speed skaters at the Albertville (France) Olympic Winter Games, only three had never trained and/or raced at the Butte facility. Bonnie Blair, America's greatest-ever female speed skater and Butte's adopted daughter, attended Montana Tech in Butte and regularly trained at the center.

montanatrivia

Chuck Kaparich, the visionary and talented woodworker behind the creation of A Carousel for Missoula, subsequently helped his boyhood home of Butte plan its Spirit of Columbia Gardens Carousel.

The oval, located at 1 Olympic Way just off Continental Drive on the south side of town, is open during the winter to public skating when not being used for competitions or training sessions. For information on using the facility and on upcoming competitions, call 494-7570 (winter only).

One of the best-hidden attractions in the Butte area is the **Granite Mountain Mine Memorial,** located off North Main up a bumpy dirt road near the neighborhood/village of **Walkerville.** The memorial marks the 1917 Speculator Mine fire, which took 168 miners' lives, making it the worst hard-rock mining disaster in American history. Not far from the memorial, you can see remaining head frames from defunct mines standing hard against the horizon, looking like skeletons of timber. They too, in fact, are memorials of a sort.

Two-hour bus tours, beginning daily June through Sept at 10 a.m. and 2 p.m. at the Butte Plaza Mall at 3100 Harrison Ave., climb 3,500 feet above town to visit one of Butte's easiest-to-spot but most difficult to access finds: **Our Lady of the Rockies.** Our Lady, a 90-foot-high statue made of concrete and metal and completed in 1985, can be seen from miles away at night, when it is brilliantly illuminated. Call 782-1221 or visit www.ourladyoftherockies.com for more details.

Before leaving what is arguably Montana's most fascinating city, stop at the Butte–Silver Bow Chamber of Commerce Visitor Center, located at 1000 George St., to find out what you have missed. It's located next to the KOA Kampground off Montana Street, north of I-90 at exit 126. To make a cyber visit to the facility, go to www.buttechamber.org. You can also call them at 723-3177.

I-15 meets I-90 a couple of miles west of Butte. A side trip of approximately 22 miles south on I-15 will lead first over the Continental Divide and then to the Moose Creek exit. Take this exit, then follow the dirt Moose Creek Road 3½ miles to the northeast, and you'll come to a trailhead for the spectacular but little-visited **Humbug Spires.**

The impressive spires, contained within an 11,175-acre Wilderness Study Area, are composed of a quartz monzonite called the Moose Creek Stock,

The Great Divide Mountain Bike Route

The **Great Divide Mountain Bike Route** is a 2,708-mile off-pavement bicycle touring, or "bikepacking," route that stretches along the **Continental Divide** from Banff, Alberta, to Antelope Wells on the New Mexico–Chihuahua border. As the route's chief architect in the early to mid-1990s, my mission was to seek out, link together, and map this puzzle of existing jeep tracks, logging roads, and single-track trails.

On entering the United States, the route climbs from the pastoral Tobacco Valley outside Eureka, Montana, into the wild Whitefish Range, through old-growth forest and much younger clear-cuts where cyclists are nearly as likely to encounter a grizzly bear as they are another human. After winding through the valley of the North Fork of the Flathead River, the route recrosses the Whitefish Range to emerge at the terrific Flathead Valley resort town of Whitefish. Over mountains and through valleys, it continues north to south in Montana; indeed, it teeter-totters with mountains and valleys throughout Idaho, Wyoming, Colorado, and New Mexico as well, crossing the Continental Divide more than two dozen times as it leads from the top to the bottom of the contiguous United States.

In Montana a few other names on the Great Divide map are the Mission Mountains and the Seeley-Swan Valley; the Swan Mountains and the Blackfoot Valley; the Pioneer Mountains and the valley of Grasshopper Creek; the Tendoy Mountains and the Red Rock River Valley; and, finally, the Centennial and Henrys Lake Mountains, the doorway to Idaho. The Great Divide also passes directly through Helena and Butte, the two largest cities on the entire route.

For information on riding the Great Divide Mountain Bike Route, contact the Missoula-based Adventure Cycling Association at 721-1776 or www.adventurecycling.org.

which was intruded into the surrounding sedimentary rock many millions of years ago. From the trailhead you can take an easy out-and-back day hike along Moose Creek to view the spires or make a longer backpacking adventure of it. Rock-climbing nuts of all skill levels—from beginning scramblers to those trained and equipped to handle 5.12-level climbs—can enjoy practicing their skills on the granite spires, part of the larger feature known as the Boulder Batholith. Small-stream fishing is another appealing option here. For additional information call the Bureau of Land Management in Butte at 533-7600 and request the Humbug Spires recreation brochure.

Anaconda was founded in 1883 when copper king Marcus Daly built the Washoe Smelter and Reduction Works. Today you can see the inactive **Anaconda Smelter Stack,** at over 585 feet high one of the tallest brick structures in the world. You can also learn about the history of smelting and railroading in the Anaconda area at the visitor center complex. The center, located at 306 East Park St., includes a replicated train depot and the historic City Hall center. Call the Anaconda Chamber of Commerce at 563-2400 or visit www .anacondamt.org/chamber.htm for information.

Also in Anaconda is the *Hearst Free Library,* built in 1889 as a gift to the Smelter City from Phoebe Apperson Hearst, mother of William Randolph Hearst. Mrs. Hearst built the library in memory of her husband, George, who was active in business with the Anaconda Company. Here, in one of the grand libraries of the West, artwork created by turn-of-the-twentieth-century masters, also presents from Mrs. Hearst, hangs on the walls. The library, located at 401 Main St., is open Mon from 9 a.m. to 5 p.m., Tues through Thurs from 10 a.m. to 8 p.m., and Fri and Sat from 9 a.m. to 5 p.m. Call 563-6932 or visit www.hearstfreelibrary.org for information.

A much newer addition to town, but one that is built with history prominently in mind: the Jack Nicklaus Signature *Old Works Golf Course,* situated at 1205 Pizzini Way, which opened to the golfing public in 1997. The first-rate eighteen-hole course, surprisingly affordable to play (GOLF Magazine named it "The number-one course in the U.S. under $50"), meanders along Warm Springs Creek, incorporating old brick walls, smokestack flues, and additional features that were either left in place or added as expressions of the area's mining heritage. Bunkers, rather than holding the typical light-colored sand, are

filled with fine black slag, a by-product of the smeltering process. To reserve a tee time, call 563-5989 or visit www .oldworks.org.

Spectacular and aptly named *Lost Creek State Park* is up a back road, off a secondary route that branches from a low-use highway coming out of a one-horse town. So, typically only those who already know about it ever make it to this spot some Native American groups considered the "Gate to Heaven." Highlights include wildlife, especially the Rocky Mountain goats that are native to the area and a herd of bighorn sheep whose predecessors were transplanted to Lost Creek in 1967 from the Sun River area west of Great Falls. Look high on the 1,200-foot-high canyon cliffs above Lost Creek to spot the critters and to view some impressive geology: Looking oddly out of place, grayish-pink granitic dikes cut diagonally across the cliffs of darker-colored limestone, the latter deposited as layers of mud at the bottom of a shallow sea more than a billion years ago. The dikes were forced as molten material into fissures in the older rock when the Rocky Mountains began to uplift much more "recently"—some seventy-five million years ago.

From where the road ends inside the park, a short, wheelchair-accessible asphalt trail leads to another highlight, cascading Lost Creek Falls. Two campgrounds with a combined total of twenty-five campsites, each with a picnic table and fire grill, await on a first-come, first-served basis. Lost Creek State Park, open May 1 through Nov 30, is 1½ miles east of Anaconda on Highway 1, then 2 miles north on Highway 273, and 6 miles west on the park road. For information call 542-5500.

The town of Philipsburg's bold description of its surroundings, "possibly the most beautiful valley in the world," may or may not be true; the verdict is in the eye of the beholder. But even if it is an exaggeration, it won't be far off the mark in anyone's view, for the valley is unquestionably alluring.

A historic mining town designated as a National Historic District in 1983, Philipsburg contains dozens of intriguing structures and is literally surrounded by old mining camps: Twenty-odd ghost towns can be found within 40 miles, including *Granite,* once among the richest silver towns in the West and home to approximately 3,000 residents in 1900.

thebasicsofamule

The terms *ass, donkey,* and *burro* are interchangeable. The basic differences between a donkey and a horse are the former's longer ears, narrower hooves, straighter back, narrower body, and cow-like tail. A mule is the offspring resulting from the mating of a male donkey, or jack, and a female horse, or mare. Mules are sterile, as a result of the different chromosome counts of the donkey and horse parents. A hinny is genetically like a mule, but it's a cross between a female donkey, or jennet, and male horse, or stallion. Donkeys are usually gray, whereas mules can run the gamut of standard horse colors.

Southwest Montana's ghost-town theme coalesces at the *Ghost Town Hall of Fame,* located in downtown *Philipsburg* in the old Courtney Hotel and Overland car dealership. The hall, actually one component of the Granite County Museum and Cultural Center, features a gallery with a respectable collection of photos depicting dozens of the old Montana mining towns at their zeniths. The museum is open daily from 10 a.m. to 5 p.m. during the summer, and by appointment the rest of the year. Admission is $3, or free for those under age 12. Call 859-3020 or visit http://philipsburgmt.com/museum for additional information.

Before moving on, appease your sweet tooth by stopping in the **Sweet Palace** at 109 E. Broadway St. in Philipsburg. The friendly folks at this emporium of sugary (and sugar-free) treats offer an amazing array of hard candies, licorice, gummies and chewies, fudge, caramels, and taffy, in an attractively renovated 1890s building. It's open year-round Sun through Fri 10 a.m. to 5 p.m. (6 p.m. in summer); call 859-3353 or visit www.sweetpalace.com for more information.

"Mountain canaries," as they were known to the miners, from throughout the Rocky Mountain states and western Canada gather in **Drummond** the second weekend in June for the annual **Montana Mule Days.** A parade with some 200 mules and donkeys marching through downtown Drummond caps the weekend, which also includes weight-pulling contests, team penning competitions, and various other events. More than 100 classes of mules and donkeys compete, ranging from miniatures to giants. Spectators are welcome and guaranteed a good time. For more information call the Stevensville-based Longears Association at 777-2331 or visit www.montanamuledays.com.

Cowboys, Cons, and the Capital

A detour off the interstate into **Deer Lodge**—birthplace of the late Janette Kelley, who became better known as General Mills' original Betty Crocker—comes highly recommended. A collection of eight unusual attractions is found in the 1100 block of Main Street, including the **Old Montana Prison,** the first territorial prison established in the western United States. Also located within the old pen, which was built by convicts and used by them until 1979, is the **Montana Law Enforcement Museum.** The entertaining **Old Prison Players** hold summer performances inside—lending new meaning to being part of a "captive audience."

Adjacent to the prison is the **Montana Auto Museum,** a collection representing Edward Towe's lifelong passion for Ford automobiles. On display are more than one hundred vintage Fords, along with Chevys and other makes, most of them in mint condition. Gracing

montanatrivia

Snags—dead, standing trees—provide homes to a wide array of Montana's cavity-nesting birds and mammals. They serve other critters, too, as hunting perches, food-cache stations, "diners" for insect-eating birds, and roosting and resting places for bats and birds of prey.

Wilbur Sanders

The house that today serves as the *Sanders Bed and Breakfast* was built in 1875 as a residence for Wilbur and Harriet Sanders, who arrived in Bannack in 1863 with the Sidney Edgerton wagon train. Edgerton, the first governor of the Montana Territory, was Wilbur Sanders's uncle. Wilbur soon began practicing law, and he was instrumental in organizing the Vigilantes Committee, the group responsible for hanging members of the Plummer gang and other road agents and for bringing some semblance of civilization to the wild Montana frontier . . . often using surreptitious and scarcely legal means themselves to do so.

These activities helped launch a political career for Sanders, which culminated in his becoming one of the state's first two U.S. senators when Montana gained statehood in 1889. He served in many other civil and official capacities and was founder of the Montana Historical Society, of which he was president for twenty-six years. Wife Harriet, also politically active, was a painter. Her work still hangs in the living room at the Sanders.

the showroom are models dating from 1903 to the 1960s, including a Lincoln once owned by Henry Ford himself.

Two newer components of the museum complex are the *Frontier Montana Museum,* added in 1994, and *Lil' Joe,* a 270-ton electric locomotive residing in the parking lot outside. Lil' Joe was one of several similar locomotives built during the last stages of World War II by General Electric for Josef Stalin's Trans-Siberian Railway. The Cold War quickly heated up during this period, however, and the engines never made it to the Soviet Union. Instead, the Milwaukee Road picked them up at bargain-basement prices, and Lil' Joe and his kin ran the rails between Harlowton, Montana, and Avery, Idaho, until the railroad discontinued its electric operations in 1974.

You can visit all of the museums by purchasing one ticket that also will get you into the nearby *Yesterday's Playthings,* a doll and toy museum. Rounding out the attractions are the historic Cottonwood City, the Powell County Museum, and Desert John's Museum. Admission fees and hours of operation vary with the museums and the time of year. For detailed information call 846-3111 or go to www.pcmaf.org.

There's a lot to see and do in *Helena,* the Montana state capital. Gold was discovered here in 1864 at *Last Chance Gulch,* and today the gulch (Main Street) is a mall between Sixth and Wong Streets that holds all sorts of shopping and eating possibilities.

Located a few short blocks from Last Chance Gulch and dozens of other Helena attractions is the charming *Sanders Bed and Breakfast.* When the wife-and-husband team of Bobbi Uecker and Rock Ringling purchased the house in 1986 to convert it into an inn, they became only the third family to have owned it during its illustrious 111-year history.

As a concession to modern sensibilities and business needs, the proprietors have added a private bath, touch-tone phone, air-conditioning, and data port to each room. Both the exterior porch and the high-ceilinged, oak-wainscoted parlor are ideal spots to relax, and the gourmet breakfast—featuring dishes like huckleberry pancakes and Grand Marnier French toast—offers the opportunity to chat with the owners and fellow guests. Additional touches include complimentary sherry and homemade cookies, and a video library.

The home's original owners, the Sanderses, were interesting, and the current ones are, too. Their flair for gracious hospitality and the personal touch is evident the minute you walk through the front door (and past Wilbur Sanders's mineral collection). Bobbi might share some tales of previous guests, who've included South Africa's late archbishop, Desmond Tutu. Rock, of the famous Ringling Brothers circus family, can relate stories about growing up on the family ranch in tiny Ringling, Montana, where elephants and other show animals were often hauled in for a little rest and relaxation. The guest inn and its seven guest rooms are appointed with many of the original owners' furnishings.

An overnight at the Sanders, located at 328 N. Ewing St. in Helena, goes for $130 double occupancy. For reservations and information call 442-3309 or visit the inn's Web site at www.sandersbb.com.

montanatrivia

Approximately one hundred Forest Service cabins and lookout towers are available for overnighting in various parts of Montana. The rental fees can range from $20 to $55 per night. For details, go to— are you ready?—www.fs.fed.us/r1/recreation_r1/cabin_dir.shtml.

A block south of the Sanders, at 304 N. Ewing St., is the *Original Governor's Mansion,* built in 1888 and resided in by Montana's chief executives from 1913 to 1959. On the guided tour of the gracious Victorian mansion, which is maintained by the Montana Historical Society, you'll see that it retains its original woodwork, wall coverings, and furniture. Tours are offered from May 1 to Sept 30, Tues through Sat, on the hour at noon and 1, 2, and 3 p.m. From Oct 1 through Apr 30, they're available Sat only, on the same hourly schedule. Admission is $4 for adults and $1 for children ($10 per family). For more information call 444-4789 or go to http://montanahistoricalsociety.org and click on "Original Governor's Mansion."

The *Museum of the Montana Historical Society* should be on every Helena visitor's itinerary. Outstanding displays include the impeccable,

10,000-square-foot "Montana Homeland" exhibit. It holds more than 2,000 arti-facts, arranged in dioramas that lead visitors through Montana's history: first, American Indians, who came into the region at least 12,000 years ago; then the earliest trappers and explorers and the first mineral exploiters; and finally, the stockmen, farmers, and others, through World War II. The display focuses on the lifestyles of the characters who have called Montana home and how they've interacted with their natural surroundings. A wonderful exhibit since summer 2005 is "Neither Empty nor Unknown: Montana at the Time of Lewis and Clark."

As outstanding as the museum is in its entirety, the chief reason many people come is to take in the *Mackay Gallery of Charles M. Russell Art.* Russell, who left his St. Louis home at age sixteen to pursue the life of a free cowboy on the open Montana plains, quickly became the state's best-known artist and one of its best-loved citizens.

The Mackay Gallery includes some two hundred Russell oils, watercol-ors, pen-and-inks, sculptures, and comical illustrated letters for which he was famous. A gallery centerpiece, one of Russell's most beautiful works in the eyes of many, is the exceptional *When the Land Belonged to God.* The broad canvas depicts a herd of bison cresting a rise above a dry-country river bottom, timbered buttes and mountains in the distant background. The painting simply looks alive, with the early-morning sun banking off the beasts and steam rising from their nostrils and off their backs.

The Museum of the Montana Historical Society is located at 225 N. Rob-erts St., directly across the street from the State Capitol building. (By the way, another famous Russell painting, the very large *Lewis and Clark Meeting the Flathead Indians at Ross' Hole,* hangs at the front of the House of Representa-tives floor in the capitol.) The museum is open year-round Mon through Sat from 9 a.m. to 5 p.m. (Thurs evening until 8 p.m.). Admission is $5 for adults and $1 for children between five and eighteen years old. Call 444-2694 or visit www.montanahistoricalsociety.org for information on guided tours.

Helena has many additional attrac-tions to see. One favorite is the *Myrna Loy Center for the Performing Arts* (443-0287, www.myrnaloycenter.com), named for Helena's celebrated home-town Hollywood girl. (Loy was actually born Myrna Adele Williams in 1905 on a ranch southeast of Helena, near the small town of Radersburg.) Entertain-ers of national repute perform in this

montanatrivia

The white steel crosses gracing certain stretches of Montana's highways were placed by Ameri-can Legion posts as memorial markers for those who've died in traffic accidents and as reminders for others to drive safely.

converted county jail. Another is the resplendent **St. Helena Cathedral** (442-5825), a replica of the formidable Votive Church in Vienna, Austria. Pews and woodwork are all of hand-carved oak, and marble statues stand throughout the beautiful house of worship.

A third is the **Archie Bray Foundation for the Ceramic Arts** (443-3502, www.archiebray.org). The grounds and gallery at this ceramic arts school of national repute are alive with the whimsical creations of both little-known and world-renowned ceramic artists (the latter includes Shoji Hamada, Peter Voulkos, and western-Montana mud-molding legend Rudy Autio). You can take a self-guided tour of the twenty-six-acre grounds, formerly the Western Clay Manufacturing Company brickyards, anytime during daylight hours, but

A Price on Their Heads

An 1887 bounty on ground squirrels and prairie dogs came close to bringing Montana's territorial treasury to its knees. Farmers, at their wits' end, early that year implored the territorial legislature to add the hole-digging little devils—called the "picturesquely pestiferous and festively fecund chipmunk" by the *New Northwest* territorial newspaper—to the list of critters that could be killed for cash.

On March 5, 1887, the Territorial Assembly bowed to that pressure, amending the existing law to offer a bounty of 10 cents for the hide of each ground squirrel killed and 5 cents for that of every prairie dog delivered to his maker. This was in addition to the higher bounties of between $1 and $3 already paid for the more traditionally bounty-hunted bears, cougars, coyotes, and wolves. Appropriating $14,000 to cover everything, the assembly members figured they had erred on the side of more than enough. They were wrong: Frontier creativity ran high, and folks found all sorts of inventive ways to kill hundreds of the rodents—including using a machine that puffed smoke into holes, "from which the squirrel soon issues in a dazed condition and is smacked senseless with a club."

According to a report issued by the territorial auditor, the amount paid in 1887 on bounties through August 21 totaled $48,012.50; of that, $41,060.05 had gone for the hides of prairie dogs and ground squirrels. Panicked, and recognizing that this couldn't go on much longer if the territory were to remain solvent, territorial governor Preston H. Leslie requested and received permission from President Grover Cleveland to convene a special session of the legislature aimed at revising the revision in the bounty law. Speaking to the gathered assembly, Governor Leslie said, "It is seen that the pathway to the treasury from the killing of the animal at his home in the mountain is easily found, is full of temptation and very dangerous to the pockets of the people."

Agreeing with the governor, the legislature repealed all bounties on all creatures, great and small.

the gallery is open only Mon through Sat year-round from 10 a.m. to 5 p.m., and, in summer only, on Sun from 1 to 5 p.m. The facility is located at 2915 Country Club Ave.

And, finally, you can visit what are reputedly the oldest octagonal house west of the Mississippi and the "largest old barn" in the United States at the **Kleffner Ranch,** now owned by Denis and Stacy Young. The three-level stone barn, built in 1888, encompasses 27,000 square feet of floor space, and today it serves as a popular spot for weddings and other events. The ranch was added to the National Register of Historic Places in 1977. To get there, take US 12 to East Helena and turn south onto Highway 518 toward Montana City, then turn right in approximately 1 mile. Call 495-9090 or visit www.kleffnerranch .com for information on tours.

To see more of Helena, including the historic Reeder's Alley, a neighborhood of restored brick miners' shanties, board the **Last Chance Tour Train** (442-1023, www.lctours.com). You can also learn more by visiting the city's chamber of commerce Web site at www.helenachamber.com.

Lincoln, 55 miles northwest of Helena, is one of those places that could just as easily have ended up a ghost town like Bannack or Elkhorn, but didn't. In the 1860s folks came to Lincoln Gulch, named in honor of the day's president, looking for gold. The only evidence remaining today of the original town, which included several log homes and stores, is the old cemetery.

Modern-day Lincoln claims about 1,100 residents (one fewer than before Unabomber Ted Kaczynski was taken into custody in 1996 after discovered to be living here). The town is home to **Hi Country Trading Post,** a surprisingly large and apparently thriving enterprise for such a tiny town. The headquarters of the employee-owned company, with its made-in-Montana gift and beef jerky sales shop, is located about 2 miles west of town on Highway 200. It's open every day of the week on a seasonally changing schedule. For more information call (800) 433-3916 or visit the Web site www.hicountry.com.

The cowboying town of **Augusta,** situated 75 miles north of Helena on the broad plains that sweep down to the east from the Rocky Mountains, holds an annual rodeo called, unabashedly, **The Wildest One Day Show on Earth.** While visiting, motor up the roads leading west into the Sun River Canyon, home to one of America's largest herds of bighorn sheep, and Beaver Creek Canyon, where you'll encounter some of the most dramatic scenery in Montana. You can also drive or ride a mountain bike through the 20,000-acre **Sun River Wildlife Management Area,** just southeast of the canyon, where grizzly bears often visit and hundreds of elk feed in the winter. For information call 562-3684.

Nestled against a backdrop of sandstone badlands and timbered arroyos, *The Bungalow* bed-and-breakfast resembles a miniature version of Yellowstone National Park's Old Faithful Inn—and with good reason: Both structures were designed by architect Robert C. Reamer. The place was built in 1911–1913 as a summer getaway for Helena entrepreneur Charles C. Power, its cedar logs hauled by rail from Sandpoint, Idaho, to Wolf Creek, then by wagon team from town to the isolated site. In 1946 the lodge and surrounding ranchlands were sold to Brian O'Connell, father of the current owner and hostess, Pat O'Connell Anderson, who has spent summers (and some winters) here most of her life. If you are lucky, Pat will haul out her files of fascinating old articles, photos, and letters, which include house-planning correspondences between Power and architect Reamer, who, it seems, was often snowbound in Yellowstone and late in getting his mail.

The Bungalow's four guest rooms go for $125 to $145 nightly; three of them have shared baths; the other boasts a private bath with what surely is one of the world's longest and deepest clawfoot tubs. Two rooms still contain furnishings personally chosen for the home by the famous designer and department-store tycoon Marshall Field. Breakfast is a scrumptious affair that typically includes homemade breads, and evenings are usually spent melting into the deep chairs and sofas surrounding the massive fireplace in the sitting room. Anglers take note: The inn is only 7 miles from some of the Missouri River's most productive trout waters. You'll find the Bungalow, which in 1995 was added to the National Register of Historic Places, hidden in the hills 4 miles north of Wolf Creek by following I-15, US 287, and a 1¼-mile-long, rutted ranch road. Call 235-4276 or e-mail bngalow@aol.com for reservations and precise directions.

Places to Stay in Gold West Country

BIG HOLE VALLEY

Beaverhead–Deerlodge National Forest Recreational Cabins
(406) 689-3243
Inexpensive

Big Hole Crossing Rental Cabin
Wisdom 59761
(406) 689-3800
Moderate

Grasshopper Inn
Box 460511
Polaris 59746
(406) 834-3456
Moderate

Jackson Hot Springs Lodge
Main Street, Box 808
Jackson 59736
(406) 834-3151
Moderate

Nez Perce Motel
Highway 43
Box 123
Wisdom 59761
(406) 689-3254
Inexpensive

DILLON

Best Western Paradise Inn
650 N. Montana St.
(406) 683-4214
Moderate

Comfort Inn
450 N. Interchange
(406) 683-6831

Sundowner Motel
500 N. Montana St.
(406) 683-2375
Inexpensive

Super 8
550 N. Montana St.
(406) 683-4288
Moderate

ENNIS

El Western Resort and Motel
US 287 South
(800) 831-2773
Moderate to expensive

Fan Mountain Inn
204 N. Main St.
(406) 682-5200
Moderate

9T9 Ranch Bed and Breakfast
99 Gravelly Range Rd.
(406) 682-7659
Expensive

Sportsman's Lodge
310 US 287 North
(406) 682-4242
Moderate

BUTTE

Comfort Inn
2777 Harrison Ave.
(406) 494-8850
Moderate

Copper King Hotel & Convention Center
4655 Harrison Ave.
(800) 332-8600,
(406) 494-6666
Expensive

Copper King Mansion Bed-and-Breakfast
219 W. Granite St.
(406) 782-7580
Moderate

Super 8
2929 Harrison Ave.
(800) 800-8000
Moderate

DEER LODGE

Scharf Motor Inn
819 Main St.
(406) 846-2810
Moderate

Super 8
1150 N. Main St.
(800) 800-8000
Moderate

Western Big Sky Inn
210 N. Main St.
(406) 846-2590
Moderate

HELENA

The Barrister Bed & Breakfast
416 N. Ewing St.
(800) 823-1148
Expensive

Days Inn
2001 Prospect Ave.
(406) 442-3280
Moderate

Holiday Inn Helena Downtown
22 N. Last Chance Gulch
(406) 443-2200
Expensive

Jorgenson's Inn & Suites
1714 Eleventh Ave.
(406) 442-1770
Moderate

The Sanders Bed and Breakfast
328 N. Ewing St.
(406) 442-3309
Expensive

VIRGINIA CITY

Cozy Cabin
110 W. Idaho St.
(406) 843-5211
Expensive

Places to Eat in Gold West Country

BIG HOLE VALLEY

Big Hole Crossing Restaurant
Wisdom
(406) 689-3800
Moderate

Elkhorn Hot Springs
Polaris
(406) 834-3434
Moderate

Jackson Hot Springs Lodge
Jackson
(406) 834-3151
Moderate

Rose's Cantina and Cafe
Jackson
(406) 834-3202
Moderate

Wise River Club
Wise River
(406) 832-3258
Inexpensive

DILLON

Lion's Den
725 N. Montana St.
(406) 683-2051
Inexpensive

Subway
Highway 41 North
(406) 683-6567
Inexpensive

ENNIS

Continental Divide
(gourmet; closed in winter)
Main Street
(406) 682-7600
Expensive

Ennis Cafe
Main Street
(406) 682-4442
Inexpensive

**Scotty's Long Branch
Supper Club**
125 E. Main St.
(406) 682-5300
Moderate

BUTTE

Joe's Pasty Shop
1641 Grand Ave.
(406) 723-9071
Inexpensive

Lydia's Supper Club
4915 Harrison Ave.
(406) 494-2000
Expensive

Matt's Place Drive-In
2339 Placer St.
(406) 782-8049
Inexpensive

Pekin Noodle Parlor
117 S. Main St.
(406) 782-2217
Moderate

Pork Chop John's
8 W. Mercury St. and
2400 Harrison Ave.
(406) 782-0812
Inexpensive

Uptown Cafe (gourmet)
47 E. Broadway St.
(406) 723-4735
Expensive

DEER LODGE

**Broken Arrow Casino
& Steak House**
317 Main St.
(406) 846-3400
Moderate

4-B's Family Restaurant
1210 N. Main St.
(406) 846-2620
Moderate

Pizza Hut
202 N. Main St.
(406) 846-2777
Moderate

**Scharf's Family
Restaurant**
819 Main St.
(406) 846-3300
Moderate

HELENA

Bert & Ernie's
361 N. Last Chance Gulch
(406) 443-5680
Moderate

Brewhouse Pub & Grille
939 Getchell St.
(406) 457-9390
Moderate

No Sweat Cafe
(breakfast and lunch)
427 N. Last Chance Gulch
(406) 442-6954
Inexpensive

On Broadway (Italian)
106 Broadway St.
(406) 443-1929
Expensive

Windbag Saloon and Grill
19 S. Last Chance Gulch
(406) 443-9669
Moderate

Wong's Chinese Kitchen
901 Euclid Ave.
(406) 442-2302
Moderate

YELLOWSTONE COUNTRY →

It is true that most of **Yellowstone National Park** lies in Wyoming, but that's certainly not to say that the Cowboy State has a monopoly on the Greater Yellowstone ecosystem's stunning scenery. In fact, many would argue that even though Wyoming's Yellowstone claims the world-famous geysers and other thermal phenomena, the really stupendous country lies to the north of the park in the Big Sky State.

You'll begin touring Yellowstone Country in the headwaters region, where three rivers merge to become the Missouri, then press on to Bozeman. From the home of Montana State University, you'll go up the Gallatin River, passing the Big Sky Ski and Summer Resort en route to West Yellowstone. From there, you'll pass into Wyoming and through the northwest corner of the world's first national park, then drop back into Montana along the Gardiner and Yellowstone Rivers. You'll then traverse the spectacular Paradise Valley to Livingston, a fun town filled with cowboys and fly fishers, before continuing on to Big Timber and Red Lodge, where a side trip leads along the world-renowned Beartooth National Scenic Byway. Finally, on your way to Custer–Missouri River Country, you can venture onto outback roads to visit the remote Pryor Mountains National Wild Horse Range.

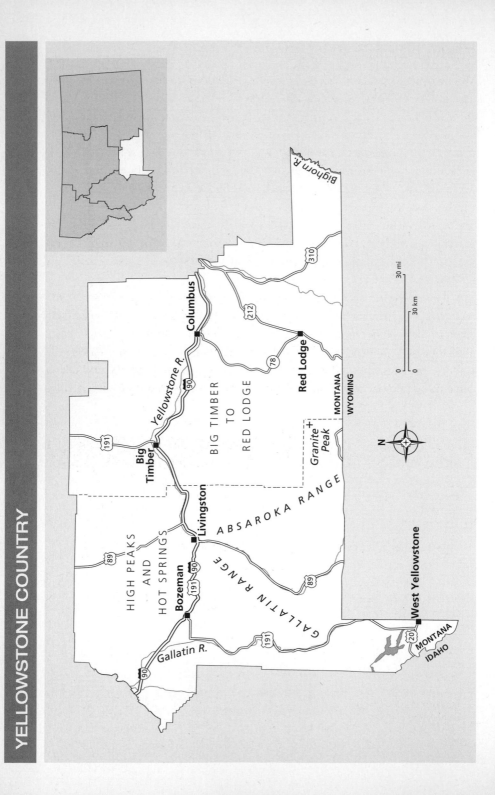

Bighorn R.

310

Columbus

212

Yellowstone R.

90

78

Red Lodge

BIG TIMBER
TO
RED LODGE

MONTANA

WYOMING

30 mi

30 km

191

Big
Timber

Granite +
Peak

N

Livingston

ABSAROKA RANGE

89

HIGH PEAKS
AND
HOT SPRINGS

GALLATIN RANGE

89

West Yellowstone

191

90

Bozeman

191

Gallatin R.

191

20

MONTANA

IDAHO

90

High Peaks and Hot Springs

The tranquil and history-rich *Missouri Headwaters State Park* lies 3 miles east of Three Forks on Highway 10, then 1½ miles north on Highway 286. Here you'll find pleasant campgrounds, displays interpreting the area's natural and human history, trails tracing the footsteps of Indians, and the ghost town remnants of *Gallatin City*. Angling is popular in the park, especially for the brown and cutthroat trout that inhabit the blue-ribbon waters of the Gallatin River. It's also a haven for bird-watchers: More than ninety species of birds can be seen throughout the seasons amid the park's rich mix of river-bottom and rocky upland habitats. Among the dozens of winged things are American goldfinches, hairy woodpeckers, yellow warblers, red-tailed hawks, and violet-green swallows. For more information on Missouri Headwaters State Park, call 285-3610 or 994-4042.

The headwaters, where three major rivers flow together to form the Missouri, was long known by American Indians as one of the most game-abundant areas in the region. During the eighteenth century the Blackfeet, Gros Ventre, Shoshoni, and Flathead tribes shared the area, but by early in the nineteenth century, the powerful and aggressive Blackfeet dominated. *Lewis and Clark* came through in 1805, naming the "three noble streams" the Madison, Gallatin,

AUTHOR'S FAVORITES

American Computer Museum
Bozeman
(406) 582-1288

Beartooth National Scenic Byway
Red Lodge
(406) 446-2103

The Bunkhouse Bed & Breakfast
outside Reedpoint
(406) 932-6537

Chico Hot Springs
Emigrant
(406) 333-4933

Gallatin Petrified Forest
Corwin Springs
(406) 848-7375

Grizzly Bar
Roscoe
(406) 328-6789

Missouri Headwaters State Park
Three Forks
(406) 994-4042

Rendezvous Ski Trails
West Yellowstone
(406) 646-7701

Torgrimson Place
Fishtail
(406) 328-6923

Willow Creek Cafe and Saloon
Willow Creek
(406) 285-3698

John Colter Run

The 7-mile *John Colter Run,* an annual institution for more than thirty-five years, is hosted in early September by Bozeman's Big Sky Wind Drinkers running club. The race celebrates John Colter's epic trek. The first year I showed up for the race, in 1993, I admit that I was relieved to find that, unlike in Colter's situation, today's contestants are permitted (in fact, required) to retain their shorts and shoes. The early autumn morning was cool, but not cold—perfect for running. After the starting gun sounded, we were off, roughly 200 strong, trotting up the paved road leading from Missouri Headwaters State Park toward the railroad siding known as Trident. Soon, though, after about a mile of level pavement, we were directed across the railroad tracks and into the hills . . . and I mean hills. On the major ascents everyone, even the leaders, I think, were reduced to walking. On the other side, descending was basically a controlled fall/slide, as competitors concentrated hard to avoid close encounters with what are, perhaps, descendants of the prickly pear cactus plants Colter had to contend with.

A half hour into the race, we were a mile-long string, with middle-of-the-pack runners diving down a steep ridge as the distant leaders inched up the next one. As the race director had prophetically informed us, "The 'iron horse' is something Colter didn't have to contend with, but it's part of the deal today." And sure enough, several of the front-runners were brought to a screeching halt just a half mile from the finish line, while they waited for a train clanking south from Trident, permitting slower runners to catch up to them.

Relief is typically the emotion one feels on nearing the end of a running race, but here relief was clouded with trepidation, for one last hurdle remained: the Gallatin River. Depending on one's height, a runner was belly- to neck-deep in the current— "the deepest I've ever seen it," according to more than one race veteran, owing to an unusually high snowpack the previous winter. Thankfully, the race organizers had secured a stout rope on opposite banks of the river and stationed hired hands dressed in wetsuits along the length of the rope to help shorter and/or spent competitors across.

H. M. Chittenden, in his seminal 1895 volume *The Yellowstone National Park,* wrote that when John Colter appeared back at Fort Remon after his eleven-day, 200-mile-plus odyssey, "The men at the fort did not recognize him at first and doubtless would not have believed his story if his terrible plight had not been proof of its truth." I can only imagine, because I know how bad I felt after just 7 miles and one hour.

For information on the John Colter Run, call Universal Athletic in Bozeman at 587-4415.

and Jefferson, after the U.S. secretary of state, secretary of the treasury, and president ("the author of our enterprize"). Not long after, trappers and traders in search of beaver pelts filtered in.

Two of the earliest into the beaver country were John Potts and the now-legendary mountain man John Colter, both formerly of the Lewis and Clark expedition. Together they were dispatched in 1808 from Manuel Lisa's trading post at the confluence of the Big Horn and Yellowstone Rivers, armed with the mission of persuading the Indians to trade at Lisa's Fort Remon. But by this time the Blackfeet, who were hostile toward white Americans, controlled the scene, and the duo unfortunately encountered a party of several hundred Piegan warriors. Legend has it that Potts was killed immediately, but Colter was given a chance for survival: After convincing the Piegan chief that he was a clumsy runner (although known among his fellow explorers as a very good one), Colter was stripped, given a head start, and permitted to run for his life, barefoot and bare naked.

The warriors chased Colter over a rough, rocky, and cactus-covered terrain, but he finally ditched them by hiding in brush along the Madison. He regained Fort Remon after an eleven-day odyssey, tattered, footsore, and hungry. The epic adventure enhanced Colter's reputation as one of the smartest and toughest of all the wild and wily mountain men.

At the corner of Main and Cedar in *Three Forks,* visit the *Headwaters Heritage Museum,* one of Montana's best small-town shrines to the past. Among the ground-floor displays is a collection of pictures taken by local photographer Niels Olson, documenting Three Forks's history during the first half of the twentieth century. Another features several hundred hand-carved miniatures created in his spare time by a local railroad engineer, many of them microscopically inscribed with his name.

Filling another case are samples of the artifacts unearthed at the Three Waters Quarry, an archaeological excavation that has served as a hands-on classroom for hundreds of Montana State University students over the past two decades. The site is in the Horseshoe Hills, close to neighboring Willow Creek. On a nearby table a scrapbook overflows with articles on the Three Forks area's past happenings—including a report on the Great American Flatboat Expedition of 1976. The expedition, one of thousands of special events that took place in the United States during our bicentennial year, began on the upper reaches of the Missouri River near here and ended in New Orleans. One article reveals that the expedition leader won the heart of a Three Forks girl, and the two later married.

Among the goodies found upstairs in the museum are collections of barbed wire and old cowboy clothes and tack. The free museum is open from June 1 through Sept 30, Mon through Sat from 9 a.m. to 5 p.m., and on Sun from 1 to 5 p.m. For more information call 285-4778.

For a look at some new clothes and tack, swing into the *Three Forks Saddlery,* the "one-stop shop for all your equine needs." But you'll enjoy this place—as fine a cowboy-outfitting store as there is north of the Pecos—even

MAJOR ATTRACTIONS WORTH SEEING

Big Sky Ski and Summer Resort
Big Sky

Museum of the Rockies
Bozeman

**Grizzly & Wolf Discovery Center and
Yellowstone IMAX Theatre**
West Yellowstone

if you have no pressing equine needs. (Perhaps you want to pick up a gift for a friend who's horsey, or you simply enjoy the smell of fresh-tanned leather.)

For more than forty years the store has outfitted area cowboys with custom chaps and saddles (you can watch 'em being made), including their popular Three Forks Team Roper and Merrill Barrel models. They also offer a full line of western hats, boots, and clothing, and books and other merchandise relating to the traditional ways of the West. The sign on the door at Three Forks Saddlery, located at 221 S. Main St., reads, COME IN AND SAY HELLO—YOU'RE ALWAYS WELCOME. Their toll-free phone number is (866) 318-2371 and their Web address is www.3forkssaddlery.com.

At the *Willow Creek Cafe and Saloon,* located 7 miles south of Three Forks in the tiny town of Willow Creek, they know how to make good coffee, and they know how to make food even better. Their sinful fresh-fruit pies and pastries are legendary in these parts; the proprietors purchase the pumpkins, huckleberries, and other ingredients from local growers and pickers. The dinner menu, with prices ranging from moderate to expensive, consists largely of sumptuous seafood, beef, and pasta dishes. The breakfasts are out of this world, and so are the lunches, which feature hearty, homemade soups.

The charming, antiques-appointed Willow Creek Cafe and Saloon sits at First and Main Streets, in a historic building once a saloon–barbershop–dance hall complex. Not only is it the town's eatery, it's also the village "chattery." Sit a spell and you're bound to hear some interesting gossip or tall tales related by an old-timer. The restaurant, legendary for its barbecued ribs, is open for lunch and dinner Tues through Sat and for all three of the day's meals on Sun (closed on Mon). For dinner reservations call 285-3698.

Just south of the Willow Creek Cafe on Main Street is a nondescript old brick building adorned with a faded mural of a bucking bronco and rider, sporting a simple blue awning on the front. On the awning, in large white letters, are the words *Willow Creek Tool & Technology,* the only clue as to what fills the building's interior.

Inside you'll find a dizzying array of some of the best woodworking tools made. The business opened in 1982, and owner David Spencer had some major-league convincing to do when citified, suit-and-tie sales reps called on his fledgling outfit in laid-back Willow Creek. But he obviously was successful, for now he sells and travels as a distributor for some of the best names in tools.

Willow Creek Tool's regular hours are 8 a.m. to 5 p.m. Mon through Fri. For more information call 285-3247.

Another surprise restaurant in the hinterland not far from Three Forks is the *Land of Magic Dinner Club,* featuring a relaxed western ambience and great steak dinners. The place is found in Logan, 6 miles east of Three Forks on the frontage road paralleling I-90. It's open for dinner seven days a week. For reservations call 284-3794.

But if you're still too full from the Willow Creek Cafe to partake of a spellbinding sirloin at Land of Magic, first motor out to visit *Madison Buffalo Jump State Park.* Here you can work on that appetite while learning about how some earlier residents procured their steak dinners.

Bone deposits, up to 60 inches deep in places, and the types of projectile points found at the site indicate that this buffalo jump, or pishkun, was active beginning at least 2,000 years ago. After being stampeded down rock-lined drive lanes by runners, herds of bison plunged over the steep cliff that rises

BEST ANNUAL EVENTS

Yellowstone Rendezvous Cross-Country Ski Race
West Yellowstone; early Mar
(406) 646-7265

Pinhead Classic Telemark Festival
Bridger Bowl (Bozeman); Mar
(406) 586-1518

Home of Champions Rodeo & Parade
Red Lodge; early July
(406) 446-2422

Summerfest
Livingston; mid-July
(406) 222-8155

Festival of Nations
Red Lodge; early Aug
(888) 281-0625

Sweet Pea Festival of the Arts
Bozeman; early Aug
(406) 586-4003

Montana Antique Aircraft Association Fly-In and Air Show
Three Forks; early Aug
(406) 586-2307

Rockin' the Rivers Music Fest
Three Forks, mid-Aug
(406) 285-0099

John Colter Run
Three Forks; early Sept
(406) 587-4415

Bridger Raptor Festival
Bozeman; early Oct
(406) 586-1518

Native to the Area

We tend to think of whites as the newcomers to Montana's plains and mountains and American Indians as having lived here forever. Of course, they haven't been here forever—"only" 12,000 years or so. Most of the tribes whose names we associate with the state today, however—the Crow, Cheyenne, Flathead, and others—are relative newcomers themselves. Archaeologists say that the first tribe whose name we recognize, the Shoshone, moved in 800 or 900 years ago and by the 1500s dominated the country east of the Continental Divide in the future state of Montana. It was they who worked the Madison Buffalo Jump during its most intensively used period.

The Shoshone began to migrate toward the southwest in the 1600s, and by the time Lewis and Clark passed through the area in 1805 and 1806, only a handful remained. Meanwhile, the Crow had moved in during the 1600s, and it was only in the late 1700s that the Blackfeet, Gros Ventre, Assiniboine, and Cheyenne established themselves in their respective portions of the state. They were greatly aided in their migrations by the horses that had arrived on the scene, obtained from tribes to the south who had, in turn, gotten theirs from early Europeans. The horse was the means to the Plains Indians' newfound mobility and to the development of an altogether different strategy for hunting bison. Pishkuns rapidly became a thing of the past.

beyond the observation deck now in place. Those only injured from the fall were quickly dispatched by hunters waiting below, and after the kill women would take over and butcher the animals. From this bounty, the Indians obtained much of their food for the winter, as well as the raw materials for clothing, tools, and shelter.

Look closely as you traverse these hills, and you'll spot stone circles, or tepee rings, and what investigators believe are eagle catch pits. After excavating a large enough hole, an Indian would hide in it beneath a cover of branches, with a rabbit or some other raptor's tasty tidbit atop the whole affair. If and when an eagle swooped down for the bait, the Indian would try to grab it by the talons and kill it. If things went according to plan, the brave became the proud owner of a new supply of valuable eagle's plumage.

As at any archaeological site, don't disturb the evidence: Even stone chippings should remain where seen on the ground. Madison Buffalo Jump State Park, open the year-round for day use only, is located 7 miles south of Logan on gravel. For more information call 994-4042.

Manhattan, Montana, received a good bit of national exposure several years ago because of its role in the "Real Beef for Real People" television ad campaign. But beef isn't the only thing raised and eaten in Manhattan; in fact, within Montana it's better known as the Seed Potato Capital. Seed potato farming began in the area around 1950, and over the years it has evolved into one of the Manhattan–Amsterdam–Churchill region's primary agricultural products. Fittingly, each August the town hosts the ***Manhattan Potato Festival*** (284-4162). The most popular event in this spud-tacular festival is the mashed-potato fight in which entrants, dressed in plastic garbage bags, line up across from one another and throw huge scoops of the mushy white stuff at each other. Now, that's real fun!

But if it's peace and quiet you're seeking, forgo the clamorous potatofest and opt instead to stay at one of several primitive ***Gallatin National Forest*** rental cabins. The forest, headquartered in Bozeman, claims some two dozen such cabins, most of them built in the 1920s and 1930s to house rangers and trail crews. They generally rent for $30 a night and come equipped with cots or bunks, wood-burning stoves, cooking gear, and tables and chairs. Overnighters haul in their own sleeping bags, food, and, in most cases, water. Visitors also are asked to replenish the wood supply from the wood pile outside (ax or splitting maul provided).

Some cabins can be reached by car; others are accessible only by trail, and some rent only during the winter. For information on the individual cabins, which are let out on a first-come, first-served basis, call the Bozeman Ranger District at 522-2520 or visit www.fs.fed.us/r1/gallatin.

Bozeman never was a boomtown of the sort that commonly popped up throughout southwest Montana. Rather, it grew slowly but surely, primarily as a commercial center for the ever-expanding Gallatin Valley agricultural trade. Helping add to that stable economic base today are major attractions like the ***Museum of the Rockies,*** considered by many to be Montana's foremost treasury of things old, some of them very old—as in dinosaurs. For more information call the Museum of the Rockies at 994-DINO (3466) or visit www.museumoftherockies.org.

One regional publication called the ***American Computer Museum,*** located in Bozeman at 2023 Stadium Dr., Suite 1-A, "an eye-opener for nine-year-olds to ninety-year-olds." Here the history of computing and computers—from the abacus (invented by the Babylonians in about 450 B.C.) to the slide rule to today's high-speed business microprocessors—is revealed in professionally prepared exhibits displayed in chronological order. Gadgets you've probably never seen, but which were common in times past, are displayed and explained. Kids, especially, will enjoy the museum's hands-on exhibits and its working robot.

An example of the little-known facts you can pick up here: Augusta Ada Byron, the only child of Lord Byron, can be considered the world's original "computer programmer," for she developed the first punch-card programs to be used with Charles Babbage's 1840s analytical engine. Another: It took seven and a half years to manually calculate the results from the 1880 U.S. Census. Thanks to a punch-card system devised by Herman Hollerith, it took only one-third the time, or two and a half years, to tabulate the results from the 1890 census. Exhibits trace the history of information storage and retrieval as far back as the Sumerians, who developed the first-known writing system, using clay tablets. The museum also displays forerunners to the computer that were important in the development of Montana—the state's oldest telephone, an early phone switchboard from Red Lodge, and an early calculator that was utilized to determine the gold content of ore from Helena-area mines.

montanatrivia

In 1989 the Nashville-based Gibson Guitar Company opened a manufacturing plant in Bozeman, where today they fashion their world-famous acoustic guitars.

Also described is the 1942 development of the first electronic digital computer, forerunner to today's personal computers, at Iowa State University. Numerous early computer models are displayed, including a massive IBM similar to the one used in putting a man on the moon in 1969. The fascinating American Computer Museum is open from 10 a.m. to 4 p.m. daily June through Aug and noon to 4 p.m. Tues through Sun the rest of the year. Admission is $5 for adults, $4 for students and seniors, and free for children under six. To learn more, call 582-1288 or visit www.compustory.com.

People from throughout Montana assemble to greet old friends and meet new ones at Bozeman's annual *Sweet Pea Festival.* First held in the early 1900s as a celebration of the Gallatin Valley's beautiful and bountiful summers, the festival went on hiatus in 1916. Resurrected in 1978, the Sweet Pea Festival now focuses on the arts and features a full slate of outdoor art shows, parades, dance and music performances by big-time names, Shakespeare in the park, and bicycle and running races. The festivities happen during early Aug, with a flurry of activities concentrated around the first weekend of the month. Call 586-4003 or go to www.sweetpeafestival.org for more information.

While in the area, consider a side trip up dazzling Bridger Canyon to partake of a good night's sleep at the *Silver Forest Inn.* Located 15 miles north of Bozeman near the Bridger Bowl alpine ski area at 15325 Bridger Canyon Rd., the inn was constructed of huge logs in the 1930s and originally served as a getaway for writers and artists. Five rooms, appointed with antiques and original western art, are available for rent, and the inn's inviting outdoor hot tub makes it tough to pass up a moonlight soak. Nightly rates range from $75

to $150; for reservations and further information, call 586-1882 or visit www
.silverforestinn.com.

Just up the way from the Silver Forest Inn, at 16621 Bridger Canyon Rd.,
is **Bohart Ranch,** a day-use cross-country ski area in winter with some 18
miles of trails groomed for both classic and skate skiing. During the snowless months the center's trails double as paths for walking, hiking, running,
and mountain biking for both leisure-
and competition-minded folks. Included
among the special events held at Bohart
throughout the year are summer biath-
lons, which combine cross-country running and target shooting. Bohart also
boasts a summer Frisbee Golf course.
Call 586-9070 for information or log on
to www.bohartranchxcski.com.

montanatrivia

Some 64,000 cattle brands are
registered in Montana. Frequently,
individuals of the same family
operation will maintain their own
personal brands.

If the air is chilly when you bid
adieu to Bozeman, it's bound to become even nippier as you near West Yellowstone. To find something cozy to ward off that chill, stop by the **Montana
Woolen Shop,** which features products at uncommonly low prices from
Amana, Woolrich, Filson, Hudson Bay, and other companies. The interior of
the small store is a fabric free-for-all, with woolen goods hanging over every
available stationary object and from every square inch of wall space. Multi-
colored blankets, robes, Navajo rugs, thousands of sweaters, and fabrics are
among the merchandise.

The Montana Woolen Shop is located west of downtown at 8703 Huffine
Lane. It's open seven days a week on a seasonally changing schedule. Call
587-8903 or visit www.montanawoolenshop.com for more information.

Proceed west from Bozeman on US 191 to Four Corners and turn south,
following US 191 and the Gallatin River. In 6 miles turn into the **Gallatin
Gateway Inn,** an opulent Spanish Colonial Revival–style structure sporting a
stucco exterior and a hard-to-miss red-tile roof. The Milwaukee Road railway
built the inn, one of the first hotels designed to serve a burgeoning number
of tourists traveling to **Yellowstone National Park**, in 1927 at the southern
end of their branch line from Three Forks. They believed that Salesville (soon
to become Gallatin Gateway) would be the ideal spot to entertain visitors who
would be traveling by bus the rest of the way to the park.

The inn features thirty-three rooms, which seems somewhat too few in
relation to its expansive dining and lounging areas. The reason: The builders
assumed that after tourists savored the inn's amenities, the majority would
return to Pullman cars to sleep. But their timing was not good, for within

a decade most were traveling to Yellowstone by car, and the venture failed. The Milwaukee Road sold the inn in the early 1950s, and not long after, it fell into disrepair.

Following an extensive renovation in the late 1980s, the Gallatin Gateway Inn has reclaimed its original grandeur and is again welcoming the Yellowstone-bound and -been. Rooms, available in a choice of single or double occupancy or two-room suites, are decorated in the subdued hues of the western landscape. The immense dining room features a menu that changes with the seasons and attracts a strong local and regional clientele, with its entrees of bison, beef, seafood, and wild game.

The high ceiling, original Polynesian mahogany woodwork, hand-carved beams, and tall windows create a distinctive atmosphere that has made the lounge and ballroom area a popular spot for weddings and other bashes. The inn also now has an outdoor pool and hot tub, a fly-casting pond, and mountain bikes available for exploring area back roads. Rooms at the Gallatin Gateway Inn range from $99 to $135 per night, depending on the time of year. For information and reservations call 763-4672. You can also learn more at the inn's Web site, www.gallatingatewayinn.com.

Continue south on US 191 up the Gallatin River, passing the entrance to the pair of mega-resorts known as *Moonlight Basin* and *Big Sky.* There's lots to do and plenty of places to dine and stay in the vicinity of the legendary newscaster Chet Huntley's dream resort—the Montana native built the formative resort in the early seventies, shortly before his death in 1974. (Huntley passed on just three days before Big Sky's official opening ceremonies.) One option, located five miles south of the Big Sky entrance junction, is *Rainbow Ranch Lodge,* where the accommodations are luxuriously rustic and intimate, and the gourmet fare served in the associated restaurant is among the most heralded (and most expensive) in the northern Rockies. The pond-side and riverside rooms go for between $215 and $385 per night. Visit www.rainbow-ranchbigsky.com or call 995-4132 to learn more.

If it's elbow room for a lot of people, rather than intimate surroundings, you're looking for, consider making reservations at the *Hud Cabin,* located on a perch at the end of Bobtail Horse Road high above Big Sky's Meadow Village. The open-air, three-level, custom log "cabin" can sleep as many as twelve, making it a fine base for a large family group wanting to sample the plethora of outdoor activities that the Big Sky area has to offer in both summer (golf, fishing, hiking, river rafting, mountain biking, zip lining, etc...)

and winter (alpine and cross-country skiing, snowboarding, snowmobiling, and more). The rental house is an enterprise of local Expressionist painter Jacqueline Rieder Hud, whose dreamy works often remind viewers of the ties that exist among the spirits of humans, horses, and other living things. With little prompting, the artist will share details about her passion for and deep involvement with Keystone Conservation, a Bozeman-based nonprofit working to protect and restore native predators and their habitats in the northern Rockies. Her pet-friendly Hud Cabin rents for around $450 per night; visit www .montanacabins.com or call 763-5215 for more information.

Skiing Yellowstone Country

Early in 2006 I was invited by the Yellowstone Country tourism region to participate in its "Ski the Fab Four" familiarization trip. Oh, darn. Well, somebody's gotta do it, I figured, so I jumped at the opportunity.

Our small group of four journalists and two guides met at the Big Sky Chamber of Commerce visitor center on a chilly Wednesday morning in late February. Our guides, Terry and Pat Abelin, informed us that they live outside Bozeman right at the base of the Bridger Bowl ski area, one of the "Fab Four." In fact, I later learned, Terry was the recently retired, longtime manager of the area.

We hit the slopes at Big Sky at about 12:30 p.m. The resort's public relations manager, an expert skier, led us to fun powder shots through recently thinned glades. The spectacular presence of 11,166-foot Lone Mountain looming above us while we skied added to the thrill.

The next day we skied Moonlight Basin. Although Big Sky and Moonlight (which opened in 2003) are distinct operations under separate ownership, it's sometimes tough for newcomers to understand exactly where one begins and the other ends. The lines were blurred even more when the resorts began offering a joint Lone Peak Pass, permitting access to all of both mountains, in the fashion of connected European ski resorts.

It was early out of bed the next morning to drive the 70 miles to Bridger Bowl and make first lift. Terry Abelin's grapevine had informed him of a foot of fresh powder overnight, on top of the 2 to 3 feet that'd fallen earlier in the week.

With 2,000 skiable acres, 2,600 vertical feet, and eight surface chairs, Bridger Bowl is destination resort in scope, yet it's operated as a community nonprofit organization. Selling real estate is not a goal at Bridger; rather, the mission there is to "provide the best possible skiing experience at a reasonable cost to local, regional, and destination skiers."

Alpine skiing simply doesn't get much better than it gets in Montana's Yellowstone Country.

Farther south, you'll pass through the northwest corner of Yellowstone National Park before coming to the junction with US 287. In another 8 miles you'll reach West Yellowstone.

Like Gallatin Gateway, **West Yellowstone** once was a terminus for a railroad spur line, but this one came from Ashton, Idaho, to the south. Check out the attractive and rustic Oregon Short Line (now the Union Pacific) Depot, built of native materials to blend into the landscape and echo the style utilized for the National Park Service buildings in Yellowstone National Park. It's located near the entrance to the park. For specific information write to 124 Yellowstone Ave., West Yellowstone 59758 or call 646-1100.

If your visit to West Yellowstone comes during the town's long and snowbound winter, try kicking and gliding along the **Rendezvous Ski Trails,** where seasoned cross-country skiers can enjoy hours of fun, and Nordic neophytes couldn't pick a better place to learn the basics.

The trail system, first carved out of Gallatin National Forest lands in the 1970s by the Neal Swanson family, has gained a reputation over the years as one of the premier ski-trail systems in the entire Rocky Mountain region (and most consistent early snow, with skiing usually available by mid-Nov). A number of foreign teams trained here for several days leading up to the 2002 Olympic Winter Games in Salt Lake City. The trails are maintained and immaculately groomed by the community for both locals and visitors. For information on the Rendezvous Ski Trails or for ski rentals, go to **Freeheel and Wheel** (646-7744, www.freeheelandwheel.com), located at 40 Yellowstone Ave. in West Yellowstone.

montanatrivia

Doug Edgerton, the magician of snow who grooms the Rendezvous Ski Trails in West Yellowstone, served as chief of grooming at the Soldier Hollow Nordic skiing venue for the 2002 Winter Olympic Games in Utah.

For lodging while in "West," as the locals call it, consider **Hibernation Station,** situated not far from the Rendezvous Trails at 212 Gray Wolf Ave. Luxurious, log-cabin accommodations— featuring classic Old West artwork and furnishings—are available year-round, with nightly rates between $119 and $299. Rooms range from single queen units to large family cabins with kitchens included. Hibernation Station also maintains a hot-tub room, and some rooms boast private hot tubs as well. Obtain additional information or make reservations by calling (800) 580-3557 or tapping in to www.hibernationstation.com.

After exploring the wonders of Yellowstone, most of which lie within the borders of Wyoming, head north from Mammoth Hot Springs back into Montana. If you're struck by the beauty of the upper Yellowstone River region, you're not the first. Consider the words Crow *Chief Arapooish* once used to describe to a white fur trader why this country, the historic home of his people since the 1600s, was so special to them:

> The Crow country is a good country. The Great Spirit has put it in exactly the right place; when you are in it you fare well; whenever you go out of it, whichever way you travel, you fare worse . . . . Everything good is to be found there. There is no country like the Crow country.

The easiest way to find the next attraction in this uncommonly good country is to backtrack from the town of Gardiner. At the second bridge spanning the river south of town, 2½ miles inside the North Entrance of the park, you'll see a parking area. Pull in, hike the half-mile trail leading down to the *Boiling River,* and enjoy a hot dip near the forty-fifth parallel, halfway between the equator and the North Pole.

Most of the park's thermal features are dangerous and therefore off-limits to swimming, but at Boiling River soaking has long been an accepted and relatively safe and common practice. Unfortunately, during the 1970s, rowdy parties also became common, culminating in two tragic drownings in 1982. This prompted the National Park Service to alter the rules at the hot springs, and today family-oriented soakers have largely supplanted the once-common party animals. Soakers are permitted in the river during daylight hours only. During spring high water, the pools are closed altogether.

If you'd prefer to soak in lavish surroundings with all the amenities at hand, keep driving north on US 89 and into the alluring Paradise Valley. Before reaching your destination, however, there are a couple of highlights you shouldn't miss.

From Gardiner it's a short side trip to *Jardine,* one of Montana's classic almost–ghost towns. Gold was first discovered in Bear Gulch in 1866, but no large-scale extracting operations were established until the turn of the cen-

montanatrivia

Teddy Roosevelt laid the cornerstone of the Roosevelt Arch in Gardiner, at the North Entrance to Yellowstone, on April 24, 1903. The inscription on the columnar-basalt structure reads, "For the benefit and enjoyment of the people," a reference to the world's first national park.

tury, when Harry Bush organized the Revenue Mining Company in 1898. The easier-to-get gold played out and Jardine nearly died, but it was resurrected in the 1920s as an arsenic-mining center. That substance's value as a pesticide lost favor in the 1940s, however, with the development of DDT, and again the town fell on hard times.

Today at Jardine, located 5 miles up Bear Gulch on the Jardine Road, you'll see the old residences of miners and the well-preserved remains of the Revenue forty-stamp gold mill. You'll also find that Jardine has yet again returned to life: In 1987 the Jardine Joint Venture began mining gold in the area. (All no trespassing signs in this area should be obeyed unquestionably because of the potentially dangerous minerals that were mined and exposed to the air.)

The phrase *hardwood forest* takes on an uncommonly literal meaning at the **Gallatin Petrified Forest,** a 26,000-acre special management zone set aside by the Forest Service in 1973. The petrified trees are the result of volcanic activity in the region some fifty million years ago, when a mixture of ash and water covered standing forests. Through the centuries, silica-containing water percolated through and turned the trees to rock, while preserving their structure. The trees of rock then were lifted high above the valley when the mountains rose approximately thirty-five million years ago.

From the Tom Miner Campground, a trail new in 1991 leads for about ½ mile up to a line of cliffs, where the remains of petrified trees can be found. A more strenuous hike of 3-miles-plus leads into the heart of the preserve, where there's much more to be seen, including tree trunks still standing. In that area it's permissible to pick up small pieces of petrified wood, provided you first obtain a free collection permit from the Forest Service office in Gardiner or Bozeman.

To find Montana's hardest hardwood forest, travel 12 miles north from Corwin Springs on US 89 and then 12 miles on the gravel road leading southwest to the Tom Miner Campground. For more information, directions, and a map detailing the longer hike, call the Gardiner Ranger District at 848-7375.

Now, 12 miles farther north along US 89, at the town of Emigrant, turn east to cross the Yellowstone River and proceed to **Chico Hot Springs Resort.** Rooms, chalets, and log cabins are available for rent, and the continental cuisine served at Chico is expensive but good—so good that the establishment is rated by many as the best restaurant in Montana. Chico also boasts of Percie's Poolside Grill, where you can enjoy ribs, a burger, pizza, and/or a salad while watching soakers soak in lusciously warm waters. Chico's western-style saloon features live dance music on weekends. For information and for dinner and lodging reservations (the wide range of rooming options available is reflected by a wide range in pricing, from $49 to $345 per night), call 333-4933 or (800) 468-9232 or go to www.chicohotsprings.com. The resort, located at 1 Old Chico Rd. in Pray, is open year-round.

Hot Springs Celebrities

Don't be surprised if, while taking in the doins' at Chico Hot Springs, you spot some-one who looks familiar, for the Paradise Valley has attracted more than its share of Hollywood celebrities. Among those who are or have been regulars at Chico: Peter Fonda, Dennis Quaid, Meg Ryan, and Jeff Bridges, who met his wife when she was working as a cocktail waitress there. Visitors of an earlier day included Steve McQueen, while yet earlier on the scene were notables such as Teddy Roosevelt and western artist Charlie Russell.

Some swear that even today you can encounter certain turn-of-the-twentieth-century Chico regulars. The ghosts of Bill and Percie Knowles, who owned the resort in 1900, reportedly still frequent the halls of the main lodge, and Percie sightings in a third-floor room have been reported by guests and employees alike. A psychic stay-ing in the lodge in the late 1980s made repeated visits to the front desk to report that the hotel was inhabited by ghosts before the staff finally convinced her that, yes, they knew that, their names are Bill and Percie, and they're already accepted as residents!

In the historic railroading and tourist-servicing town of *Livingston,* stop at the *Depot Center,* located in the imposing old Northern Pacific railroad station at 200 W. Park St. The depot was designed by the Minnesota firm of Reed and Stem, the railroad-architecture specialists responsible for Grand Central Sta-tion in New York City. Built in 1901–1902 to the tune of $75,000, the building remains one of the most impressive ever constructed in Montana.

The depot was abandoned by the railroad in the 1980s, and members of the newly created Livingston Depot Foundation took it upon themselves to raise the funds necessary to restore the building to its original splendor. They clearly were successful, and today visitors find distinctive exhibits on railroad-ing, Indian artifacts, western history and art, and more on permanent display at the Depot Center. Traveling exhibitions also are commonly shown; past shows have included an impressive traveling art show from Russia and the "Beautiful, Daring Western Girls: Women of the Wild West Shows," on loan from the Buffalo Bill Historical Center in Cody, Wyoming. (Livingston was a fitting place for this show, for past residents have included the likes of Martha "Calamity Jane" Canary.)

The museum is open Mon through Sat from 9 a.m. to 5 p.m. and Sun from 1 to 5 p.m., mid-May through late Sept, and is closed the rest of the year. Admission is $3 ($2 for kids six to twelve and for seniors). Various community events are also held at the Depot Center throughout the year. For a schedule and other information, call 222-2300 or visit www.livingstonmuseums.org/depot.

At the ***Chatham Fine Art*** gallery you'll find displayed originals by the owner, the well-known Montana writer, angler, painter, and intellectual good ol' boy Russell Chatham. Chatham's oils have captivated hundreds of worldly art collectors and scores of not-so-worldly ones, too. Also on display at Chatham Fine Art are the paintings, photographs, and handiwork of a select group of additional artists from the region. The gallery is located at 120 N. Main St. For information on hours of operation, call 222-1566; to view an array of Russell Chatham's works, visit www.russellchatham.com.

Up Mission Canyon, approximately 12 miles southeast of Livingston at the base of the glorious Absaroka Range's Elephant Head Mountain, awaits an enterprise straight out of the Old West. The ***Sixty Three Ranch,*** a Montana dude ranch of proud tradition, began operations in 1863 (hence its name),

Home on the Range

After making reservations to stay a Saturday night in late September at Livingston's historic *Murray Hotel,* I informed Nancy that I'd been told we might be holing up in the Sam Peckinpah Room. Peckinpah, the late movie director known for his bloody westerns and other violent flicks, stayed often at the Murray; in fact, he considered the hotel one of his homes away from home.

Naturally, I had in mind a room with a masculine decor, featuring plenty of dark-stained woodwork, leather furniture, and paintings of things like mallards and moose. As soon as we walked into our suite, though, Nancy began laughing loudly. It was as frilly a place as we'd ever seen, brimming with lace and trimmed with a color scheme that I'm certain Peckinpah would not have selected. I still don't know if that's the Sam Peckinpah Room—but if it is, I'd say it must have him rolling around in his grave at a pretty good clip.

In the mezzanine above the lobby, we discovered a display featuring the paintings of Parks Reece, whose work reminded me of a cross between Gary Larson's *(The Far Side)* and that of Missoula's popular Monte Dolack. Hilarious stuff, and great to look at, too. (Reece subsequently established his own gallery in Livingston, which you can visit at 119 S. Main St., Suite A3.)

After arriving late that afternoon, it had been difficult even making it to the registration desk; because of street barricades, we'd been forced to park 2 blocks away. The reason: Unbeknownst to us it was the day and evening of Livingston's annual Oktoberfest, and the celebrating was centered right in the lobby of the Murray and on the surrounding streets. Microbrew and bratwurst vendors were doing brisk businesses in the cold evening air. Cowboys and non-cowboys alike were keeping warm by dipping and twirling in the crowded, vibrant streets, to the sounds of a hard-core country band. All in all, it was wild, and definitely a "Livingston Saturday Night" that would have done Jimmy Buffett proud.

and since 1929—that's 80 years—it has been in the hands of members of the Christensen family. Still a working cattle spread in addition to its guest-serving function, in 1982 the Sixty Three became the first dude ranch in Montana to be listed as a National Historic Site.

Trail rides, hiking, photography workshops, pack trips into the Absarokas, bird-watching, and fishing on Mission Creek, which rambles through the ranch for a lengthy 3½ miles, are popular outdoor pursuits at the Sixty Three.

Activities guests can pursue in or close to the lodge include volleyball, horseshoes, billiards, square dancing, and "sweat-lodging." Rates include a private cabin, three meals daily for seven days, and the use of a saddle horse and all ranch facilities. A week at the Sixty Three goes for $1,780 per adult, $1,580495 per child six to eleven, and $200 for kids five and under (no horse included). The rates include all gratuities and service charges. For reservations call (888) 395-5151 or go to www.sixtythree.com.

Big Timber to Red Lodge

Downtown **Big Timber** is interesting for its abundance of historic masonry buildings constructed toward the end of the Victorian Age. The **Grand Hotel Bed and Breakfast,** once a center of social activity for Big Timber, served turn-of-the-twentieth-century travelers who arrived in town on the railroad. The inn was recently renovated and now features a dozen rooms, some with shared bath, which rent for $65 to $165 per night. The rate includes a hearty breakfast. The old hotel includes a first-rate supper club as well, featuring Montana-grown beef, bison, and lamb. Call 932-4459 for reservations or visit www.thegrand-hotel.com to learn more about the Grand, which proudly boasts of "Serving Cattlemen, Cowboys, Sheepherders, and Travelers Since 1890."

The name may stink, but the food is hot and tasty at the **Road Kill Cafe.** "From your grill to ours" is the slogan at the tongue-in-cheek eatery, where patrons are reminded, "This is not Burger King and you cannot have it your way."

Delicious sandwiches, including buffalo burgers and elk burgers, top the lunch menu, while for dinner you can order a steak or seafood meal. Rest assured that as you dine, local cowboys and the occasional celebrity—the Boulder Valley is another hot spot for the stars, and Tom Brokaw, Brooke Shields, Michael Keaton, and others have built places nearby—will keep the adjacent McLeod Bar lively and the jukebox loud.

The false-fronted Road Kill is the real rural-Montana thing. Open Wed through Sun for lunch and dinner, it's located near the tiny town of **McLeod,**

16 miles south of Big Timber on Highway 298. Even if you're not hungry for road kill, the drive up the Boulder River, a nationally famous trout stream, is well worth the time spent. As you head upstream, you'll notice that fingers of timber begin reaching down from the slopes above as the mountains claim more and more cropland. Watch for deer on the road—the valley is swarming with them—or you may fashion new fodder for the cafe! The Road Kill Cafe can be reached by calling 932-6174.

Twelve miles south of McLeod on Highway 298 is **Natural Bridge State Monument,** whose name is now a misnomer, for the great arch that once spanned the Boulder River collapsed in 1988. But the 100-foot-high waterfall still flows strong, and the spot is as serene and seductive as ever. Trails radiate out from the parking area, leading to viewing sites above the falls, and a picnic area is available for day use. Call 932-5155 to learn more.

If you leave I-90 at exit 384 a few miles west of Reed Point and head south on gravel up the canyon of Bridger Creek, in 3½ miles you'll arrive at the **Bunkhouse Bed & Breakfast.** You'd be hard pressed to find a prettier and more isolated piece of overnighting property anywhere. Horseback riding and fishing are popular activities for those bedding down in one of two attractive log cabins, which can sleep up to six and include washrooms and basic kitchen facilities. A gourmet breakfast, served in the adjacent main ranch house's sunroom or dining room, features fresh strawberries and raspberries from the enterprise's own garden, when in season. (The attractive ranch house has been featured in several national publications, including the June 1997 issue of *Log Home Living.*) Nightly rates range from $100 to $200. Call 932-6537 to make reservations or request further information, or check out their Web site at www.bunkhouse.biz.

montanatrivia

Five varieties of falcon call Montana home: the prairie falcon, peregrine falcon, kestrel, merlin, and gyrfalcon.

In **Columbus**, the **New Atlas Bar,** situated at 528 East Pike Ave. is an ancient masonry structure housing a collection of more mounted animal heads than Teddy Roosevelt could have shaken his big stick at. The interior of the old place, which turned one hundred in 2006, is smoky, yellowed, and grimy, in need of a good bath, but consider stopping in for a cool drink anyway. Among the dead critters on display are an albino deer, a two-headed calf, and a pair of battling bobcats, frozen in action.

For an altogether relaxing experience, arrange to stay at the **Torgrimson Place,** located on the Bench Ranch a few miles south of **Fishtail.** (Fishtail is 20 miles southwest of Columbus on Highways 78 and 419.) From the outside, the guesthouse still looks like what it was: an old log cabin built in 1904. Only its sound roof, new white chinking, and unbroken windows distinguish it from a hundred other homesteaders' cabins in the region.

But on the inside of this old cabin, you'll discover a touch of the modern West and what might be termed *lavish-rustic* accommodations. Jack and Susan Heyneman, owners of the Bench Ranch, and their five sons have surely performed a little miracle in creating this sanctuary.

You'll have the run of most of the Bench Ranch's 5,000 acres when staying over. The Heynemans, who operate the ranch under a conservation easement with the Montana Land Reliance, abide by the practices of Holistic Resource Management. In order to preserve the resources and protect the ecosystem for all living things, they use no chemical fertilizers or herbicides in raising their sheep and acclaimed red Angus cattle. (You can read more about the Bench Ranch in the Crow Country section of Wallace and Page Stegner's book, *American Places.*)

Careful Where You Drive

The puns run as wild as the wool-bearing beasts in Reed Point at the annual **Great Montana Sheep Drive,** where in years past celebrities and characters including Meryl Sheep and Rambo have been spotted. The event began as a spoofy spin-off of the well-publicized Montana Centennial Cattle Drive of 1989, but that first summer's sheep drive was successful beyond anyone's wildest dreams: It raised nearly $12,000—twice what organizers had optimistically expected and enough to add a wing to the town's library. "And I don't think we fleeced anybody," said one official.

Originally envisioned as a one-time happening, the unexpected success of the premiere event prompted a "rebleat performance" in 1990. That summer the Associated Press reported: "They're ba-a-a-c-k . . . . While coyotes salivate in the hills, hundreds of sturdy Montana-bred woolies will charge down the six blocks of Main Street in an event some say is matched only by the running of the bulls in Pamplona, Spain."

The sheep drive now draws a crowd of thousands who come to witness the wooly wonder of countless sheep darting through the streets of tiny Reed Point, population two hundred (give or take a few). The theme of one recent drive, in honor of the upcoming November elections, was "Ewe've got to be kidding." Several Montana political candidates were there, providing the voters in attendance with an opportunity to decide in person—in the words of another event organizer—"who's trying to pull the wool over their eyes."

Also on the roster at the annual event are a sheepherder poetry reading, a sheep-shearing contest, a street dance and barbecue, and competitions for the ugliest sheep, prettiest ewe, and smelliest sheepherder. The Big Montana Sheep Drive is held in Reed Point on the Sunday before Labor Day. Call 326-2315 for additional details.

A stone's throw from the cabin is the sparkling West Rosebud River, perfect for tube-floating or fly fishing (catch-and-release only on the ranch). And rising abruptly to the south are the crags of the Beartooth Range, the highest mountains in all of mountain-filled Montana.

The Torgrimson Place features two bedrooms with big, log-frame feather beds, a completely equipped kitchen, a living room with a wood fireplace, and plenty of western art on the walls and books on the shelves. And, as the Heynemans like to boast, no TV. For one full day the place rents for $225 ($250 for three people or more; it'll sleep up to six). You can also rent the cabin for an entire week—after which you will most certainly not want to leave. Call 328-6923 or visit www.benchranch.com for reservations or more information, such as precise directions to the remote outpost.

Two bar-restaurant combinations within only a few miles of the Torgrimson Place could readily throw your taste buds into a tug-of-war. It's a toss-up as to which is the better; perhaps the only way—or at least the best way—for you to decide is to stay at the Torgrimson Place for two days minimum and sample supper at both.

Montana Hanna's Trout Hole Restaurant is found southwest of Fishtail along Highway 419. The soups, seafood, and steaks are great at this out-of-the-way eatery, open for dinner Thurs through Sun. Vintage snowshoes, skis, and fly-fishing gear adorn the walls, making the place feel downright Montana homey. Call 328-7400 for information and reservations. The adjacent Stillwater Saloon is open seven days a week.

Option number two is the ***Grizzly Bar,*** at the prominent address of 1 Main St. in ***Roscoe***, whose regulars for years have included local sheep and cattle ranchers and others from far afield and all walks of life. The interior is classic West, with cattle brands burned into the woodwork, while outside the East Rosebud River rushes by under a cover of huge cottonwoods, and a life-size grizzly bear roars down from the roof at those entering. If you're a truly committed carnivore, you may want to try tackling one of the Grizzly's legendary, two-pound-plus "I dare ya!" steaks. The establishment is open daily, serving meals from noon to 9 p.m.; call 328-6789 for reservations.

From Roscoe, to experience some real Montana backcountry, wend your way toward ***Red Lodge*** along the gravel roads paralleling Highway 78. The roads are poorly marked—they're mostly for the benefit of local ranchers who already know where they are—so you may become temporarily lost here or there. If so, just ask a local for directions.

The annual ***Festival of Nations*** has been staged in the mountain town of Red Lodge for more than fifty years. Conducted in early August, the festival is dedicated to promoting peace and goodwill among the citizens of all countries of the world. Ethnic crafts, foods, and music are featured throughout the three-day event. Nearly 15,000 visitors participate in the sing-alongs, street dances, and dozens of other activities. You can find out more about the Festival of Nations by calling the Red Lodge Chamber of Commerce at 446-1718 or logging on to the event's Web site, www.festivalofnations.us.

Red Lodge, which started life as a coal-mining town, is a favorite destination year-round, with downhill and Nordic skiing popular during winter and dozens of diversions readily at hand in the summer. Like most tourist-serving towns, Red Lodge has spawned its share of restaurants, T-shirt shops, gift stores, and other businesses, some more unusual and interesting than others. Among the more interesting is *Kibler & Kirch,* found at 101 N. Broadway Ave., where you'll want to stop in to lust over the wide selection of lavish furnishings. Most of the merchandise sports a uniquely Montana flair: log and iron furniture, original sculptures, willow baskets, classy picture frames featuring classic cowboy scenes, and a whole lot more. The women who own the shop also offer a full range of home and business decorating services.

This store somehow appeals even to those of us who aren't natural-born shoppers. For more information on *Kibler & Kirch,* open daily, call 446-2226 or visit www.kiblerandkirch.com.

Another shop worth visiting is *Magpie Toymakers,* located at 115 N. Broadway Ave. The front of the store is dedicated to the dozens of toys on display, handmade and otherwise, many of them wonderfully whimsical. The back half is shop space, where visitors can watch toymakers creating their articles of amusement. You can call Magpie Toymakers at 446-3044.

Finally, before heading up the big hill, appease your sweet tooth by swinging into the *Montana Candy Emporium* (446-1119), housed in the 1925 Iris Theater at 7 S. Broadway Ave. The large assortment of

longinthe beartooth

Early in the twentieth century, a group of Red Lodge–vicinity citizens, headed by a medical doctor named Dr. J. C. F. Siegfriedt, dreamed of building a new road to Yellowstone, an attraction that would bring in an influx of sorely needed tourism dollars. The vision of the physician and his fellows came true in 1931, thanks largely to their lobbying, when President Hoover signed into law the Leavitt Bill, which included the Park Approach Act. Crews from the Civilian Conservation Corps and a number of private contractors commenced construction, finishing their astounding, $2.5 million task in June 1936. The full length of the Beartooth Highway they constructed extends 68 miles, from Red Lodge to the Northeast Entrance of Yellowstone.

candy—more than 2,000 varieties!—inside is reason enough to wander into the old building, but once there you may be drawn away from the candy containers to the wall filled with historic photos and posters. The wall honors Red Lodge–area rodeo stars, including the celebrated Greenough and Linderman families, both of which claim national champions among their clans—and are responsible for garnering Red Lodge its nickname, the "Home of Champions."

If the rodeo display intrigues you, you'll find more about the Greenough family and Red Lodge rodeoing at the **Carbon County Historical Museum** (446-3914; www.carboncountyhistory.com), located at 224 N. Broadway Ave. and open Memorial Day through Labor Day, Mon through Sat from 10 a.m. to 6 p.m. and Sun from 11 a.m. to 3 p.m. The rest of the year's it's open Thurs and Fri 10 a.m. to 5 p.m. and Sat 11 a.m. to 3 p.m. Admission is $5 for adults and $3 for students.

Also on display outside the Red Lodge Chamber of Commerce visitor center, situated at the north end of Broadway Avenue, is the intact homestead cabin of legendary mountain man John Johnston, better known as **"Liver Eatin' Johnston,"** who served for a spell as the first constable of Red Lodge. Johnston, aka John Garrison, was reputedly the inspiration for the character played by Robert Redford on the wide screen in the 1972 mountain-man classic Jeremiah Johnson.

Don't leave Yellowstone Country before negotiating the **Beartooth National Scenic Byway,** arguably the most beautiful and exciting roadway in America. In a typical year, the lofty, 10,947-foot Beartooth Pass is open to cars from Memorial Day through mid-Oct (and to snowmobiles the remainder of the year), although brief snowstorms can cause temporary closures even in the middle of summer. If you tackle the byway in early summer, in places you'll be driving through a virtual tunnel of snow, with high snowbanks lining both sides of the road. Kids will get a kick out of battling it out with snowballs in late June.

montanatrivia

Montana's high point is 12,799-foot Granite Peak, located in the Beartooth Range of Yellowstone Country.

Once you reach the high, treeless alpine realm of the Hellroaring Plateau, trails beckon. The broad and surprisingly gentle landscape is dotted with small lakes, many of them brimming with golden, brook, and cutthroat trout. Dozens of varieties of tiny, colorful wildflowers blanket the ground during the short growing season; you might also notice polygons formed in the ground's surface, the product of constant freezing and thawing.

From Red Lodge, the 68-mile Beartooth Highway switchbacks its way up, up, up. It dips into Wyoming before veering north to return to Montana and then connects with the isolated outpost of Cooke City, Montana, and the Northeast Entrance into *Yellowstone National Park.* For more information on the roadway, call the Custer National Forest at 446-2103.

The remote *Pryor Mountain National Wild Horse Range* occupies the extreme southeast corner of Carbon County and an adjacent chunk of Wyoming. The secretary of the interior in 1968 designated this 30,000-acre area as the first federal wild-horse range.

Some believe the resident horses are direct descendants of the mustangs brought to North America by the Spanish conquistadors in the 1500s, and that the isolation provided by the area's deep canyons and remote mountains has kept them genetically pure. Others, typically those less fond of wild horses, are quick to argue that the horses descend from domesticated stock that escaped or was released back into the wild, and that they're no more closely related to the Spanish mustangs than are the horses seen in every farmer's pasture. Lending credence to the former theory is the fact that some of the Pryor Mountain horses lack the sixth lumbar vertebra, as the Spanish mustangs did.

Regardless of their genetic heritage, horses run wild along the eastern and southern fringes of the Custer National Forest and on adjacent Bureau of Land Management lands. In the past, the isolated Pryor Mountains also have been home during parts of the year to the Crow Indians and to a rich legacy of Native Americans preceding them. It's estimated that more than a thousand cultural sites are hidden in these hills, so watch closely for evidence of prehistoric human beings.

The range is reachable by dirt roads, some impassable when wet, leading southeast from the town of *Warren.* If you prefer to get there entirely on pavement, first go to Lovell, Wyoming, and then negotiate the 25-mile Bad Pass Road between that town and Barry's Landing, Montana. (Lovell is the location of the *Pryor Mountain Wild Mustang Center,* which you can visit online at www.pryormustangs.org.) Bighorn sheep can often be seen close to the Bad Pass Road in the fall, near the Devil Canyon Overlook. Another good strategy for viewing bighorn sheep and wild horses: Hike into the juniper-studded canyon behind the Hough Creek Ranger Station, where a natural spring attracts the animals.

This is exceedingly remote country, so obtain good travel directions and stock up on water, gas, and provisions before striking out. Call the Bureau of

montanatrivia

Columbus, the seat of Stillwater County, was originally known as Sheep Dip.

Land Management at 896-5013 for maps and additional information. Inquire also about **Petroglyph Canyon,** a tough-to-find site that you'll come quite close to on the route from Warren. Located on Bureau of Land Management lands, the prehistoric aboriginal carvings were added to the National Register of Historic Places in 1975.

Places to Stay in Yellowstone Country

THREE FORKS

Broken Spur Motel
124 W. Elm St.
(888) 354-3048
Moderate

Bud Lilly's Angler's Retreat
16 W. Birch St.
(406) 285-6690
Moderate

Fort Three Forks Motel
10776 US 287
(406) 285-3233
Moderate

Sacajawea Hotel
corner of Main and Ash
Streets
(406) 285-6515
Expensive

BOZEMAN

Fairfield Inn by Marriott
828 Wheat Dr.
(406) 587-2222
Moderate

Gallatin Gateway Inn
12 miles southwest of
Bozeman
76405 Gallatin Rd.
(US 191)
P.O. Box 376, Gallatin
Gateway 59730
(406) 763-4672
Expensive

**Gallatin National Forest
Recreational Cabins**
various locations
(406) 522-2520
Inexpensive

Holiday Inn
5 Baxter Lane
(406) 587-4561
Expensive

**Lehrkind Mansion
Bed & Breakfast**
corner of East Aspen Street
and North Wallace Avenue
(800) 992-6932
Expensive

Silver Forest Inn
15325 Bridger Canyon Rd.
(406) 586-1882
Expensive

Voss Inn
319 S. Willson Ave.
(406) 587-0982
Expensive

WEST YELLOWSTONE

Comfort Inn
638 Madison Ave.
(406) 646-4212
Moderate

Firehole Ranch
11500 Hebgen Lake Rd.
(406) 646-7294
Expensive

**Holiday Inn Sunspree
Resort West Yellowstone**
315 Yellowstone Ave.
(406) 646-7365
Expensive

Stage Coach Inn
209 Madison Ave.
(800) 842-2882
Expensive

Three Bear Lodge
217 Yellowstone Ave.
(406) 646-7353
Moderate

GARDINER

**Headwaters
of the Yellowstone
Bed & Breakfast**
northwest of Gardiner
(406) 848-7073
Expensive

Yellowstone River Motel
14 Park St.
(406) 848-7303
Moderate

LIVINGSTON

**Blue Winged Olive
Bed & Breakfast**
5157 US 89 South
(800) 471-1141
Expensive

Comfort Inn
114 Loves Lane
(406) 222-4400
Moderate

The Murray Hotel
201 W. Park St.
(406) 222-1350
Expensive

Super 8
105 Centennial Dr.
(800) 800-8000
Moderate

**Yellowstone Expeditions
Bed & Breakfast**
4996 US 89 South
(406) 222-4614
Expensive

RED LODGE

Pitcher Guest House
call for location and
reservations
(406) 446-2859
Expensive

The Pollard Hotel
2 N. Broadway Ave.
(406) 446-0001
Expensive

Rock Creek Resort
4 miles south on US 12
(406) 446-1111
Expensive

Super 8
1223 S. Broadway Ave.
(800) 800-8000
Moderate

Yodeler Motel
601 S. Broadway Ave.
(406) 446-1435
Moderate

Places to Eat in Yellowstone Country

THREE FORKS

Headwaters Restaurant
105 S. Main St.
(406) 285-4511
Moderate

**Land of Magic Dinner
Club**
6 miles east of Three Forks
in Logan
(406) 284-3794
Expensive

**Willow Creek Cafe
and Saloon**
7 miles south of Three
Forks in Willow Creek at
21 Main St.
(406) 285-3698
Moderate

BOZEMAN

Azteca (Mexican)
134 E. Main St.
(406) 586-5181
Moderate

The Baxter
(Italian and other)
105 W. Main St.
(406) 586-1314
Moderate

Cafe Zydeco
1520 W. Main St.
(406) 994-0188
Moderate

John Bozeman's Bistro
125 W. Main St.
(406) 587-4100

**MacKenzie River
Pizza Co.**
232 E. Main St.
(406) 587-0055
Moderate

Montana Ale Works
611 E. Main St.
(406) 587-7700
Moderate

Pickle Barrel
East Main Street downtown
and in the university area at
809 W. College St.
(406) 587-2411
Inexpensive

WEST YELLOWSTONE

The Gusher (pizza, etc.)
corner of Madison Avenue
and Dunraven Street
(406) 646-9050
Moderate

Old Town Cafe
128 Madison Ave.
(406) 646-0126
Inexpensive

**Oregon Short Line
Restaurant**
315 Yellowstone Ave.
(in the West Yellowstone
Conference Hotel)
(406) 646-7365
Moderate

Stage Coach Inn
209 Madison Ave.
(406) 646-7381
Moderate

Three Bear Restaurant
205 Yellowstone Ave.
(406) 646-7811
Moderate

LIVINGSTON

Adagio
101 North Main St.
(406) 222-7400
Expensive

2nd Street Bistro
123 N. Second St.
(406) 222-9463
Moderate

Northern Pacific Beanery
108 W. Park St.
(406) 222-7288
Moderate

Pickle Barrel of Livingston
31 S. Main St.
(406) 222-5469
Inexpensive

RED LODGE

Bogart's
11 S. Broadway Ave.
(406) 446-1784
Moderate

Bridge Creek Backcountry Kitchen & Wine Bar
116 S. Broadway Ave.
(406) 446-9900
Moderate

Café Regis
(breakfast and lunch)
corner of West Sixteenth St. and South Ward Avenue
(406) 446-1941
Inexpensive

Old Piney Dell Restaurant
at the Rock Creek Resort
(406) 446-1111
Expensive

Red Lodge Pizza Co.
115 S. Broadway Ave.
(406) 446-3333
Moderate

CUSTER–MISSOURI RIVER COUNTRY →

Custer Country and Missouri River Country encompass two of the state's designated travel regions. Combined, the two "countries" cover the eastern third of Montana, a region teeming with wide-open vistas and creatures such as mule deer and pronghorns, but lacking in humans. The twenty-one counties included are inhabited by roughly 200,000 people—a figure that is particularly impressive once you consider that nearly half of them live in Billings, the state's largest city. So, as you can imagine, the twenty counties excluding Yellowstone County, in which Billings is located, offer some uncrowded possibilities, indeed.

This route begins in that major city of Billings, with side trips leading east to Pompeys Pillar, north to Roundup, and south to the Crow Indian Reservation and Bighorn Canyon National Recreation Area. From Hardin you'll travel to the outback of extreme southeast Montana. Miles City, Baker, Ekalaka, and Glendive, towns you may or may not have heard of, are the major "metropolitan areas" in this part of the state. From there you'll drive to the Big Open, the most remote and least visited region of this immense state. From Jordan, after leading you on a loop around the northeast

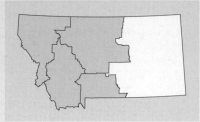

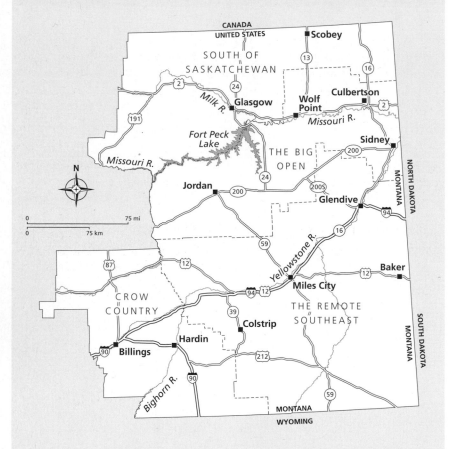

CANADA
UNITED STATES
Scobey

SOUTH OF
SASKATCHEWAN

13

16

Milk R.
24
Glasgow
Wolf Point
Culbertson
2
2

Missouri R.

Fort Peck Lake

191

Missouri R.

THE BIG OPEN

Sidney
200

NORTH DAKOTA

24

Jordan
200
200S
Glendive
94

MONTANA

N

0   75 mi
0   75 km

59

Yellowstone R.
16

87
12
Baker
12
94   12
Miles City

CROW COUNTRY

59

Colstrip
THE REMOTE SOUTHEAST

SOUTH DAKOTA

Hardin
90   Billings
212
MONTANA

90

Bighorn R.

MONTANA
WYOMING

59

corner of Montana—through towns that include Circle, Sidney, Culbertson, and Plentywood—the route covers the country north of monstrous Fort Peck Lake, where settlements with names like Glasgow and Saco grace the broad prairie expanses.

Crow Country

It is easy to draw generalizations about Montana's larger towns: Missoula, for instance, is a timber and university town, while Butte's economy is based on mineral extraction, and Bozeman is an agricultural and higher-learning center. *Billings,* nestled against the rimrocks carved by the Yellowstone River, has perhaps the most diverse economy of any city in Montana, with an emphasis on cattle, farming, and minerals—specifically, oil.

You might begin touring the Magic City by driving up to the rimrocks via Twenty-seventh Street, then turning east onto Highway 3 and, in 1 mile, right onto the Black Otter Trail. As you bang along this chuckholed road, you'll catch breath-stealing glimpses of the river basin below. At just over 2 miles is a turnaround; as you circle a knob in another ¾ mile, stop at *Yellowstone Kelly's Grave,* which is set off by a split-rail cedar fence.

AUTHOR'S FAVORITES

Chief Plenty Coups State Park
Pryor
(406) 252-1289

Evelyn Cameron Gallery
Terry
(406) 635-4040

Fort Union Trading Post National Historic Site
Fairview
(701) 572-9083
(visitor center is in North Dakota)

Granrud's Lefse Shack
Opheim
(406) 762-3250

Makoshika State Park
Glendive
(406) 377-6256

Medicine Lake National Wildlife Refuge
Medicine Lake
(406) 789-2305

Medicine Rocks State Park
Ekalaka
(406) 234-0926

Range Riders Museum and Memorial Hall
Miles City
(406) 232-4483

Rosebud Battlefield State Monument
between Busby and Decker
(406) 234-0900

Sleeping Buffalo Hot Springs
Saco
(406) 527-3370

A sign at Kelly's gravesite reads:

A LONG BREACH-LOADING SPRINGFIELD RIFLE COVERED FROM MUZZLE TO STOCK WITH THE SKIN OF A HUGE BULLSNAKE WAS CARRIED BY MAJOR LUTHER SAGE 'YELLOWSTONE' KELLY, SHAKESPEARE-QUOTING INDIAN FIGHTER AND SCOUT. KELLY, A NEW YORKER BORN APRIL 19, 1849, AND CIVIL WAR VETERAN, GUIDED GOVERNMENT EXPEDITIONS IN THE 1870S AND '80S IN THE YELLOWSTONE RIVER VALLEY. HE LATER SERVED WITH THE MILITARY IN ALASKA AND THE PHILIP-PINES AND THEN RETIRED TO CALIFORNIA BEFORE HIS DEATH DECEMBER 17, 1928. HE ASKED TO BE BURIED ON THIS POINT OVERLOOKING THE AREA HE HAD SCOUTED. . . . YELLOWSTONE KELLY WAS THE LITTLE BIG MAN WITH A BIG HEART.

You can appreciate why Kelly so loved this spot, for the view is splendid (the smoke-belching refinery immediately below notwithstanding): the city, the Yellowstone River Valley, the Pryor Mountains, and, beyond, the distant Beartooths, Bighorns, and other ranges. Early morning is the best time to visit the tranquil spot, before the city below has awakened.

The **Moss Mansion,** at 914 Division St. in Billings, is a piece of opu-lent evidence left behind by one who profited handsomely from the natural wealth of this country. The veritable castle of stone-block construction, with its red-tiled roof, remains nearly unchanged from the day in 1903 when the Preston B. Moss family moved into their new domicile. It cost $105,000 to build the mansion—this at a time when the price for an average house was about $3,000.

Moss, who moved to Billings in 1892, became president and owner of the First National Bank and delved into numerous other enterprises, including the hotel, utilities, and publishing businesses. Many of his family's original furnish-ings decorate the ornate rooms of the three-story house, which was designed by famous turn-of-the-twentieth-century architect Henry Janeway Harden-bergh. Finely woven Persian rugs, stained glass, and woodwork of polished mahogany, oak, and red birch were all used extensively, lending rich tones and a vibrancy to the library, lounge, and other rooms.

MAJOR ATTRACTIONS WORTH SEEING

Little Bighorn Battlefield National Monument
Hardin

ZooMontana
Billings

For decades the mansion was cloaked in secrecy, as Miss Melville Moss continued living there alone after the rest of her family had passed away. A hedge eventually covered the lower level, so that only second- and third-story windows were visible to those passing by, and rarely was anyone seen being admitted into the house by its lone resident. Miss Moss died at the age of eighty-eight in 1984, and soon thereafter Billings residents finally had the opportunity to view what lay inside the mansion long camouflaged by brush and ivy vines. Its elegance stunned visitors, and a community-wide determination quickly mounted to save the grand home.

montanatrivia

Torres Mexican Products, family-owned for nearly half a century, creates handmade tortillas and salsas Tuesday through Saturday at their cafe/kitchen at 6200 S. Frontage Rd. in Billings. You can call ahead for orders at 652-8426.

No secret today, the Moss Mansion has even been discovered by Hollywood. Several scenes of *Son of the Morning Star,* a television miniseries about George Armstrong Custer, were shot in its interior.

The mansion is owned by the Montana Historical Society, while the nonprofit Billings Preservation Society administers it and raises funds for maintenance. Guided tours are offered on the hour in summer from 9 a.m. to 4 p.m. Mon through Sat and 1 to 3 p.m. on Sun. The rest of the year they're available seven days a week from 1 to 3 p.m. Admission is $7 for adults, $5 for students and seniors, and $3 for children ages six to twelve. For information on the many seasonal events held at the Moss Mansion, call 256-5100 or go to www .mossmansion.com.

Duffers will find a most unusual course at the **Circle Inn Golf Links,** located behind the Circle Inn restaurant at 1029 Main St. The entire nine-hole course is less than 800 yards long, or about one-quarter as long as a typical course. The average hole is only 89 yards, and the par is just 27. A round takes less than an hour, and even novices will have a good time without holding up the players behind.

A round of golf, cocktails, and dinner at the Circle Inn, featuring some of the best beef cuts to be found in this beef eater's town, is a popular way for Billings residents to while away a summer evening, when lights permit play to continue until past midnight. Greens

montanatrivia

Kampgrounds of America, better known as KOA, established its first campground along the Yellowstone River in 1962 in Billings, where the company is still headquartered.

fees are $6 for nine or eighteen holes ($7 after 6 p.m.), and you can rent the two or three clubs needed. For dinner reservations and more information, call 248-4202.

Billings citizens are justifiably proud of their **Riverfront Park**, a greenbelt featuring a system of trails and recreation sites surrounding two small lakes. One of them, Lake Josephine, was named after the stern-wheeler Josephine, which reached Billings in June 1875—the farthest upstream a steamboat ever made it on the Yellowstone River. Cycling, canoeing, picnicking, bird-watching, and fishing are all popular activities in the summer, while ice-skating on the lakes and cross-country skiing on the 2-mile Lake Loop and 3-mile Forest Loop trails gain favor in the colder months. The park, open from 5 a.m. to 10 p.m. daily, is located on South Billings Boulevard (exit 447) on I-90. Turn left before reaching the South Bridge. A sign indicates the park.

Before leaving the Billings area, take a trip along the scenic, 5-mile back road leading to **Pictograph Cave State Historic Site**, where some of Montana's most significant archaeological finds, dating back some 4,500 years, have been unearthed. Take the Lockwood interchange on I-90 (exit 452) and turn right at the stoplight and then immediately right again at the sign pointing toward the pictographs. In 2¼ miles the road turns to gravel and descends into a dramatic, sandstone-rim canyon, punctuated with stands of ponderosa pine. After 2¾ miles of gravel you'll reach the parking area, from which a narrow asphalt trail winds steeply up into the caves.

Pictograph Cave was named a National Historic Landmark in 1964, and in 1969 the Montana Department of Fish, Wildlife and Parks assumed responsibility for its protection. It's now open to visitors May 1 through Sept 30 from 8 a.m. to 8 p.m. at an admission fee of $4 per car for nonresidents, while those calling Montana home are admitted for free. For more information call 247-2940 or visit www.pictographcave.org.

From 5 miles north of Billings on US 87, turn east onto old Highway 10 and take a side trip through the verdant portion of the Yellowstone River Valley known as the Huntley Project, a shortening of the official moniker, Huntley Irrigation Project. The Bureau of Reclamation opened the headgates for the irrigation project in 1907, making it one of the first of its kind after Congress passed the Reclamation Act of 1902. The project comprises four towns—Huntley, Ballantine, Worden, and Pompeys Pillar.

"A thousand smiles and a million memories" await those who visit the **Huntley Project Museum of Irrigated Agriculture** (348-2533; http://huntleyprojectmuseum.org), at the site of the former town of Osborn in Homesteader Park, 3 miles east of Huntley. The museum, featuring eighteen homestead buildings and artifacts used in the early days of farming and

Prehistoric Montana

There's not a lot of evidence remaining at Pictograph Cave of the early Americans who once resided there, but by using one's imagination it's not hard to picture a place swarming with early human activity.

Amid the harsh environment of the prehistoric plains, the surrounding area was an unusually attractive spot to reside. Water was abundant, and the caves are situated such that they are protected from cold northerly winds and hit full-force by the sun's warming rays during the short days of winter. Moreover, the point where Bitter Creek, the stream just below the parking lot, empties into the Yellowstone River was a natural river ford; for millennia animals traveled the route, and for centuries people followed.

Dozens of edible foods were available in the pine- and bramble-filled ravines surrounding the caves: fruits like chokecherry, wild grape, gooseberry, currant, and buffalo berry; and roots, bulbs, and herbs, such as arrow-leaf balsam root, wild onion, asparagus, wild turnip, and yucca.

The three rock overhangs lining the Eagle Sandstone cliffs are known as Ghost Cave, Pictograph Cave, and the smaller and shallower Middle Cave. The floors of Ghost and Pictograph were excavated by a Works Progress Administration crew in 1937; 30,000 artifacts were recovered at several distinct levels of occupation. Projectile points, stone knives, and animal bones were dug from as deep as 40 feet below the ground surface in Pictograph, the largest of the three caves. Among the most significant finds unearthed were the rock paintings, also of various ages, on the wall of Pictograph. (Although badly faded, some of these can still be made out.)

In 1940 William T. Mulloy, a doctoral candidate at the University of Chicago, took over the project. Most of the excavations were already completed, so Mulloy's primary task was to inspect and interpret what had been found. He concluded that the Empty Gulch area had been occupied during four distinct periods, ranging from around 2600 B.C. to historic times. The chronology Mulloy devised to relate specific artifacts to particular time periods became the standard still used to date artifacts found throughout the Great Plains. Mulloy went on to a long and distinguished career at the University of Wyoming and became well known in the archaeological world for additional works on the plains and on isolated Easter Island in the Pacific Ocean.

irrigation, details the way in which this dry country was converted into the lush, crop-filled valley seen today. May through Sept the museum is open from 10 a.m. to 4 p.m. Tues through Sat; in winter it's open the same hours on Mon and Tues only (or by appointment). Perhaps the best time to visit is on the second weekend in July, when the Huntley Project Lions Club hosts the celebration known as *Homesteader Days* at Homesteader Park.

The town of Pompeys Pillar, at the eastern end of the Huntley Project, was named after *Pompeys Pillar National Historic Landmark,* the nearby, prominent sandstone butte. On his trip back east through the Yellowstone River Valley in 1806, Capt. William Clark carved his name on the face of the butte, where it can still be seen today. This is significant because it's the only known physical evidence remaining of the expedition along the entire *Lewis and Clark National Historic Trail.*

Long before Captain Clark visited on July 25, 1806, the butte was known by American Indians as a good camping spot, and Clark found that numerous petroglyphs had been carved into its face by his predecessors. Quite taken with the view after climbing to the summit, Clark wrote that he could see the snow-capped Rockies to the southwest and the Bull Mountains to the northwest, while huge numbers of buffalo, elk, and wolves meandered about the prairie before him.

Clark called the feature "Pompy's Tower" in honor of Baptiste Charbonneau, Sacajawea's young son, whom Clark had nicknamed Pompy, or "little chief" in Shoshonean. The name was changed to Pompeys Pillar when the journals of Lewis and Clark were published in 1814.

The pillar figured heavily for the next several decades as a landmark for trappers and explorers and as a campsite for both Indians and U.S. troops. With the completion of the Northern Pacific Railroad in 1882, Pompeys Pillar became a popular stopover, and the railroad eventually placed a protective grate over Clark's signature. The landmark was privately held from 1906 until 1991, when it and the surrounding 366 acres were purchased for just under $900,000 by the Bureau of Land Management. Today's visitor can climb a 200-step boardwalk to view Clark's signature and then continue to the mesa top. The site is open to the public at $7 per car Memorial Day through Labor Day from 8 a.m. to 8 p.m. daily and Labor Day through mid-Oct from 9 a.m. to 4

Big Pie Country

There are a lot of places to order up a great slice of homemade pie in Montana. Here's a small sampling of ten favorites:

Log Cabin Family Restaurant, Choteau	Yesterday's Cafe, Dell
Bridger Cafe, Bridger	Book 'n' Bear, Glendive
Home Cafe, Conrad	Libby Cafe, Libby
Glen's Cafe, Florence	The Shack, Missoula
Three Forks Cafe, Three Forks	Stella's Kitchen, Billings

p.m. daily. (Admission is free with Golden Age, Golden Access, and Golden Eagle Passports.) Walk-in visits are permitted the rest of the year. For information call 875-2400 or 896-5013 or visit the Web site at www.pompeyspillar.org.

Before heading south to the Crow and Cheyenne reservations, consider a loop trip north to the broad sweep of rolling farm and ranch country surrounding the Musselshell River. Begin the 120-mile route by going northwest on Highway 3 through Acton and Broadview, then cross the Musselshell and turn east onto US 12 at Lavina. In another 20 miles you'll arrive at **Roundup,** which served as the kick-off point for the **Great Centennial Cattle Drive** of 1989. Thousands of head of cattle were moved to Billings by some 3,500 drive participants, who ranged from saddle-sure wranglers to saddle-sore greenhorns.

A few miles northwest of Roundup is the three-unit **Lake Mason National Wildlife Refuge,** totaling 16,000 acres of prairie marsh and adjacent uplands that provide ample opportunity to see an assortment of critters. Migrating waterfowl, like Canada geese and white pelicans, are common during the spring and fall, and nesting shorebirds, such as avocets and sandpipers, can be seen during the summer. Watch also for pronghorn antelope, coyotes, and red fox.

The verdant scent of the marsh and its buzz of activity, especially during the evening and early morning, make the place seem uncommonly alive in contrast with the surrounding dry and quiet prairie. To reach the refuge, take Golf Course Road west from town, turn right in about 6 miles, and arrive at Lake Mason in another 3 miles. Call 538-8706 for more information.

From Roundup, US 87 leads south over the Bull Mountains and back to Montana's largest city. From the I-90 Lockwood interchange (exit 452), go south for ½ mile and turn right onto Old Pryor Road. The road soon rolls into a stunning landscape of timbered buttes, sandstone cliffs, and bottomlands brimming with hayfields and huge cottonwoods—in all, some of southeast Montana's prettiest country. From the ridgetops along the route, you'll earn long-range vistas of this land, historic home to the nomadic Plains Indians and to endless herds of buffalo.

After 10 miles, turn right, following Old Pryor Road. On reaching the Crow Indian village of **Pryor** in another 23 miles, turn right at the stop sign, go ¾ mile and turn in to **Chief Plenty Coups State Park.** This park celebrates *Aleck-chea-ahoosh*—which translates to "Many Achievements" or "Plenty Coups"—the last great war chief of the Crow. It's a wonderfully peaceful place: The Castle Rocks of the Pryor Mountains rise to the south, and Pryor Creek gurgles below a stand of box elders near the base of a protective sandstone rim on the north. Black-capped chickadees, revealed through Plenty Coups's dreams as his own good medicine, flutter about.

Plenty Coups

Chief Plenty Coups was born near present-day Billings in 1848 and died in 1932. Inviting, grassy picnic sites surround his grave, where Strikes the Iron and Kills Together, two of Plenty Coups's wives, also are buried. (In Crow fashion, after the death of Kills Together, Plenty Coups took her sister, Strikes the Iron, as his next wife.) An American flag flutters atop a tall pole, reminding us that here lies not only a great Indian chief but also an American hero.

When chosen to represent all Indians of the Americas in a ceremony at the Tomb of the Unknown Soldier in 1921, Plenty Coups's brief but stirring speech was said to have brought tears to the eyes of more than one old hard-edged cavalry man: "For the Indians of America I call upon the Great Spirit . . . that the dead should not have died in vain, the war might end and peace be purchased by the blood of red men and white." It was on this trip east that Plenty Coups visited George Washington's Mount Vernon, instilling in him the idea of donating his home as a historic site for the enjoyment of the American people.

Plenty Coups was a proud Indian who had come to terms with the whites, realizing that to continue fighting them would do more harm than good to the Crows. A proponent of goodwill among all people, when deeding his property to the nation in 1928, Plenty Coups asserted that it must be a park for all people to use together. "My people—the Crow nation—have not always been treated fairly," he said. "They hold no hate. Today I, who have been called the chief of chiefs among red men, present to all the children of our great white father this land, where the snows of more than fifty winters have fallen on my tepee. This park is not to be a memorial to me but to the Crow nation. It is given as a token of my friendship for all people, both red and white . . . "

The park museum houses Plenty Coups's personal items and additional displays examining the Crow culture, and nearby is the chief's stout, square-hewn log house. The original central section of the house was built around 1885, the eastern portion in 1906, and the west wing was added at an unknown date; its fireplace was constructed of bricks salvaged from Fort Custer, which was situated near present-day Hardin. It is said that Plenty Coups drank daily from the Medicine Springs, still flowing beneath the huge cottonwoods next to his house, the waters of which he considered a source of strength and power.

Chief Plenty Coups State Park is open from 8 a.m. to 8 p.m. daily (with the museum open 10 a.m. to 5 p.m.) May through Sept, and between Oct and Apr by appointment. Admission for nonresident visitors is $5 per vehicle; for more information call 252-1289 or visit http://fwp.mt.gov/lands/site_283264 .aspx.

Follow the paved road leading east from Pryor for some 35 miles to Saint Xavier, then turn south onto Highway 313, and shortly you'll arrive at the **Bighorn Canyon National Recreation Area.** Most of the 63,000-acre recreational haven straddling the Montana-Wyoming border is easily reachable only by boat, on the waters of 60-mile-long Bighorn Lake. The northernmost 55 miles of the reservoir lap against the walls of the dazzling, multihued Bighorn Canyon, considered by many as this region's small-scale version of the Grand Canyon.

Afterbay Reservoir, the 2-mile stretch of water between Yellowtail Dam and the much smaller Afterbay Dam, has garnered a reputation as an extraordinary spot for winter bird-watching. Meanwhile, the waters downstream from Afterbay Dam are a nationally known, blue-ribbon trout fishery.

At the **Yellowtail Dam Visitor Center,** operated by the National Park Service for the Bureau of Reclamation, you'll find displays on Crow tribal history and the Yellowtail Dam, which was constructed in the late 1960s, as well as exhibits explaining how the project helps to serve the irrigation, hydroelectric, recreation, and flood control needs of the region. You'll also learn about the rich natural history and prehistory of the region, and perhaps pick up a tip on where to hike to find an ancient buffalo jump or vision-quest site. Inquire here also about arranging a ranger-led tour to the site of Fort C. E. Smith (now on private land), established in 1866 to protect gold prospectors traveling the Bozeman Trail from attack by Sioux Indians. The visitor center is open daily from 9 a.m. to 5 p.m. Memorial Day through late Aug, and Thurs through Mon from 9 a.m. to 5 p.m. through late Sept (closed the rest of the year). Admission is $5 per vehicle. Call 666-2412 or tap into www.nps.gov/bica for additional information.

As you drive through this area, gaze up at the cliffs above the Grapevine Creek Drainage. According to Crow Indian history and also to the journal of trapper Zenas Leonard, these hills hosted an unusually ferocious and bloody battle in 1834 between two Indian tribes. A band of Piegan (Blackfeet) warriors who had strayed far from their homeland (which ranged between present-day Browning, Montana, and Calgary, Alberta) surely knew they were treading on dangerous ground in this Crow territory. And they were. A group of Crows attacked and annihilated the band of Piegan, but not before at least thirty Crows were killed.

Crow Fair, held the third weekend in August at **Crow Agency** (the "Teepee Capital of the World"), boasts one of the biggest rodeos in Montana, a horse-fest including bareback show riding by Crows—known as the best riders among the Plains Indians—and horse racing with pari-mutuel betting. Crow Fair is one of the preeminent powwows for all of North America's

Indians, and members of tribes throughout the United States and Canada come for the dance competitions, parades, and other events. Neophyte attendees are coached by announcers at the various events regarding what actions are expected or are taboo. Crow Fair is held at the tribal campgrounds along the Little Bighorn River. You can't miss it—just look for the sea of tepees flooding the bottomlands. Call 638-3700 or tap into http://crowfair.crowtribe.com to learn more.

Before heading east, consider taking a side trip 13 miles north to Hardin to visit the **Big Horn County Historical Museum and Visitor Center.** First opened in 1979, the museum complex incorporates two dozen historic structures along with a handful of new buildings on twenty-two acres of grounds. Within view is the site of old Fort Custer, presently a wheat field but once one of the most modern of the frontier forts. A number of abodes and places of business, worship, and schooling have been moved from various outlying locations to the museum grounds. Some are filled with old-time goodies, such as farm machinery and railroad memorabilia, designed to lend the visitor a sense of what life on the frontier must have been like for white settlers.

montanatrivia

Reportedly, the largest snowflake ever recorded in the United States fell at Fort Keogh (Miles City) in 1887. It was 15 inches across.

The free-to-enter museum, located just off I-90 at exit 497 (go 3 blocks south to Third Street), is open daily 8 a.m. to 5 p.m. May 1 through Sept 30. The rest of the year, the visitor center operates weekdays only on the same hourly schedule (the historic buildings are closed during this time). Call 665-1671 or visit www.bighorncountymuseum.org for further information.

The Remote Southeast

US 212 heads east into the 444,000-acre **Northern Cheyenne Indian Reservation,** home to around 3,500 Cheyenne Indians. For a decade, beginning in 1874, the Northern Cheyenne were a homeless people. First uprooted from the Black Hills and southeastern Montana when gold fever hit the region, they were shuffled off to the valleys of the Tongue and Powder Rivers; then they were sent to live in Indian Territory (present-day Oklahoma) with the Southern Cheyenne. In 1878, on a heroic journey poignantly documented in Mari Sandoz's book, *Cheyenne Autumn,* Northern Cheyenne chiefs Little Wolf and Dull Knife struck out to lead their people back to the north country they loved. En route, they were trapped by soldiers and incarcerated at Fort Robinson,

Nebraska, then moved to the Sioux reservation at Pine Ridge, South Dakota, where they spent several years. Finally, in 1884, they returned home to the newly designated Northern Cheyenne Indian Reservation.

From Lame Deer, 42 miles east of Crow Agency, travel 21 miles east on US 212 to the town of Ashland. The *St. Labre Mission* and *Cheyenne Indian Museum* offer visitors the chance to gain a better appreciation for the enduring spirit of the Morning Star People. Free tours of the mission, the museum, and the St. Labre Indian School, founded in 1884—all located at the edge of town—are available from 8 a.m. to 5:30 p.m. daily, Memorial Day through Labor Day. (Management requests that bus-tour operators call in advance to ensure that enough staff members are on duty.) For more information call 784-4500 or go to www.stlabre.org.

Broadus, located 35 miles east of Ashland on US 212, is home to the *Powder River Historical Museum & Mac's Museum.* Displayed inside are a lot of things, including a real surprise, considering that Broadus is situated high and dry hundreds of miles from the nearest ocean: one of the largest private collections of seashells in the world. The approximately 22,000 seashells and other marine life specimens were collected by the late R. D. "Mac" MacCurdy, who homesteaded in the area but obviously spent a lot of time oceanside. The museum (436-2977), located at 102 W. Wilson St., is open Mon through Sat 9 a.m. to 5 p.m. from Memorial Day through the end of Sept, and by appointment the rest of the year.

Colstrip, 22 miles north of Lame Deer on Highway 39, is "the town that coal built." The Northern Pacific Railway established Colstrip in 1923 to house the workers the company had employed to mine the local coal to fuel its locomotives. By 1959, however, diesel had replaced coal as the preferred fuel for powering trains, and Colstrip was sold to the Montana Power Company. During the construction of two gargantuan power plants in the 1980s, the town's population mushroomed to more than 8,000 but has since leveled off to 2,300. Well-planned and unexpectedly attractive, Colstrip is obviously a company town, although most of the businesses and residences are privately owned. If desiring overnight accommodations in the area, consider the *Lakeview Bed and Breakfast,* situated on a slope overlooking Castle Rock Lake. The inn has six guest rooms, three of which face the picturesque body of water. Rates range from $98 to $138 per night. For reservations or more information call 748-3653 or visit www.lakeviewbnb.com.

In the county seat of Forsyth—tucked into a pretty, protected setting below pine-studded bluffs—stop by to see the *Rosebud County Courthouse,* a grand neoclassical building capped with an ornate copper dome and listed in the National Register of Historic Places. The top floor of the building explodes in a colorful display of murals and stained glass. Next door you'll find the **Rosebud County Pioneer Museum,** worth visiting while in the neighborhood. The museum (356-7547) is open May 1 through Sept 15, 9 a.m. to 6 p.m., Mon through Sat, and on Sun from 1 to 6 p.m. The address is 1331 Main St.

Before heading eastward along I-90, consider making the 40-mile side trip northwest on US 12 to the far-from-anywhere settlement of **Ingomar.** The town once was a major wool-shipping railhead along the now-defunct Milwaukee Road, boasting nearly fifty businesses. Some 2,500 homestead claims were filed in the area between 1911 and 1917. But today the spot in the road is all but a ghost town. Of what remains, the surprising **Jersey Lilly Cafe** is known throughout Montana for a plate of beans considered by some the best in the West. The restaurant (358-2278) is open daily from 7 a.m. until midnight. There are also RV hookups at the enterprise.

In **Miles City** shoot straight for the **Range Riders Museum and Memorial Hall,** a monument dedicated to the great American cowboy and cowgirl. Miles City, the oldest white settlement in this part of Montana, became its primary cowtown after the Northern Pacific Railway pushed through in 1881. Herds were driven hundreds of miles from the central and eastern ranges of Montana and beyond to the railhead here. (The popular TV miniseries *Lonesome Dove* was based on a fictional cattle drive that takes place between Texas and Miles City.) Lending the downtown color today are classic western taverns, with names like Range Rider Bar, Montana Bar, and Log Cabin Saloon, all aglow in bright neon.

Cattle and horses meant cowboys, of course, and the area produced some of the country's best bronc riders. Realizing the significance of what already in 1938 was a colorful history, a group of **Miles City** stock growers and fellow townspeople formed the organization now known as the Range Riders. Their first facility was constructed of logs cut in western Montana and shipped to town, gratis, by the Northern Pacific Railroad. It was situated near where the Tongue River empties into the Yellowstone—fittingly, the very site where some sixty years earlier Gen. Nelson A.

montanatrivia

Garryowen, a name attached to a small town near the Little Bighorn Battlefield National Monument, is taken from a popular Irish tune that served as the official song of George Custer's 7th Cavalry.

Miles had constructed Cantonment 1, a temporary quarters for soldiers waiting for the completion of nearby **Fort Keogh.** Miles had been dispatched, in the wake of **Custer**'s defeat at the Little Bighorn, to establish this fort—named after Capt. Myles Keogh, who was killed at the Little Bighorn—along the Yellowstone River to serve as a headquarters for the Indian campaign.

The Range Riders' original log building now serves as the hub of a complex of buildings gracing the museum grounds. There's a lot to be seen. Memorial Hall features plaques honoring some 500 pioneering range riders. These plaques include a brief biography of each honoree's life. Found inside

Up Rosebud Creek

Another battle, much better known and documented than the Crow–Piegan skirmish of 1834, took place about 30 miles away as the raven flies at the **Little Bighorn Battlefield National Monument**. At this major attraction the National Park Service maintains outstanding interpretive displays and facilities. Yet another battle—somewhere between these two in importance and public awareness—exploded several miles southeast of the Little Bighorn. It was the Battle of the Rosebud, where Gen. George Crook and forces were attacked on June 17, 1876, by the same Sioux and Cheyenne warriors who annihilated Custer and his troops eight days later along the Little Bighorn.

Crook's army consisted of 1,000 cavalry and infantry troops, along with roughly 450 Crow and Shoshone warriors and aides. Among the warriors: a twenty-eight-year-old Crow Indian named Plenty Coups. Crook, an old-hat Indian fighter, was moving his men north from Fort Fetterman, Wyoming, as one line of a huge military operation designed to close in on "hostiles" along the Bighorn, Tongue, and Powder Rivers. However, before nearing the other two parties, which were coming in from central Montana and Bismarck, Dakota Territory, Crook was trapped and repeatedly attacked on Rosebud Creek by Crazy Horse and his warriors.

Although Crook later maintained that he won the battle, just about anyone who was there would have said otherwise. The Cheyenne-Sioux victory at Rosebud Creek readied the Indians mentally and physically for the battle a week later, in which George Armstrong Custer and his detachment out of Bismarck were decimated. Not incidentally, when Custer attacked the Indian encampment on the Little Bighorn, he fully believed Crook's soldiers and warriors were still heading in his direction and that they would be there to provide backup if needed. In reality, they'd been repelled at the Battle of the Rosebud and had retreated into Wyoming.

Today at **Rosebud Battlefield National Historic Landmark**, you'll find a preserved buffalo jump, displays on pioneer cattle-ranching efforts in the area, and a self-guiding tour interpreting the battle's back-and-forth action. Quiet and remote, the 3,000-acre park also includes the homestead ranch of the Kobold family. To get there, from I-90 go east on US 212 for approximately 25 miles. Just inside the Northern Cheyenne Indian Reservation, but before reaching Busby, turn south onto CR 314. You'll come to the battlefield site in about 20 miles. Don't look for a water supply, but do keep your eyes peeled for rattlesnakes. For additional information you can call Montana Fish, Wildlife and Parks in Miles City at 234–0900.

the vaultlike Gun Building is a priceless, 500-piece collection of firearms donated in 1987 by the Bert Clark family. The guns span at least 300 years of history and include an early wick-ignition, matchlock Arabian rifle; models of the guns that won the West; and World War I and World War II weapons.

Additional buildings house the Wilson Photo Collection of Old Timers, the Fort Keogh Officers' Quarters, and the Homestead House. The museum, found at the west end of Main Street just over the Tongue River Bridge, is open between Apr 1 and Oct 31 from 8 a.m. to 6 p.m. daily. The admission fee is $5 for adults, $4 for seniors, $1 for high-school and college students, 50 cents for elementary-school students, and free for children six and under. For more details call 232-6146.

An event not unrelated to the community's vivid cowboying past is the **World Famous Miles City Bucking Horse Sale,** held every third weekend in May. The town pulls out all the stops for this one, and the partying contin-ues without break from Fri through Sun. Festivities include a wild-horse drive, street dances, cowboy poetry readings, barbecues, the always-popular rodeo, and much more. "Buck-outs" are contested, with the wildest, buckingest horses drawing top dollar from rodeo-stock contractors from throughout North Amer-ica. Wedged between buck-outs are somewhat more tame but no less exciting thoroughbred horse races, with pari-mutuel betting offered.

The Bucking Horse Sale is a popular and nationally known event. Since beginning in 1950, it's attracted a lot of well-known personalities—including Ted Kennedy, who, when campaigning for brother John in 1960, lasted about five seconds on a wild bronc. For information on the popular Bucking Horse Sale, call the Miles City Chamber of Commerce at 234-2890 or go to www .buckinghorsesale.com. Make your reservations early!

Ekalaka, named for the Sioux Indian bride of early settler David Harrison Russell, is not on the road to anywhere. It's one of those places to which you must intend to go in order to ever get there. Either that or you have become incredibly lost.

To get to Ekalaka entirely on paved roads, drive the 77 desolate miles of piney hills and rolling grasslands separating Miles City and Baker, then turn south onto Highway 7 and continue for 35 miles. (At the **O'Fallon Historical Museum** in Baker, you might be able to coax directions out of an old-timer for side trips to prehistoric human sites or ruts carved by wagon trains passing through the area. The museum's phone number is 778-3265.)

Why bother going to Ekalaka? Well, it's one of the most marvelously empty corners of Montana; other than that, perhaps the best excuse is the **Carter County Museum,** located at 306 North Main St. Montana's first county-run museum houses a large collection of fossils and artifacts found throughout the area, including a complete skeleton of an Anatosaurus, or duck-billed dino-saur— the Montana State Fossil—dug in 1937 just a few miles from town. Also on display are Triceratops skulls and a mammoth skeleton. The museum build-ing itself is a fossil of sorts, with its construction of native stone and petrified wood. It's open year-round Tues through Fri 9 a.m. to 5 p.m. and weekends 1 to 5 p.m. Admission is free. For more information call 775-6886 or visit www .cartercountymuseum.com.

On your way to Ekalaka perhaps you noticed protruding from the roll-ing prairie and pine-covered hills the pockmarked pillars of *Medicine Rocks State Park.* On the way back north, stop and have a look, as Teddy Roosevelt did in 1883. Of his camping trip here, Roosevelt later wrote, "Altogether it was

Where Have All the Horses Gone?

In the 1930s a Midwest-based outfit called Chappel Brothers Company (CBC) employed dozens of Montana cowboys, who were assigned to riding the ranges sur-rounding Miles City. These cowboys should have been called horseboys, however, because it was equines and not bovines that they spent their days herding and tend-ing to.

Across hundreds of acres of open range, much of it composed of former home-steads abandoned by their settlers, the cowboys grazed thousands of horses. The best of the bunch were sold to the U.S. Army as cavalry mounts, but most of the horses wound up at a cannery in Rockford, Illinois, where they were butchered. The finer cuts were sold to European markets for human consumption, while the trimmings went into Ken-L Ration dog food. At one point CBC was the second-biggest user of tin cans in the United States, runner-up only to the Campbell Soup Company. "I think they fed practically the whole dog population of Philadelphia with those trimmings," said Phil Rich, an Ohio business executive who attended a 1994 gathering of former CBC riders, bosses, and descendants of those who worked for the company during the era. The group congregated at the Range Riders Museum in Miles City during the forty-fourth annual Bucking Horse Sale festivities.

Responding to a recent publication that had included an article erroneously say-ing that CBC stood for Christian Brothers Company, master of ceremonies John L. Moore, a rancher whose father worked for the company, said, "The North Side [range north of Miles City, that is] was not a monastery, Sid Vollin [one of the CBC trail bosses] was not a monk, and the last time I checked, the Christian Brothers were making wine, not horseflesh."

A growing network of roads in the Midwest had led to a decline in the number of horses in that region, which is what persuaded CBC to expand its range into Mon-tana. CBC got out of the horse business after selling Ken-L Ration to Quaker Oats in 1943.

as fantastically beautiful a place as I have ever seen; it seemed impossible that the hand of man should not have something to do with the formation."

Native Americans, conversely, held that the unearthly landscape must have been created by the Great Spirit. Historically, the area has been of spiritual significance to the Cheyenne and Sioux, who held spirit-renewal ceremonies at these rocks containing "big medicine." Many stone circles and other prehistoric artifacts have been found at Medicine Rocks, indicating that it was also an important spot for the nomadic groups preceding the Sioux and Cheyenne.

TOP ANNUAL EVENTS

Montana Outdoor Recreation Expo
Billings; Mar
(406) 657-1200

Eastern Montana Celtic Festival
Glendive; Mar
(406) 377-6690

Miles City Bucking Horse Sale
Miles City; mid-May
(406) 232-7700

Custer's Last Stand Reenactment and Little Big Horn Days
Hardin; late June
(406) 234–2890

Fort Union Rendezvous
Sidney; late June
(406) 433-1916

Longest Dam Run
Glasgow; mid-June
(406) 228-2222

Governor's Cup Walleye Tournament
Glasgow; early July
(406) 228-2222

Wild Horse Stampede
Wolf Point; early July
(406) 653-2012

Wahcinca Dakota Oyate Celebration
Poplar; mid-July
(406) 768-5186

Magic City Hot Air Balloon Rally
Billings; late July
(406) 671-3104

Hispanic Fiesta
Billings; early Aug
(406) 248-8492

Northeast Montana Fair
Glasgow; mid-Aug
(406) 228-6266

Montana Fair
Billings; mid-Aug
(406) 256-2400

Eastern Montana Fair
Miles City; late Aug
(406) 234–3848

Crow Fair
Crow Agency; late Aug
(406) 638-3700

Northeast Montana Threshing Bee
Culbertson; late Sept
(406) 787-5265

NILE Stock Show and Rodeo
Billings; Oct
(406) 256-2495

Alzada Cowboy Poetry Show
Alzada; Oct
(406) 828-4517

You, too, may find the remote and unusual park, 10 miles north of Ekalaka on Highway 7, a magical place. Free camping is available; for more information call 234-0926.

From Ekalaka, return to Baker and continue north on Highway 7 for 45 miles to I-94. Go west on I-94 for 25 miles to *Glendive,* where, at the southeast edge of town, you'll find yet another starkly spectacular parcel of lands administered by Montana Fish, Wildlife and Parks: *Makoshika State Park. Makoshika* means "bad country" or "badlands" in Sioux, a name you'll appreciate after traversing the fantastically eroded, pine- and juniper-studded wildlands. The park is brimming with hogbacks, fluted ridges, pinnacles, hoodoos, and other oddly shaped sandstone buttes capped and protected by harder rock.

Camping, picnicking, and exploring the scenic roadways and nature trails are among the most popular activities at Makoshika. Although it's Montana's largest state park, it covers only about one-fifth of the 56,000-acre Makoshika badlands area. Most of the park's geological strata belong to the sixty-five-million-year-old Hell Creek Formation, which formed from decaying vegetation in a verdant coastal swamp where ancestors of today's sequoia, magnolia, oak, and palm trees thrived. This was the Age of Reptiles, and the Hell Creek Formation is world renowned for its abundance of dinosaur fossils. No fewer than ten species are found in the formation, including the notable Triceratops and Tyrannosaurus rex.

montanatrivia

In 1928 John Phillip Sousa and his band performed a concert for a crowd of some 2,000 in Glendive's Ford garage. Sousa also led the local school band in a rendition of his march, "King Cotton."

In recent years folks have been coming from throughout the country to help dig dinosaurs at Makoshika, paying handsomely for the privilege of working hard under the hot eastern Montana sun, under the auspices of the Milwaukee (Wisconsin) Public Museum and the Museum of the Rockies in Bozeman. Findings from their work have lent support to the theory that dinosaurs perished in a cataclysmic event, such as a meteor crashing into Earth. You can also learn more about this area by visiting the Museum of the Rockies' Web site at www.museumoftherockies.org.

It's illegal for private parties to remove fossilized animals or plants, but you are asked to report to park headquarters any that you come across. The park is open all year and charges nonresidents of Montana an entrance fee of $5 per car; for information call 377-6256 or visit www.makoshika.org. (Visit in early June and you can take part in *Buzzard Day,* celebrating the return of turkey vultures and spring.) Campgrounds are located throughout the park, or you can stay indoors at the Glendive Noon Lions Camp, a privately owned facility within the boundaries of Makoshika. Call 377-2556 to learn more about that option. When gawking at dinosaurs or sampling caviar *a la Montana,* consider holing up at the **Charley Montana Bed & Breakfast,** an imposing brick structure built in 1907 for rancher Charley Krug and his family, and now listed in the National Register of Historic Places. Hosts Kevin and Sonja Maxwell welcome overnighters, who share a reading hall, parlor, sitting rooms, formal dining room, and more. Five guest rooms, all with private baths, air-conditioning, and queen-size beds, rent nightly for between $95 and $105. For more information on the inn, located at 103 North Douglas St., call 365-3207 or tap in to www.charley-montana.com.

montanatrivia

The tiny town of Ismay, located 30 miles northwest of Baker, was temporarily rechristened "Joe, Montana" in a professional-football publicity stunt several years back.

Two champion rodeo riders of the 1920s—Paddy Ryan and Bob Askin—came from Ismay. Both are Cowboy Hall of Fame inductees.

In **Terry,** 35 miles southwest of Glendive on I-94, be sure to take in the captivating **Evelyn Cameron Gallery,** located beside the Prairie County Museum. The museum is housed in the attractive, marble-floored 1915 State Bank of Terry building.

Evelyn Cameron, an Englishwoman, came to the Terry area in 1889 to ranch with her naturalist husband, Ewen. (He's known, among other things, for killing the Boone and Crockett Club record grizzly bear for Montana, in 1890, at the Missouri Breaks.) Lady Cameron took up photography in 1894 and for more than thirty years lugged her 5x7 Graflex camera and associated paraphernalia around the prairie, incessantly photographing the eastern Montana landscape and its homesteads, wildlife, and legion of characters. Under the watchful eye of her neighbor and friend, Janet Williams, more than 1,400 of Cameron's glass-plate and nitrate negatives survived the years following her death. In 1990 they were donated to the Montana Historical Society by the Williams family.

Excerpts from the celebrated biography of Lady Cameron, *Photographing Montana (1894-1928): The Life and*

montanatrivia

Steer Montana, "the world's largest steer" at 3,980 pounds, was reared in the 1920s and '30s in Baker. When the Roan Polled Shorthorn steer died, in a roundabout way both his skeleton and stuffed hide ended up at the O'Fallon Historical Museum in Baker.

The Paddlefish

The odd paddlefish *(Polyodon spathula)* is a living fossil of sorts. Also known as the spoon-billed catfish, the paddlefish possesses sharklike fins and a long snout that looks like a paddle. They can grow to be 3 feet long, weigh 140 pounds, and live to be thirty years old. This ancient and unlikely bottom-feeder, or some reasonable ancestral facsimile, has swum the waters of the region for millions of years. Thought to be extinct in the United States since 1912, one of the monsters was pulled from the Yellowstone River near Glendive in 1962, and since then their numbers have been increasing.

Therefore, the May and June **Paddlefish Spawning Run** is cause for great celebration in Glendive. In 1989 the Montana legislature revised a state law prohibiting the use of game fish parts for commercial use, expressly so that the Glendive Chamber of Commerce could collect paddlefish roe, process it, and sell it as caviar! The ruling forbids the chamber to pay for the eggs; rather, they must be donated. So, they're collected from among the 3,000 or so anglers who gather May 16 through June 30 for the spawning run at the diversion dam at Intake, 16 miles northeast of town. In turn, the anglers benefit by having their fish cleaned free of charge by chamber-hired employees. (Formerly, the eggs would simply have been tossed aside after an angler snagged one of the beasts and tugged it to shore.)

The eggs are washed, salted, cooled, and then packaged for sale. The snagged paddlefish seems to be the only party who doesn't profit from the arrangement, for money raised through caviar sales is split evenly between the chamber and the state, which uses its portion to improve eastern Montana fisheries. The chamber uses its share to enhance local recreational opportunities. And, in what might be thought of as one prehistoric beast coming to the aid of another, some of the funds have helped to finance the community's Triceratops project. Curious? Call the chamber of commerce at 377-5601 to find out more.

Works of Evelyn Cameron, by Donna Lucey, appear alongside the strikingly sharp photographs of cowboys, wolves, sheepherders, badlands, wagon trains, and other turn-of-the-twentieth-century eastern Montana subjects. The Prairie County Museum—where you'll find, among other things, a steam-heated outhouse—is located at 103 South Logan Ave. It's open Memorial Day through Labor Day, weekdays (except Tues) 9 a.m. to 3 p.m. and weekends 1 to 4 p.m.; admission is free. During the off-season you can visit by appointment; call 635-4040 to make one.

The Big Open

From Miles City pull onto long and lonesome Highway 59 going northwest and proceed to that part of Montana known as The Big Dry or *The Big Open.* For

Big Open Debate

The Big Open encompasses a vast spread of wild, wide-open spaces. Here refuges teem with bird and animal life, and signs of prehistoric human beings are abundant— and so is evidence of failed homesteads.

Even for those homesteaders who managed to hang on, life in the Big Open typically has been tough. By 1930, after twenty years of settlement by homesteaders, only 25 of Garfield County's more than 1,000 farms had piped-in water. Electricity came to Jordan in 1951, and telephone service five years later. The long-awaited railroad never made it there.

This hard living in a lonely land has spawned a fiercely independent spirit. You may recall that in the mid-1990s, Jordan was the site of the infamous "Freemen" stand-off. Several years prior to that event, a group of romantics and visionaries, under the auspices of Missoula's Institute of the Rockies, proposed that residents of the 15,000-square-mile Big Open (which includes all of Garfield County and portions of several others) should consider a new way to make ends meet. Because raising cattle and wheat are such marginal endeavors in this harsh country, they maintained, native species should be returned in great numbers—75,000 bison, for instance, and 40,000 elk—while domestic stock and grain are phased out. Landowners would keep their land and simply change jobs: Basically, they would become outfitters, guiding tourists on hunting, photography, and wildlife-viewing expeditions into the Big Open Great Plains Wildlife Range, Montana's answer to Africa's Serengeti.

For many the idea was compelling, but it wasn't exactly met with a resounding "Let's do it!" by the folks living there. "Bizarre," "outrageous," "insulting," and "monstrous" are adjectives one Montana newspaper quoted residents as using when voicing their opinions of the plan.

Their sentiment was perhaps best summed up in a counterproposal offered by a group of Big Open citizens: Why not build a huge dam on the Clark Fork River downstream from Missoula, causing the immense basin occupied by prehistoric Lake Missoula to fill again? The new mega-lake would create hundreds of recreation-oriented jobs and also rid Montana of its worst pollution and congestion problem— Missoula (while also ridding the free-minded Big Open residents of meddling western Montanans).

many, the greatest attraction here is the very lack of attractions, of the modern, human-made variety.

Jordan, the most isolated county seat in the lower forty-eight states, is Garfield County's center of enterprise. Several Tyrannosaurus rex skeletons have been taken from the Hell Creek Formation in the surrounding hills, including specimens that for decades were displayed at the American Museum of Natural History in New York City and the Carnegie Museum in Pittsburgh. At the *Garfield County Museum* you can learn about the area's numerous excavations and view some of the fossils found nearby. You can also check out displays of old photographs, antique farm machinery, and the Pioneer Room's Wall of Fame, featuring early area homesteaders. The museum is open weekdays 1 to 5 p.m. June 1 through Labor Day. To learn more, call 557-2517.

Hell Creek State Park and Marina is situated on the Hell Creek Arm of formidable Fort Peck Lake. As you traverse the 26-mile road leading north from Jordan through the Missouri Breaks country, you'll suspect that you're headed to the middle of nowhere (or maybe you already thought you were there when in Jordan!). Wild turkey, pronghorns, golden eagles, and mule deer are commonly seen along the route.

At your destination, however, you'll discover a buzzing oasis of activity. There's a campground, grocery and concession stores, boat rentals (Fort Peck Lake is known for its world-class walleye fishing), and more. For information on the park, open year-round, call 234-0900; to find out more about the marina, call 557-2345 or visit www.hellcreekmarina.com.

It'll probably never gain the notoriety of the Baseball Hall of Fame in Cooperstown, New York, but nevertheless at the McCone County Museum in Circle, you'll find the **Montana Sheepherders Hall of Fame.** Outside the entryway stands a life-size concrete statue of a sheepherder holding a lamb, and inside are listed the names of more than 300 local sheep growers, many displayed with their brands. (Circle was named for a cattle brand, by the way.) Also within the museum are farming implements, Indian artifacts, and the wildlife collection of the Orville Quick family. The animal mounts, accumulated over the span of forty years, include more than 200 birds in dioramas resembling their natural habitats.

The **McCone County Museum,** located at 801 First Ave. South in Circle, is open weekdays May 1 through Sept 30, from 9 a.m. to 5 p.m. Call 485-2414 or visit www.mccone.mt.gov/museum.html for more information.

A great deal of work has gone into creating the **MonDak Heritage Center** in **Sidney,** a well-above-average museum and art center. The pride of the museum is its two galleries, where monthly revolving shows from throughout the country are displayed. Exhibits beyond the galleries include a large archive of regional photographs and Pioneer Town, the former shack of homesteader Donald Baue that was moved into the lower level of the complex before construction was completed. The MonDak Heritage Center, located at 120 Third Ave. Southeast, is open from 10 a.m. to 4 p.m. Tues through Fri (with the hours extended to 7 p.m. on Thurs) and 1 to 4 p.m. Sat; closed in Jan. Admission is free. Call 433-3500 or tap into www.mondakheritagecenter.org for more information.

What remains of **Fort Union Trading Post** is found 23 miles northeast of Sidney, astride the Montana–North Dakota border. Traders and settlers became interested in the area when William Clark, of the Lewis and Clark expedition, wrote in his journal that whoever came to control the confluence of the Missouri and Yellowstone Rivers would probably command the fur trade of the entire Northwest.

montanatrivia

Schmeckfest, a fund-raiser for the nondenominational Lustre Christian High School, happens in tiny Lustre, located within the Fort Peck Indian Reservation, in late March. Among the goodies baked or otherwise cooked by the ladies of Lustre one year were 108 dozen *perishke* (fruit pockets), 95 dozen *portzilke* (New Year cookies), 2,400 cheese pockets, and 900 cabbage rolls. To learn about this year's Schmeckfest, aka the "German Festival of Tasting," call 392-5735 or visit www.lustrechristian.org.

The Canadians beat the Americans to the punch when, in the late 1820s, Kenneth McKenzie built his namesake Fort McKenzie. The American Fur Company's John Jacob Astor was close behind, and in 1829 he built Fort Union at the confluence of the great rivers. For two decades thereafter Fort Union was the center of the upper Missouri fur trade. Assiniboine Indians from the north, Crow from the south, Blackfeet from the Missouri headwaters, and additional tribes from elsewhere brought beaver pelts and buffalo hides to trade. At its zenith, the fort employed some one hundred workers, many of them with Indian wives and families. Men from throughout the world found their way here; inhabitants included Americans (black, white, and Native), Russians, Spaniards, Italians, Germans, Englishmen, Frenchmen, and others.

By the mid-1830s, the demand for beaver was tapering off in Europe and on the East Coast, as silk replaced fur as the favored material for men's hats. Simultaneously, the market for tanned buffalo robes burgeoned, and trade at Fort Union remained brisk until late in the 1830s, when a smallpox epidemic arrived via the steamboat St. Peter and decimated some of the Indian tribes. Trade slowed for a while and then again picked up, until another smallpox scourge hit in 1857. By the time the Civil War heated up, trade at Fort Union was sluggish and the post was badly in need of repair. Most of the buildings were dismantled in the 1860s by federal soldiers, and the logs were moved a mile downstream to be used in constructing Fort Buford.

Recent National Park Service archaeological excavations have turned up scores of valuable artifacts and shed new light on Fort Union's past. The efforts have resulted in the reconstruction of portions of the fort's stone bastions, the

Indian trade house, and the Bourgeois House, the imposing former quarters of the post commander. The lofty exterior of the house now looks much as it did in 1850, and the interior serves as a visitor center and reference library.

Fort Union Trading Post National Historic Site is located at 15550 Highway 1804 (not coincidentally, the year the Lewis and Clark expedition wintered in North Dakota). To get there, go northeast from Sidney on Highway 200 for 14 miles; after crossing the North Dakota border just past Fairview, turn north onto Highway 1804 and continue for 8 miles. The free-to-visit site is open Memorial Day through Labor Day from 8 a.m. to 8 p.m. (central time, because the visitor center is on the North Dakota side of the complex). During the remainder of the year, it's open from 9 a.m. to 5:30 p.m. For more information call (701) 572-9083 or go to www.nps.gov/fous.

montanatrivia

Fairview, Montana, straddles the Montana–North Dakota state line, lies partly in the mountain time zone and partly in the central time zone, and claims to be the Sugar Beet Capital of both Montana and North Dakota.

In *Wolf Point,* 21 miles west of Poplar, cowboys and cowgirls whoop it up at the granddaddy of Montana rodeos, the *Wild Horse Stampede,* first held early in the twentieth century. In the wild horse race, an unusual addition to the more typical rodeo events, teams of three cowboys compete to be the first to saddle and ride a wild horse across the finish line. Held on the second full weekend in July, the three days of rodeoing and revelry also include a carnival, parades, and Indian cultural displays. For more information you can call the Wolf Point Chamber of Commerce at 653-2012 or visit their Web site at www.wolfpointchamber.org.

South of Saskatchewan

A mile south of the town of *Medicine Lake* (which is 25 miles north of Culbertson) on Highway 16 lies an immense diamond in the rough: the *Medicine Lake National Wildlife Refuge.* The refuge, established in 1935 under the management of the U.S. Fish and Wildlife Service, contains a proliferation of potholes and swamps left behind when the last great glacier retreated. In all, 40 percent of its 31,000 acres is covered by lakes, ponds, and marshes, with the remainder in prairie and meadow. The largest body of water, 8,700-acre Medicine Lake, enjoys added protection as the centerpiece of the two-tract, 11,370-acre Medicine Lake Wilderness. The wilderness also contains the Sand Hills, 2,320 acres of rolling hills, native grasses, and remnant groves of quaking aspen.

Prairie Beauty

I spent most of the summer of 1979 living in a motel room in *Sidney.* From there I ventured to the surrounding prairies of Montana and North Dakota to survey proposed oil-well sites for evidence of prehistoric artifacts. For a fellow accustomed to living in the Rocky Mountains, the days were relentlessly hot in that country, and the nights weren't all that cool, either. I remember listening to the radio early in the mornings, when the mercury often had already climbed to around seventy degrees, and hearing reports of temperatures in the forties back in Missoula. It made me want to go home.

But I did see some amazing things as I walked through those unpeopled badlands fashioned by the erosive action of wind and water. Much of the country bordered on the Little Missouri—the river responsible for carving the maze of terrain known as Theodore Roosevelt National Park, which I often worked in close proximity to. As the summer wore on, I learned that the prairie possesses a brand of beauty unlike any I'd previously known. Occasionally, when I was assigned to survey a particularly remote site, a Shell Oil Company helicopter would deliver me there in the morning and return to retrieve me at day's end. I felt like it was just me and the mule deer, alone on the Great Plains . . . along with the occasional rattlesnake.

Two things from that summer particularly stand out: a full skeleton of a prehistoric bison that I found eroding out of the cut banks of Bennie Peer Creek; and the drive across the extraordinary Fairview Bridge. The bridge, located 3 miles east of Fairview, has railroad tracks running the length of its driving surface. The only lift bridge on the Yellowstone River, it once carried both car and train traffic across the river . . . but not at the same time, one supposes (actually, a watchman was stationed at the bridge entrance to prevent automobiles and trains from colliding).

Like other national wildlife refuges, Medicine Lake is financed largely through the sale of migratory bird stamps, or "duck stamps," which waterfowl hunters must purchase annually. A staggering variety of birds—as many as 75,000 at a time—call the place home: Canada geese, double-crested cormorants, grebes, ruddy ducks, yellow-headed blackbirds, American bitterns, and sharp-tailed grouse, to name only a few. The refuge is important both as a stopover for migrating birds and as a breeding ground for dozens of species.

The headquarters, with mounted birds and prehistoric artifacts on display, is open from 7 a.m. to 3:30 p.m. Mon through Fri, and during other daylight hours visitors are welcome to stop at employees' residences to make inquiries. At the office you can obtain a key to the 100-foot-high viewing tower; be sure also to pick up an interpretive brochure for the 14-mile car tour. Destinations include the Bridgerman Point observation deck, where the largest colonies of white pelicans in the United States can be viewed. The refuge also features an observation blind in close proximity to a sharp-tailed grouse dancing ground, which provides an outstanding opportunity to get an close-up view of one of nature's most fascinating rituals (early Apr through late May). The brochure pinpoints where you can expect to see many other bird species, as well.

Glaciers aren't all that left evidence after passing. Surrounding Medicine Lake, and included in the scenic drive, are the **Tipi Hills,** listed in the National Register of Historic Places because of the dozens of tepee rings found there (tepee rings are circles of stones that once held down the edges of tepee skins). Clearly the area was an animal-abundant hunting ground in prehistoric times and served as a "wildlife refuge" long before the U.S. government desig-

montanatrivia

Brush Lake, just two miles from the North Dakota border, in 2003 became Montana's fiftieth state park. It owns the distinction of becoming the first state park in the extreme northeast corner of the state.

nated it so. For more information on Medicine Lake National Wildlife Refuge, call the visitor center at 789-2305 or go to http://medicinelake.fws.gov.

Sitting Bull, the prominent Sioux chief, surrendered to U.S. troops in July of 1881 near present-day **Plentywood,** 22 miles north of Medicine Lake on Highway 16. A monument to him now stands just outside the **Sheridan County Museum,** located along Highway 16 at the entrance to the county fairgrounds. Near the museum in the Civic Center, you'll find one of the longest murals in Montana, a 74-foot canvas by local artist Bob Southland depicting the county's history, from the days of the prehistoric Americans to the present in this corner of Montana that was the last part of the state to be settled. Also on the fairgrounds you'll see the Old Tractor Club's collection of some thirty threshers, eighty-five tractors, and an array of plows, wagons, and other pioneer farming artifacts from Sheridan County.

Not long after Sitting Bull and his people were subdued, outlaws—including Butch Cassidy's infamous Wild Bunch—traveled through this area on the Outlaw Trail, occasionally hiding out in the rough breaks of the Big Muddy River Valley. You can find out more about the region's Indians, outlaws, and homesteaders at the museum (765-2420 summer; 765-3411 off-season), which opens daily 1 to 5 p.m. Memorial Day through Labor Day, and by appointment at other times of the year.

In **Daniels County,** dozens of decaying cabins attest to the fact that many hundreds more people than reside here now once tried their hands at eking out a living in the challenging conditions of this portion of the Big Sky State. Of the hundreds of would-be dryland farmers who moved to Daniels County

The Missouri Coteau

The town of **Westby,** situated 26 miles east of Plentywood, occupies a wetlands-filled corner of Montana that's within the **Missouri Coteau.** This glacier-created landscape of rolling hills and prairie potholes stretches from northern South Dakota into Saskatchewan. The Missouri Coteau (*coteau* is French for "hill") provides vital nesting grounds for a large number of species of passerines, or perching songbirds. Their annual migrations have turned isolated Westby, nestled against the North Dakota border, into somewhat of a mecca for bird-watchers from throughout the country. The Missouri Coteau also contains some of the richest prairies of native mixed grasses remaining on the Great Plains, making the region an early summer haven for fans of wildflowers, too.

during the homesteading boom of 1910–1920, it's estimated that only about 15 percent stuck it out. In 1963 the town of Scobey pulled out all the stops to celebrate that minority at the Homesteaders' Golden Jubilee.

The festival spawned the notion of building a monument of permanence to the past. The idea matured and grew into the twenty-acre **Pioneer Town and Museum,** found today 7 blocks west of Main Street on Second Avenue in **Scobey**, a small plains town situated at the junction of Highways 5 and 13, 41 miles west of Plentywood. Some three dozen buildings, most of them reconstructed and spilling over with artifacts, line the streets—a blacksmith shop, one-room school, general store, completely furnished homestead shack, and many others. An extensive collection of early-day farm equipment is featured, and approximately fifty restored antique automobiles fill two adjacent buildings. The museum visitor center holds additional displays, such as antique lamp and gun collections.

montanatrivia

Two former Chicago White Sox players, ejected from the major leagues for fixing 1919 World Series games (the movie *Eight Men Out* was based on the event), were recruited to play for a Scobey baseball team. With "Swede" Risberg and "Happy" Felsch on the team, Scobey's rivals stood little chance of winning, and they didn't.

At the Rex Theatre on the museum grounds, various shows are given throughout the summer, including the annual performance by the Dirty Shame Belles and Dixieland Band, held during Pioneer Days on the last weekend in June. Tours of the museum complex are conducted daily between 12:30 and 4:30 p.m. from Memorial Day through Labor Day. Winter hours are 1 to 4 p.m. Fri or by appointment. Admission is $5 for adults and $2.50 for kids. Call 487-5965 for information.

In the late 1970s, at a Lutheran Church lutefisk dinner, Glasgow gift-shop owner Marge Forum sampled some of the hand-rolled *lefse* produced by Myrt Granrud and her friend, Arlene Larson. Their lefse, a tortilla-like Scandinavian Christmas treat made of potatoes, cream, and butter, was so good that Marge convinced the two ladies to make more to sell at her shop. It went over even bigger than Marge had anticipated, and soon the ladies couldn't make enough to keep up with demand.

So Myrt's husband, Evan, began helping to roll out mashed potatoes in the evenings after returning from work at the Opheim radar station. Although the ladies at first maintained that hand-driven rolling pins were the only acceptable means by which to roll out the dough, Evan finally convinced them otherwise by tinkering away in his shop and devising an ingenious, automated rolling pin. The rest, as they say, is history.

Today **Granrud's Lefse Shack** operates out of **Opheim,** a tiny burg found 46 miles west of Scobey on Highway 248. (The Granruds sold the business in 2005 to their managers of four years, Alice Redfield and Twyla Anderson.) Potatoes are cooked, twenty-five pounds at a time, mixed, chilled in ice cream buckets, and packed into round cylinders. Evan's machines then kick into action and roll out the rounds, and the lefse is cooked on griddles.

montanatrivia

Steve Reeves was a native of *Glasgow* who became a world-famous bodybuilder—among his many titles were Mr. America and Mr. Universe—and the best-remembered portrayer of Hercules on the silver screen. After he passed away in 2000, Reeves's wishes were granted when he was returned to Montana. Some of his ashes were scattered over the Big Snowy Mountains outside Lewistown, with the balance of his remains laid to rest next to those of his father at the cemetery in Scobey.

The shop turns out many tons of lefse in a season. Approximately 1,200 pounds of potatoes—a combination of reds and whites—are cooked in a typical day, and in an average week, they go through 6 gallons of cream, 40 pounds of butter and 300 pounds of margarine. The operation is as large as the owners want it, fearing that additional growth would mean losing control of quality. The lefse is sold primarily in stores in Montana and North Dakota and through a mail-order operation. They advertise very little, depending instead on word of watering mouth to get the message out.

The key to running a successful operation in tiny Opheim? Timing, according to Evan. "We started at about the time all of the old-time Scandinavian grandmas were either gone or had arthritis in their hands. Twenty years ago people made their own lefse, but a lot of the wives are working now and don't have the time."

Visit during the lefse-making season (fall and early winter), and you'll be impressed by the friendliness of the staff of approximately ten and the laid-back yet industrious atmosphere. You'll also be treated to hot-off-the-griddle lefse with your choice of white or brown sugar. Call 762-3250 or visit www .lefseshack.com to find out more.

"From Dinosaur Bones to Moon Walk" is the theme at the **Valley County Pioneer Museum** in **Glasgow,** 50 miles south of Opheim on Highway 24. The eclectic collection includes area fossils, the late Chief Wetsit's original tepee (made from twenty-three elk hides), an outdoor machinery exhibition, wood carvings by the late master carver Frank Lafournaise (including what Ripley's Believe It or Not! once recognized as the world's tiniest workable violin), a miniature model of the 1930s Fort Peck Dam project, and a display on the history of aviation in Valley County.

The museum showpiece, to which an entire large room is dedicated, is the **Stan Kalinski Collection.** For years on display at Stan's Bar on Front Street, the collection includes some 300 mounted animals, such as an albino deer; an extinct Audubon sheep; many reptiles, birds, and mammals from the far corners of the earth; and a bison that was butchered for a feast honoring President Franklin D. Roosevelt when he visited Glasgow in the 1930s. Stan's ornate Buffalo Bill Cody bar—bullet hole and all—resides here, too.

montanatrivia

In addition to Bergie's in Nashua, traditional soda fountains in Montana well worth investigating include the Bon Ton in Lewistown, Olson's Drug in Conrad, and Chapin's Drug in Circle.

The Valley County Pioneer Museum is open daily from Memorial Day through Labor Day, 9 a.m. to 8 p.m. and by special arrangement the rest of the year. Admission is $3 for adults and $2 for those age 7 through 21. Located on US 2 West in **Glasgow,** it's tough to miss—it is the only building in the vicinity with an Air Force jet in the front yard. For more information call 228-8692 or visit www.valleycounty museum.com.

People drive from afar to the tiny town of Nashua, 12 miles southeast of Glasgow on US 2, to enjoy **Bergie's** homemade ice cream. Housed in a nondescript structure at 410 Sargent St., the place is a northeast Montana institution. It had been in business as a Miller Drug Store for decades prior to 1985, when Larry and Jeannie Bergstrom bought it, even though they already had jobs, in order to prevent it from closing for good. Over the antique marble counter, ice-cream aficionados can order one of seven flavors, several of which change with the seasons (chokecherry and rhubarb are popular in summer). Sodas, sundaes, and milk shakes are staples at Bergie's, too. For more information call 746-3441.

When informed in 1932 by U.S. Army Corps of Engineers officials of their intention to build a dam across the Missouri River a few miles south of his town, Glasgow mayor Leo B. Coleman is reported to have exclaimed, "My God, man! It would cost a million dollars to build a dam across there!"

But President Franklin D. Roosevelt gave the go-ahead in 1933, and over the span of six years, the *Fort Peck Dam* was erected. Even today it is the largest earth-filled dam in the United States—with embankments reaching 4 miles across the Missouri River—and ranks sixth among dams in the world in the volume of water impounded.

The stated purposes for the dam were to aid in flood control and to make the Missouri River more navigable, but even more important at the time was the creation of jobs. Montana was reeling from the effects of the Great Depression and several straight years of drought. The Fort Peck public works project was a godsend: Construction at its peak provided jobs for nearly 11,000 individuals. Eighteen boomtowns, with a combined population of nearly 40,000, buzzed where months before only a few hundred people had quietly resided. It was the Wild West all over again, a sight that moved Pulitzer Prize–winner Ernie Pyle to write, "You have to see the town of Wheeler to believe it . . . it is today the wildest wild-west town in North America. Except for the autos, it is a genuine throwback to the '80s, to Tombstone and Dodge City." (Wheeler was a small, makeshift town that no longer exists.)

montanatrivia

Some town names in eastern Montana hint at their isolation: for instance, Lonesome, located south of Malta, and Faranuf, south of Glasgow.

The Fort Peck Dam backs up the waters of the Missouri into its main valley and dozens of side drainages to create *Fort Peck Lake,* which at full pool is 134 miles long and claims an astounding 1,520 miles of shoreline. The lake is entirely surrounded by the public lands of the equally formidable *Charles M. Russell National Wildlife Refuge* (538-8706, http://cmr.fws.gov). At 1.1 million acres, C. M. Russell is the largest contiguous wildlife refuge in the lower forty-eight states and the most untrammeled stretch of the northern Great Plains remaining. It encompasses the native prairie, badlands, timbered coulees, and bottomlands so often depicted in the works of the cowboy-turned-painter for whom the refuge was named.

Incidentally, little did Mayor Coleman know that eventually the project would cost not one million dollars but nearly $150 million, along with the lives of six men killed in a slide (they are still buried in the dam today). Guided tours of the Fort Peck Dam and surroundings can be arranged between Memorial Day and Labor Day by calling the Corps of Engineers at 526-3431. An ambitious new museum and interpretive center are there for visitors' enjoyment, as well. You can learn a lot more about the area's present and past at www.fortpeckdam.com, a Web site privately maintained by a man named Rafe Sigmundstad.

montanatrivia

In January 2001, bison returned home to northeastern Montana's Fort Peck Indian Reservation for the first time since late in the nineteenth century.

The **Fort Peck Theatre,** listed in the National Register of Historic Places, is a beautiful wooden structure built in the style of a large Swiss chalet. It, too, was constructed in the 1930s, designed for showing movies to the dam workers and their families. The 1,100-seat structure now houses the Fort Peck Summer Theatre, presenting professional shows from late May through early Sept on Fri and Sat at 8 p.m. and Sun at 4 p.m. Reservations are not needed, and the box office opens at 7 p.m. (3 p.m. on Sun). For more details call 526-9943 or visit www.fortpecktheatre.org.

Natural hot springs aren't common in the eastern reaches of Montana, so why is there one near **Saco,** 60 miles northwest of Fort Peck on Highway 24 and US 2? Well, it's not exactly natural, but at least at **Sleeping Buffalo Resort** the water is naturally heated. In 1922 a wildcatter exploring for oil hit a fantastic flow of gushing hot mineral water at about 3,200 feet below the ground's surface. Allegedly, he proceeded to go broke trying to cap the flow!

Luckily, he wasn't successful. During Franklin D. Roosevelt's presidency, the Soil Conservation Service joined with the Phillips County American Legion to develop a complex around the springs, and the Work Projects Administration built several rock buildings at the "Saco Health Plunge." In 1958 a new well was drilled after a flow stoppage occurred; unfortunately, the following summer the Madison Canyon earthquake struck near far-off Yellowstone, causing the ground here to shift and break the casing. So another new well was drilled.

The history continues, but what is really important is what you'll find today at Sleeping Buffalo Hot Springs (renamed in honor of a particular bison-resembling boulder located in the area). Two indoor pools, one as toasty as 106 degrees and the other maintained at around 90 degrees, await soakers all year round. Some 600,000 gallons of freshwater flow through the pools every day. Because the water contains unusually high concentrations of minerals, it's purported to possess therapeutic value for those suffering from arthritis and similar ailments.

Probably not even the buffalo slept on the summer day in 1992 at the resort when Butte native **Robbie Knievel** flew on his motorcycle over a 125-foot line of twenty covered wagons—arm in a cast, no less, owing to a broken bone suffered from a fall in another recent stunt.

Sleeping Buffalo Hot Springs, open year-round, features rustic cabins and both new and vinatage hotel rooms, a cafe, and a gift shop. The pools are open daily 7 a.m. to 9 p.m. The resort is located 10 miles west of Saco on US 2, near the Nelson Reservoir. Call 527-3370 or visit http://sleepingbuffalo .blogspot.com for more information.

Finally, a couple of museums you might want to take in before continuing into Russell Country: the one-room **Huntley School,** situated in the town park in **Saco,** where the late television newsman Chet Huntley began his education; and the **Phillips County Historical Museum** (654-1037; www.phillipscoun-tymuseum.org), open year-round from 10 a.m. to 5 p.m. Mon through Sat and 12:30 to 5 p.m. Sun at its facility on US 2 East in Malta (watch for the dinosaur silhouette marking the adjacent Great Plains Dinosaur Museum). Admission to the museum is $5 for adults and $3 for kids over five. And just east of Malta you'll pass the turn into **Bowdoin National Wildlife Refuge** (654-2863, http://bowdoin.fws.gov), a marshland environment where you can spot pelicans, white-faced ibises, and a noisy cast of other winged things.

Places to Stay in Custer–Missouri River Country

BILLINGS

Best Western Clock Tower Inn
downtown at 2511 First Ave. North
(406) 259-5511
Expensive

Billings Super 8
5400 Southgate Dr.
(406) 248-8842
Moderate

Dude Rancher Lodge
415 N. Twenty-ninth St.
(406) 259-5561
Moderate

The Josephine Bed & Breakfast
514 N. Twenty-ninth St.
(406) 248-5898
Expensive

Crown Plaza Billings
27 N. Twenty-seventh St.
(888) 444-0401
Expensive

HARDIN

American Inn
1324 N. Crawford Ave.
(406) 665-1870
Moderate

Hardin Super 8
201 W. Fourteenth St.
(406) 665-1700
Moderate

MILES CITY

Best Western War Bonnet Inn
1015 S. Haynes Ave.
(406) 234-4560
Moderate

Comfort Inn
1615 S. Haynes Ave.
(406) 234-3141
Moderate

Historic Olive Hotel
501 Main St.
(406) 234-2450
Moderate

Motel 6
1314 S. Haynes Ave.
(406) 232-7040
Inexpensive

BAKER

Montana Motel
716 E. Montana Ave.
(406) 778-3315
Inexpensive

Sagebrush Inn
518 W. Montana Ave.
(406) 778-3341
Inexpensive

GLENDIVE

Best Western Glendive Inn
222 N. Kendrick Ave.
(406) 377-5555
Moderate

Days Inn
2000 N. Merrill Ave.
(406) 365-6011
Moderate

Super 8
1904 N. Merrill Ave.
(406) 365-5671
Moderate

JORDAN

Fellman's Motel
Highway 200
(406) 557-2209
Inexpensive

Garfield Hotel & Motel
Highway 200
(406) 557-6215
Inexpensive

SIDNEY

Lone Tree Motor Inn
900 S. Central Ave.
(406) 433-4520
Moderate

Park Plaza Motel
601 S. Central Ave.
(406) 433-1520
Moderate

Richland Motor Inn
1200 S. Central Ave.
(406) 433-6400
Moderate

PLENTYWOOD

Sherwood Inn
515 W. First Ave.
(406) 765-2810
Moderate

GLASGOW

Campbell Lodge
534 3rd Ave. South
(406) 228-9328
Moderate

Cottonwood Inn
US 2 East
(406) 228-8213
Moderate

Historic Fort Peck Hotel
18 miles southeast
of Glasgow
175 S. Missouri St.
Box 168
Fort Peck 59223
(800) 560-4931
Inexpensive

Star Lodge Motel
1023 US 2 West
(406) 228-2494
Moderate

MALTA

Great Northern Motel
2 S. 1st Ave.
(406) 654-2100
Inexpensive

Riverside Motel
8 N. Central Ave.
(406) 654-2310
Inexpensive

Sleeping Buffalo Hot Springs
18 miles northeast of Malta
HC 75 Box 460
Saco 59261
(406) 527-3370
Inexpensive

Sportsman Motel
231 N. 1st St. East
(406) 654-2300

Places to Eat in Custer–Missouri River Country

BILLINGS

The Granary
1500 Poly Dr.
(406) 259-3488
Moderate

Juliano's
2917 7th Ave. North
(406) 248-6400
Expensive

Montana Brewing Company
113 N. Broadway
(406) 252-9200
Moderate

Nara Oriental Restaurant
109 N. 28th St.
(406) 256-0809
Moderate

Torres Cafe
6200 S. Frontage Rd.
(406) 652-8426
Moderate

Walker's Grill
301 N. 27th St.
(406) 245-9291
Moderate

MILES CITY

Boardwalk Restaurant
906 S. Haynes Ave.
(406) 234-0195
Moderate

Club 519
519 Main St.
(406) 232-5133
Expensive

Historic Olive Hotel
501 Main St.
(406) 234-2450
Moderate

Hole in the Wall
602 Main St.
(406) 234-9887
Inexpensive

600 Cafe
600 Main St.
(406) 234-3860
Inexpensive

BAKER

Big K Drive-In
409 W. Montana Ave.
(406) 778-3731
Inexpensive

Sakelaris's Kitchen
Lake City Shopping Center
(406) 778-2202
Inexpensive

GLENDIVE

CC's Family Cafe
1902 N. Merrill Ave.
(406) 377-8926
Inexpensive

Li's Chinese Restaurant
1615 W. Towne St.
(406) 377-5135
Moderate

JORDAN

Hilltop Cafe
Jct. of Highways 59
and 200
(406) 557-6287
Inexpensive

M & M Snack Shack
613 Jordan Ave.
(406) 557-2883
Inexpensive

SIDNEY

Footers Pizza & Subs
616 S. Central Ave.
(406) 433-7827
Moderate

Gullivers
120 E. Main St.
(406) 433-5175
Inexpensive

New China Restaurant
821 S. Central Ave.
(406) 488-6188
Moderate

The South 40
207 2nd Ave.
Northwest
(406) 433–4999
Moderate

PLENTYWOOD

Cousins Family Restaurant
564 W. 1st Ave.
(406) 765-1690
Inexpensive

Randy's Restaurant
323 1st Ave. West
(406) 765-1661
Inexpensive

GLASGOW

Hong Kong Restaurant
411 1st Ave. South
(406) 228-8383
Moderate

Johnnie cCafe
433 1st Ave. South
(406) 228-4222
Inexpensive

Sam's Supper Club
307 1st Ave. North
(406) 228-4614
Moderate

MALTA

Great Northern Hotel
2 South 1st St. East
(406) 654-2100
Moderate

Stockman Bar & Steakhouse
64 S. 1st Ave. East
(406) 654-1919
Moderate

Westside Cafe
US 2 West
(406) 654-1555
Inexpensive

RUSSELL COUNTRY

→

Russell Country encompasses the high plains, tall buttes, and muddy waters of north-central Montana, a landscape depicted often in the evocative works of "America's cowboy artist" Charlie Russell. The region also holds a lot of flat farming country, lying north of the Missouri River, as well as a broad sweep of the Rocky Mountain Front, where massive mountains give way to the endless Great Plains.

From southwest of Malta you'll wind along the Missouri Breaks Back Country Byway to Lewistown, an attractive, midsize community that serves as the geographical hub of Montana. From there you'll head northwest to *Fort Benton,* a town that, arguably, played a more important role than any other in the taming of Montana. From Havre, situated northeast of Fort Benton, US 2 leads west along the Hi-Line to Shelby; from there it is on to the Rocky Mountain Front settlement of *Choteau.* US 89 will then lead you to Great Falls, where history buffs can fill up on the lore of Lewis and Clark. Next, heading southeast on US 87, you'll turn south onto US 191 before regaining Lewistown and continuing on to Harlowton. Finally, a trip heading west along US 12 leads to White Sulphur Springs by way of the interesting spots in the road known as Twodot and Martinsdale.

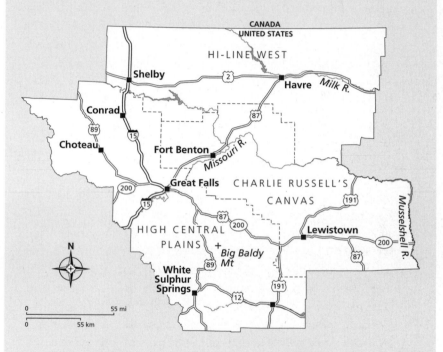

CANADA
UNITED STATES

HI-LINE WEST

Shelby

Havre

Milk R.

Conrad

Choteau

Fort Benton

Missouri R.

Great Falls

CHARLIE RUSSELL'S
CANVAS

Musselshell R.

HIGH CENTRAL
PLAINS

Lewistown

Big Baldy
Mt

White
Sulphur
Springs

N

0   55 mi
0   55 km

Charlie Russell's Canvas

Nature clocked eons of overtime in fashioning the jumble of geology known as the Missouri Breaks, described by Lewis and Clark as "the deserts of America." Seventy miles southwest of Malta on US 191, at *James Kipp Park* (just south of the Fred Robinson Bridge), you'll find the kick-off point for the *Missouri Breaks Back Country Byway.*

The river and adjacent floodplains, timbered coulees, and prairie comprise a diverse range of habitats, and perhaps nowhere in the contiguous United States can such a medley of wildlife be met (outside of Yellowstone National Park, anyway, and you'll definitely see fewer tourists here than there). More than 60 species of mammals, 200 varieties of birds, and 20 types of reptiles and amphibians have been identified in the Breaks. Along the eastern portions of the Lower Two Calf Road, for instance, you've a good chance of spotting prairie elk in the river bottoms. Bighorn sheep also are regularly seen atop the ridges and in the coulees of this area—not the Audubon bighorn described by Lewis and Clark (which has since become extinct) but the introduced and apparently thriving Rocky Mountain bighorn.

From James Kipp Park head west on the Knox Ridge Road. After 27 miles turn north onto the Lower Two Calf Road, which loops back east, eventually

AUTHOR'S FAVORITES

Bear Paw Battlefield
Chinook
(406) 357-3130

Bonanza Creek Country Guest Ranch
Lennep
(800) 476-6045

Charles M. Bair Family Museum
Martinsdale
(406) 572-3650

Charlie Russell Chew Choo
Lewistown
(406) 535–5436

Havre Beneath the Streets
Havre
(406) 265-8888

Heaven on Earth Ranch
Ulm
(406) 866-3316

Missouri River Back Country Byway
Lewistown
(406) 538-7461

Montana Agricultural Center and Museum of the Northern Great Plains
Fort Benton
(406) 622-5316

Pine Butte Swamp Preserve
Choteau
(406) 466-5526

Square Butte
Square Butte
(406) 538-7461

rejoining the Knox Ridge Road 4 miles west of the beginning point. Along the 34-mile Lower Two Calf Road are several spur roads leading to overlooks and river-bottom sites.

The entire loop, sans side trips, is about 65 miles long. All of the Knox Ridge Road, except for its easternmost 4-mile portion, is surfaced for all-weather travel, while long stretches of Lower Two Calf Road are unsurfaced. The gumbo clay of the Missouri Breaks is notorious for becoming absolutely impassable when wet, so keep a close eye on the weather or you may spend more time in the Breaks than planned.

If the weather is dry and has been for some time, with little chance of rain in the forecast, you'll probably do fine in a passenger car, although a high-clearance vehicle is recommended. Because of the isolated nature of the country, go equipped with plenty of provisions and water. For more information on how to prepare and for detailed maps and brochures, call the Bureau of Land Management in Lewistown at 538-7461, or go to www.mt.blm.gov.

montanatrivia

In 1992 Bureau of Land Management archaeologists reported finding near Lewistown two human face masks carved from large seashells. Thought to have been fabricated prior to 1600, the masks are similar to ones discovered in the southeastern United States.

Lewistown, sitting at the center of Montana, is a popular spot for rockhounding for Yogo sapphires, one of Montana's two state gemstones, and for world-class fishing and big-game and bird hunting. To get there from James Kipp Park, follow US 191 south for 20 miles, and then continue south along Highway 19 for 21 miles. Turn west onto US 87 near Grass Range and proceed across the southern flank of the Judith Mountains, earning a good view of attractive Lewistown just before dropping into it.

Considering that it's smack in the middle of central Montana's arid plains, Lewistown in summer is a surprisingly verdant spot. The town's storm-attracting location along the base of the *Judith Mountains* is responsible. In an average year Lewistown receives half again as much rainfall as Missoula, for instance, which sits west of the Continental Divide, commonly regarded as the "wet" side of the divide.

The Judith Basin is nothing if not cowboy country; it was here that Charlie Russell came as a kid to learn the ways of the range. Cowboy poetry, a unique art form, expounds on the life of the open-range rider, and the emotions it triggers range from joy to heartbreak. If you've never had the opportunity to hear it read by those who write it, consider making the annual *Montana Cowboy Poetry Gathering,* convening in Lewistown in mid-Aug at the Yogo Inn convention center. Rhymin' wranglers from throughout Montana and beyond gather to share their poetry and music and to participate in workshops, jam-session readings, and social activities. Past performers have included the well-known (in cowboy poetry circles) Wally McRae, Hank Real Bird, and Sandy Seaton. Sessions are conducted for cowboy poetry neophytes and old-timers alike. Call 535–8278 or visit the chamber's Web site at www.lewistownchamber .com for more information.

One of the world's largest freshwater springs feeds **Big Springs State Hatchery** and also provides Lewistown's delicious supply of 99.9 percent pure drinking water. Flowing at over 3 million gallons per hour at Big Springs, the water originates in the nearby Big Snowy Mountains. Several strains of rainbow and other types of trout are raised at the facility, and lots of them: Big Springs supplies approximately half of all trout stocked in Montana lakes each year. An idyllic picnic ground, maintained by the Department of Fish, Wildlife and Parks and the local Lions Club, sits adjacent to the placid pools fed by the spring.

montanatrivia

Until 1959, the year the Fred Robinson Bridge northeast of Lewistown was completed, ferries provided the only transportation across the Missouri River between Fort Benton and the Fort Peck Dam, a distance of some 200 miles.

In 1968 a nineteen-pound brown trout was taken from Spring Creek, downstream from the hatchery. For an idea of just how big a fish that was, glimpse into the open-air pond filled with giant trout, many of them in the twelve-to-sixteen-pound range. By dropping a coin into the nearby "candy machine," you can obtain a handful of stinky treats to feed the fish. Toss some food into the tank and then stand back, or prepare to get wet as a consequence of the splashing feeding frenzy you've incited.

Big Springs State Hatchery is located 6½ miles south of Lewistown on Spring Creek Road. (En route to the primary unit, you'll go by the hatchery's lower component.) Group tours are available on request; call 538-5588 for more information.

The **Charlie Russell Chew Choo** dinner train departs from the Kingston Junction depot 10 miles northwest of Lewistown on Saturday evening throughout the summer and early fall. Boasting "the best prime rib east of the Rockies," the three-hour excursion also promises bountiful wildlife viewing, thrilling trestles and tunnels . . . and the very real possibility of being chased down and robbed by the Denton Gang. The cost for the outing, which follows the old Milwaukee Road line (now operated by Central Montana Rail), is $90 per adult and $50 for kids twelve and under. Call (800) 860-9646 or visit www.yogoinn.com for reservations and information on special hotel/ train packages.

Several gold-mining camps lie rotting in the ranges surrounding Lewistown, the most accessible being **Maiden Ghost Town.** Although gold prospectors had been interested in the Judith Basin country for years, fear of hostile Indians precluded their exploring too far afield. It wasn't until the early 1880s, by which time the Indian wars had ended, that claims began appearing and makeshift towns popping up in the Judith and North Moccasin Mountains.

In 1885 Maiden claimed around 700 residents and 150 buildings. The Spotted Horse, the most important mine in the area, paid out more than $2 million in gold over the years. Among the things still to be seen there is the foundation of the Spotted Horse's gold-stamp mill, found just east of Maiden on Warm Springs Road. To get to Maiden, go north from Lewistown on US 191 for 9 miles to its junction with Highway 81, and then turn east onto Warm Springs Canyon Road and continue for 9 miles.

At the junction of Highway 81 and US 191, turn west onto Highway 81. This low-traffic road dips and twists through the heart of the Judith Basin country, possibly the prettiest blend of mountains and plains you'll ever lay eyes on. (Judith is a big name in these parts: Judith River, Judith Basin, Judith Mountains. The river was first to receive the name—Capt. William Clark named it in honor of his bride-to-be.) But know that the wind is free to blow without obstruction here, so beware of opening both front car doors at the same time, or you may lose anything not tied down!

Five miles west of the junction of US 191 and Highway 81, note the sign on the north side of the road reading **Gigantic Warm Springs.** What you'll find is definitely gigantic, but "warm" might be stretching things a bit, since the water maintains a constant cool temperature of 68 degrees (so it's best visited on a warm summer day). Follow the gravel road for a mile to the Dave Vanek Ranch, pay the $4 fee, and head on down to the pool, which holds warm water diverted from nearby Warm Springs Creek. The springs formerly provided the water for the mining town of Kendall, using a system of ditches and viaducts. A pleasant picnic ground sits beside the waters, open to the public between 10 a.m. and dark. Call 538-9825 for more information.

The imposing feature known as **Square Butte,** located between Lewistown and Fort Benton on Highway 80, is home to a whopping variety of four-legged and two-winged creatures and was used prehistorically as a vision-quest site by American Indians. The Bureau of Land Management has designated Square Butte an "outstanding natural area" and protects it for its extraordinary geological, historical, and scenic attributes.

Square Butte is a volcanic pillar—technically a *laccolith,* or huge, solidified bubble of molten rock—that stands at an elevation of 5,684 feet, or more than 2,000 feet above the surrounding prairie. Raptors such as golden eagles, prairie falcons, and great horned owls nest in the butte's protected alcoves, while pronghorns, deer, and occasionally elk are seen around the base. A herd of shaggy, white mountain goats resides on top and along the vertical cliffs below. The goats were moved here in the 1970s to replace a herd transplanted three decades earlier. The earlier herd abandoned the butte in the 1960s, apparently concluding that the nearby Highwood Mountains looked like a preferable place to call home.

From the town of Square Butte, 64 miles northwest of Lewistown, turn onto the gravel road leading west and go 1 mile. At a ranch entrance you'll find a sign describing the butte; be sure to follow the posted instructions, for public access to the butte is permitted only through the kindness of the ranch owner.

"Hay There, Travelers!"

The Utica Road (Highways 541 and 239) connects the small towns of Hobson and Windham, en route meandering around the upper Judith River Valley and passing through tiny Utica. To the sides of the road, on a specified weekend early each September, some fifty local ranchers create strange and wonderful things out of hay, as they vie to bring home the prize money in the "What the Hay?" competition. The contest, sponsored by the Utica Rod and Gun Club, transforms the normally sleepy byway into a road brimming with rigs, as folks travel from miles around to crane their necks and see what sorts of whimsical and hilarious sculptures have been piled up this year.

A few past entries have included a likeness of the national bird, the Baled Eagle, the Cook-hay Monster, and The Lone RaHAYnger . . . replete with the slogan "Hay-Ho-Silver."

Although the works of hay art are often conceived weeks, even months, in advance, the ranchers-turned-artists wait until the last minute to build the creations, in order to keep their plans secret. The sculptures usually remain standing for a few days after the official day of competition, until the wind blows them over or the local bovine population discovers and then devours them.

Once on top of Square Butte you'll notice charred evidence of the light-ning fire that raged through in 1956. The views of the surrounding country-side are stunning: To the west are the Highwood Mountains and the nearby, smaller laccolith known as Round Butte; far to the north and east are the Bear's Paw and Little Rocky Mountains; to the southeast and southwest, the Snowy Mountains and the Little Belts.

For maps or for more information call the Bureau of Land Management in Lewistown at 538-7461.

Fort Benton, 35 miles northwest of Square Butte on Highway 80, was once known as "Chicago of the Plains," "the world's most inland port," and by less complimentary names such as "the home of cutthroats and horse thieves" and "the bloodiest block in the West." More recently it was nicknamed the "Birthplace of Montana." From the 1830s until the 1850s, steamboats ventured up the Missouri only as far as Fort Union, which straddles the present-day Montana–North Dakota border. But a new design of broad-bottom steamboats appeared in the 1850s, permitting travel into the treacherous upper reaches of the river. By the mid-1860s, Fort Benton was a primary port, controlling the trade between the eastern markets and the goldfields of southwest Montana.

There's much to be seen in the small town today. Fort Benton's main street, which fronts the river responsible for the town's very being, is the put-in for the float along the **Upper Missouri National Wild and Scenic River,** so designated in 1976 and now the heart of the new Upper Missouri River Breaks National Monument. Most parties take seven days to cover the 149 river miles between here and the Fred Robinson Bridge on US 191. (For information on guided historic river tours, which can include overnights in restored home-stead cabins, call the **Missouri River Canoe Company** in nearby Virgelle at 800-426-2926, or go to the Web site http://paddlemontana.com.) The swath of wild country traversed remains much as it was when Lewis and Clark passed through in 1805, minus a few grizzly bears and bison and a large share of its timber: In twenty-four hours of chug-ging, a steamboat burned as much as

montanatrivia

Montana is home to eleven Indian tribes, occupying a total of seven reservations: the Blackfeet, Chip-pewa, Cree, Crow, Northern Chey-enne, Assiniboine, Sioux, Gros Ventre, Salish, Kootenai, and Little Shell tribes.

montanatrivia

Big Sandy, a burg of around 750 people located midway between Havre and Fort Benton, is the hometown of Pearl Jam bass gui-tarist Jeff Ament. He participated in football, basketball, and track while attending Big Sandy High School.

That's the Breaks

In one of his final acts as president of the United States, Bill Clinton on January 17, 2001, designated the **Upper Missouri River Breaks National Monument.** Clinton's action came on the heels of a recommendation by his secretary of the interior, Bruce Babbitt, who had toured the area by canoe in May 1999 with Sen. Max Baucus (D, Montana) and renowned authors and Lewis and Clark experts Dayton Duncan (Out West) and the late Stephen Ambrose (Undaunted Courage). Clinton signed the proclamation creating the monument in the East Room of the White House, the same quarters where 200 years earlier Thomas Jefferson had toiled while plotting out plans for his Corps of Discovery's expedition.

The more than 375,000 acres of public lands involved were deemed worthy of national monument status because of their extreme historic, cultural, scenic, and natural significance. The lifeblood of the monument is the Upper Missouri National Wild and Scenic River, a 149-mile stretch of the Missouri whose relatively unaltered condition makes it more like the river experienced by Lewis and Clark than any other long stretch remaining. That wide and winding, cottonwood-embraced waterway runs top and center in Montana, from the vicinity of Fort Benton to the Charles M. Russell National Wildlife Refuge northeast of Lewistown. It gives way to high cliffs of various hues and to deep, steep, juniper- and yucca-peppered side coulees, which provide food and shelter for mule deer, elk, and hundreds of other varieties of wildlife, both winged and wingless.

Place names in the monument that are still foreign to most but becoming better known include the Bullwhacker area, the White Cliffs, Coal Banks Landing, and the Cow Creek Area of Critical Environmental Concern.

twenty-five cords of wood, cut and supplied by "woodhawks" working the banks of the river.

The intrepid explorers, along with their female Shoshone Indian interpreter and ambassador, still stand sentinel over the river. The **Lewis and Clark State Memorial,** commissioned for the Bicentennial celebration in 1976, is one of the finest works by the late master western sculptor and Browning resident Bob Scriver. Cast larger than life, Clark, Lewis, and a sitting Sacajawea gaze out over the waterway they traced westward for so many hundreds of miles. (Incidentally, it's said that more statues of Sacajawea have been erected in the United States than of any other woman.)

Directly in front of the Lewis and Clark State Memorial, mired in the river's mud, lie the sunken remains of the *Baby Rose,* one of the last steamboats to wend its way to Fort Benton. Also nearby, and more visible, is the full-scale replica of the keelboat *Mandan,* built for the filming of the movie based on A. B. Guthrie's *The Way West.*

Tree-canopied **Old Fort Park** in **Fort Benton** is a museum of sorts, as the locations of the various structures of the original fort—first a fur-trading post and later an army garrison—are marked with interpretive signs. The entire riverside length of the fort has undergone extensive reconstruction; you can visit the trade store, warehouse, blacksmith and carpenter's shop, and more. Guided tours of the fort originate at the adjacent **Museum of the Upper Missouri,** open daily Memorial Day through Sept 30, 10 a.m. to 4 p.m. (noon to 4 p.m. on Sun). Admission is $5, a fee that will get you a pass good at other museums in town (see www.fortbenton.com/museums) for two consecutive days.

As you head out of Fort Benton and before you pass the burial place of world-famous Shep the dog (an interpretive monument to Shep, explaining his story, is located on Main Street), stop in at the **Museum of the Northern Great Plains,** the official state agricultural museum. Top-notch displays take up where the Museum of the Upper Missouri leaves off—that is, after the railroad came through and the tough prairie sod began being ripped open by those attempting to scrape out a livelihood by farming the arid land.

The museum focuses on the equipment, culture, and economy of the region from the time of the first homesteaders, around 1910, to the mid-1970s. In a newer museum area—a wing officially known as the Hornaday/Smithsonian Buffalo and Western Art Gallery—you'll find the six bison mounted in 1886 by William T. Hornaday, then chief taxidermist for the U.S. National Museum in Washington, D.C. The sextet, for years displayed together at the

BEST ANNUAL EVENTS

C. M. Russell Art
Great Falls; late Mar
(406) 761-6453

Ice Breaker Road Race
Great Falls; late Apr
(406) 771-1265

Whoop–up Days and Rhubarb Festival
Conrad; early June
(406) 271–7791

Fort Benton Summer Celebration
Fort Benton; late June
(406) 622-5166

Montana State Fair
Great Falls; late July
(406) 727-8900

Rocky Boy's Pow Wow
Box Elder; early Aug
(406) 395-4282

Montana Cowboy Poetry Gathering
Lewistown; late Aug
(406) 538-5436

Montana State Chokecherry Festival
Lewistown; early Sept
(406) 538-5436

The Big Sky

Pulitzer Prize–winning author **A. B. "Bud" Guthrie,** born in 1901, grew up in and around Choteau, Montana. After earning a degree in journalism in 1923 at the University of Montana, Guthrie launched a successful newspaper career that culminated in his being named executive editor of Kentucky's *Lexington Leader.* By the time the mid-1940s rolled around, Guthrie was serving as a Nieman Fellow at Harvard, where he wrote *The Big Sky,* his most famous work. The widely read novel's success gave him the means and impetus to move back to Montana, where he continued writing.

Guthrie became to Montana what Steinbeck is to California's Salinas Valley, what Faulkner is to Mississippi. Concerning *The Big Sky,* he wrote: "I had a theme, not original, that each man kills the thing he loves. If it had any originality at all, it was only that a band of men, the fur-hunters, killed the life they loved and killed it with a thoughtless prodigality perhaps unmatched." Although Guthrie's words make it sound as if *The Big Sky* is a depressing read, it is in fact an exultation: of the free trapper, of the Native American, and of the broad Montana landscape. His five books that followed, including *The Way West* (winner of the 1950 Pulitzer Prize for Fiction) and *These Thousand Hills,* continued the saga of the settling of Montana, whose nickname derived from Guthrie's most enduring story. (He once joked that he ought to receive royalties from the sale of Montana license plates, which are emblazoned with the words "Big Sky," just as he did from his books.) He also wrote screenplays for westerns, including *Shane,* considered by some critics the best of its genre.

In his later years, Guthrie, living outside Choteau—where he was surrounded by ranchers and mineral exploiters—was an outspoken conservationist, as he continued seeing evidence of the truth in the theme on which he based *The Big Sky.* "There are too many among us who think first and only of the immediate personal profit, not of the long-term and irreparable loss," he wrote. "They figure that posterity never did anything for them and to hell with it." Yet he also wrote that "not everything is lost. The air around my old home is still clean and tonic; Ear Mountain still stands and I imagine industrious boys can still find fish, and in the fall see a cottontail sitting."

Bud Guthrie passed away in 1991.

Smithsonian, were refurbished in the mid-1990s by a Butte taxidermist; now, for the first time since 1955—when the display at the National Museum was dismantled—the six bison are together again. The big bull of this group is the most celebrated buffalo of all time: His likeness appears on the U.S. buffalo head nickel, the National Park Service ranger badge, several postage stamps, and elsewhere.

The museum and adjacent Schwinden Library and Archives are open from 10 a.m. to 4 p.m. daily (noon to 4 p.m. on Sun) Memorial Day through

Sept 30. The complex is at Twentieth and St. Charles Streets, next to the high school playing field (just watch for the colorful farming mural adorning the side of a long metal building). The $5 ticket will also get you into other museums, as explained above. Call 622-5316 or visit www.fortbenton.com for more information.

The welcome sign on the outskirts of tiny *Loma,* 11 miles northeast of Fort Benton, reads, TAKE A BREAK: LEWIS & CLARK DID IN 1805. How could one pass up an invitation like that?

To take that break, head down to the nearby confluence of the Marias and Missouri Rivers, where you can enjoy watching the proliferation of bird life at the 3,300-acre *Richard E. Wood Watchable Wildlife Area.* Watch for bald and/or golden eagles perched on the limbs of cottonwood trees. You may also glimpse deer, fox, coyotes, and other critters.

It was at this confluence, at "Decision Point," that in early June 1805 Lewis and Clark faced a world-class conundrum: The river they'd been following since St. Louis split into two forks of nearly equal size. The expedition established a base camp at the confluence for more than a week, making exploratory trips up both forks to try to solve the puzzle. Initially, Lewis and six companions went up the right-hand fork; Clark, with five men, explored the south. The captains both concluded that the northerly fork was not the Missouri; most everyone else in their company, however, insisted it *was.* For one thing, the north fork was the muddier of the two, much more similar in appearance to the Missouri they had grown accustomed to. However, Lewis

montanatrivia

According to the MontanaKids .com Web site, the greatest temperature change within a twenty-four-hour period ever recorded in the world took place at Loma on January 15, 1972. The temperature rose 103 degrees, from 54 degrees below zero to 49 above.

and Clark astutely deduced that the Missouri *should* begin running clearer, as they knew they were nearing the mountains. After the two parties regrouped, Lewis and four companions set off again, pushing farther up the south fork than Clark had initially traveled. Three days later they reached the great falls, a major hurdle on the Missouri that Mandan Indians had forewarned the explorers about. The expedition leaders were correct: the south fork was the Missouri River. The other stream Lewis christened Maria's River, after his obviously lovely cousin, Maria Wood, about whom he wrote:" . . . it is true that the hue of the waters of this turbulent and troubled stream but illy comport with the pure celestial virtues and amiable qualifications of that loved fair one . . ."

Hi-Line West

The territory north of the Missouri River and east of the Rocky Mountains in Montana is known as the *Hi-Line,* a term used variously to describe the Great Northern Railway, the rairoad's route, and the surrounding countryside.

At the western edge of *Havre,* the Hi-Line's version of a metropolis (population 9,621), is the 2,000 year-old *Wahkpa Chu'gn (walk-pa-chew-gun) Archaeological Site.* The Indian words translate to something akin to "too close for comfort." Perhaps by this the Assiniboine Indians were describing their own position in relation to dozens of massive, charging bison.

The site, used throughout prehistory by at least three distinct cultures, includes a combination of a traditional buffalo jump, or *pishkun,* and a pound. Basically, pounds were traps—sometimes outfitted with sharpened, upward-pointing sticks for impaling the animals—which the Indians probably used to trap smaller herds. Recent improvements at the site include a paved system of paths, as well as stairs leading down into the heart of the buffalo kill. Hour-long guided tours are available June 1 through Labor Day, daily between 9 a.m. and 2 p.m. If you can't make it during these hours, you can arrange for a special tour later in the day or evening. Tours start at the site, located behind the Holiday Village Mall. The cost is $6 for adults, $5 for seniors, and $3 for students. For more information call 265-6417 or visit www.buffalojump.org.

montanatrivia

In 1991 the U.S. Coast Guard established a LORAN–C post north of Havre. It's as unlikely a location as you'll ever find Coast Guard personnel on duty, some 700 miles from the nearest ocean.

On display at the *H. Earl Clack Museum* in Havre, you'll find artifacts from Wahkpa Chu'gn, an exhibit on the Minnesota-Montana homesteading migration, details of the early Signal Corps Weather Station at Fort Assiniboine, and a brief history of the Prohibition-era Bootlegger Trail chain, which connected the Havre area with Canada. Also on display are dinosaur eggs and embroyos found in the Judith River formation. The museum, located at the Holiday Village Mall, is open in the summer daily from 11 a.m. to 6 p.m. (noon to 5 p.m. Sun) and from 1 to 5 p.m. Wed through Sun the rest of the year. For information call the museum at 265-4000.

Not so much off the beaten path as *under* it: *Havre Beneath the Streets.* Some of the popular pursuits in a youthful Havre, when the turn-of-the-twentieth-century town served as an important regional railroad and ranching center, took place underground, both literally and figuratively. Today a subterranean mall underlying a full city block of downtown features basements connected by walkways. In these dark depths thrived opium dens, bordellos, honky tonks, and other sorts of enterprises, both above and below the law. The rooms are packed with high-quality displays, vividly bringing those days to life. "People don't realize the magnitude of this project, nor did they expect to see what they saw," Havre resident Frank DeRosa, considered the father of Havre's underground movement, told a Spokane *Spokesman Review* travel editor. Havre's underground stands above those in other cities, wrote Graham Vink, because of its "quantity and quality— all authentic, all loaned and donated by residents of Havre and surrounding communities." Havre Beneath the Streets is open daily throughout the summer from 9 a.m. to 5 p.m., with tours given on the half hour from 9:30 a.m. to 3:30 p.m. In the winter it's open Mon through Sat from 10 a.m. to 4 p.m. Tours cost $10 for adults, $9 for seniors, and $7 for kids seven and older; for children six and under, they're free. The ticket office is located on Third Avenue, south of Norman's Ranch Wear. Call 265-8888 for more information or to make reservations for a tour.

> ### montanatrivia
>
> Beaver Creek Park near Havre, some 10,000 acres in area, is the largest county park in the United States.

An unexpected find rising from the flat Hi-Line country is the weather-beaten volcanic **Bear's Paw Mountains** and **Beaver Creek Park** (395-4565). Beaver Creek begins 12 miles south of Havre on Highway 234 and runs south for 15 miles, encompassing some 10,000 acres. Hundreds of campsites await in the park, and good fishing and hiking abound.

Toward its southern end, Highway 234 enters the **Rocky Boy's Indian Reservation** and continues to the **Bear Paw Ski Bowl** (265-8404, www .skibearpaw.com), a low-key resort with low-priced lift tickets to match. The Indian reservation, the smallest of the seven in Montana, was the last to be created (1916). Two groups of Indians who had wandered down from Canada in the 1880s, Chief Rocky Boy's band of Chippewa and a group of Cree led by Little Bear, were still roaming the high plains of northern Montana well into the twentieth century. Determined lobbying by Charlie Russell and other concerned Montanans resulted in the federal government taking 55,000 acres of surplus

> ### montanatrivia
>
> Wylie Gustafson, who grew up in and around Conrad, is known as one of the best yodelers in America. While you may not know his name, you know his voice: It's the "Yahoo-oo-oo" behind the Yahoo search engine ads.

land from the Fort Assiniboine Military Reserve and setting it aside as a home for these landless and destitute native people.

On October 5, 1877, one of the most valiant treks in American history ended at Snake Creek in the Bear's Paw Mountains, at the site known today as the **Bear Paw Battlefield. Chief Joseph** of the Nez Perce had seen enough of death and bloodshed, and it was here that he spoke the stirring words, "It is cold and we have no blankets. The little children are freezing to death. . . . Hear me, my chiefs! I am tired. My heart is sick and sad. From where the sun now stands, I will fight no more forever."

When the Nez Perce surrendered to Col. Nelson A. Miles at Snake Creek, it ended a journey of nearly 1,200 miles, at times arduous, at times remarkable. The trek began in Oregon's Wallowa Valley, passed through northern Idaho, and then wound through Montana's Bitterroot and Big Hole Valleys, into Yellowstone National Park and back into Montana. After failing to gain sanctuary from the Crow, a traditional ally of the Nez Perce, Chief Joseph continued north, intending ultimately to join **Sitting Bull** in Canada.

But they were caught in the Bear's Paw Mountains, 40 miles short of the border. After several days of fighting, the Indians were still holding off the soldiers, but the chiefs couldn't agree on their next move. Eventually, some 300 Nez Perce followed Chief Looking Glass to Canada, and Chief Joseph surrendered for the rest.

Sixteen miles south of Chinook (a town whose name comes from an Indian word meaning "warm wind") on Highway 240 you can visit the Bear Paw Battlefield, one of thirty-eight components of the Nez Perce National Historical Park (www.nps.gov/nepe), which stretches across four states. The battlefield looks much as it did in 1877: Snake Creek still twists across the swath of treeless prairie, cutting steep side coulees, and willow thickets crowd its banks.

montanatrivia

Stockman and old-timey cowboy singer Ken Overcast ranches north of Chinook on Lodge Creek. Weekly, he also broadcasts his nationally syndicated radio program, *The Cowboy Show with Ken Overcast.*

Until relatively recently the site was administered by the Montana Department of Fish, Wildlife and Parks, and therefore was the only one of four major Nez Perce War battle sites not included in the Nez Perce National Historic Park. A movement to change the situation was successful; technically, however, the state still owns the land, due to an old law prohibiting the state of Montana from selling off its lands. But the National Park Service is the only bureaucratic presence you'll find there. To learn more about the Bear Paw Battlefield,

A Taste of Montana

The Sweetgrass Hills, encompassing East Butte, Middle Butte, and West Butte, make up a tiny mountain range rising against the skyline north of the highway between Chester and Shelby. Composed of 50-million-year-old igneous intrusions and the sedimentary rocks surrounding them, geologically the Sweetgrass Hills are closely related to the Judith and Moccasin Mountains outside Lewistown.

I'm not sure what it is the deer in that country eat—other than farmers' grain crops—but the flavor of their venison is out of this world. Almost every fall our good friends from Missoula, Peggy, Robin, and son Ian, mount a hunting trip to the Sweetgrass Hills (Peggy grew up on a farm in nearby Rudyard), and Nancy and I are usually the lucky recipients of some of their bounty. The barbecued backstrap of a Sweetgrass Hills mule deer is a taste of Montana as sure as huckleberry hotcakes.

open daily throughout the year during daylight hours, call the **Blaine County Museum** in Chinook at 357-2590. The museum offers tours to the site and also presents an outstanding multimedia show on the battle, entitled "*40 Miles to Freedom.*" The free-to-visit museum, located at 501 Indiana St., is open in summer Mon through Sat from 8 a.m. to 5 p.m., and Sun from noon to 5 p.m. In Sept and May it's open Mon through Fri from 8 a.m. to 5 p.m., and the rest of the year Mon through Fri from 1 to 5 p.m.

Heading west from Havre along US 2, you'll pass through a string of Hi-Line wheat-farming towns: Kremlin, Gildford, Hingham, Rudyard, Inverness, Joplin. Classic T-shaped railroad towns, each has its own depot and set of grain elevators, creating the top of the T, and a business strip, forming the stem of the letter.

In **Shelby,** visit the **Marias Museum of History and Art,** where you'll learn about a lot of things, including the Dempsey-Gibbons World Championship Heavyweight Fight. On July 4, 1923, nearly 25,000 spectators crammed into the small town to watch the match, in which Jack Dempsey outlasted Tommy Gibbons for fifteen rounds. The museum contains fight artifacts, photos, and displays, as well as exhibits on other Toole County historical happenings. Located at the corner of Twelfth Avenue and First Street North, across from the city park and swimming pool, the museum is free to visit and open June, July, and Aug, Mon through Fri from 1 to 5 p.m. and 7 to 9 p.m., and Sat from 1 to 4 p.m. The rest of the year it's open Tues only from noon to 4 p.m., or by calling 424-2551 and making an appointment.

High Central Plains

Stop first in *Choteau* at the *Old Trail Museum* complex, located along US 287 at the northern outskirts of town. Among the many displays of minerals and fossils in the museum's dinosaur grounds are photos and castings of the dinosaur nests for which nearby Egg Mountain has become renowned in dino-digging circles.

Museum of the Rockies and Montana State University paleontologist Jack Horner (who later served as a technical advisor for the film *Jurassic Park)* was first led to the Egg Mountain site in 1978 by rock-shop owners John and Marian Brandvold. In the mudstone of Egg Mountain, Horner located more than a dozen 6-foot-wide nests of duck-billed dinosaurs, with fossilized skeletons of baby dinosaurs still in them. The findings set the paleontological world on its ear: It had always been believed that dinosaurs were cold-blooded, solitary beasts with little intelligence. But here was proof, Jack Horner asserted, that these were warm-blooded, intelligent herd animals who cared for their young long after birth.

The species of duck-billed dinosaur first found by Marian Brandvold was named *Maiasaura peeblesorum,* or "Good Mother Lizard," and has since been named the Montana state fossil.

The museum also features exhibits on the late local author Bud Guthrie, "homestead justice," the Old North Trail, and Choteau history in general in the new "A Walk Through Time" exhibit. It is open daily Memorial Day weekend through Labor Day, 10 a.m. to 6 p.m. (10 a.m. to 3 p.m. Tues through Sat the rest of the year). For more information, call 466-5332 or visit www.theoldtrailmuseum.com. (The Old Trail Museum is one of fifteen components in the statewide *Montana Dinosaur Trail,* which also encompasses several other museums featured in this book. For more information on it, visit http://mtdinotrail.org.)

Egg Mountain is contained within the Nature Conservancy's unique, 18,000-acre *Pine Butte Swamp Preserve* (although the Conservancy sold the dig site to the Museum of the Rockies in 2005). Also within the preserve is the 4,000-acre Pine Butte Swamp—a "boreal fen," technically—along with thousands of acres of foothills and rolling grassland. Part-time and year-round inhabitants include no fewer than 43 species of mammals and 150 varieties of birds. Pine Butte, rising some 500 feet above its surroundings, is a fine place to hike to earn an overall view of the area.

To find the preserve entrance, go north on US 89 from Choteau for 5 miles and then turn west onto Teton Canyon Road. This is where the plains sweep up to marry the mountains; as you approach the stunning, hard-rock front,

The Prairie Cathedral

Often the only feature disrupting the rolling perfection of the central and northern Montana plains is the distant grain elevator, the ubiquitous "prairie cathedral." Abandoned, weathered, and leaning precariously with the prevailing winds, more of these historic grain-storing ghosts disappear every year.

During the homesteading boom in the early part of the twentieth century, thousands of new farms popped up on the face of the Montana prairies. At harvest, which usually occurred late in August, farmers were compelled to make dozens of trips to haul to the nearest elevator their bounties of hundreds of bushels of grain. As a result, more and more railside elevators emerged throughout grain country. The structures, which typically held between 10,000 and 30,000 bushels, served not only as grain-collection sites at harvest time, but also in other seasons as gathering places where far-removed neighbors would catch up with one another. Once the big grain companies came into the country, the small elevators could no longer compete, and they were rapidly abandoned by the score. But those who spent time in elevators say they can never forget the clamor, the dust, and the earthy essence of drying grain.

you'll notice pockets of ancient limber pine claiming more and more of the windswept plains. In 15 miles turn south and continue for about 4 miles until you see the information sign.

Access onto Pine Butte Swamp Preserve is limited in order to better protect its features and creatures. To obtain permission to hike in the swamp area or up onto the butte, call 466-2158. Here you also can request information about Conservancy-guided summer tours and natural history workshops conducted at the preserve.

No doubt the best way to see and learn about the preserve is to arrange a stay at the Nature Conservancy's nearby *Pine Butte Guest Ranch* (from 1930 until 1978 the privately owned Circle 8 Ranch). From May through Sept the ranch offers lodging for up to twenty-five guests in rustic, comfortable cabins set amidst stands of aspen, cottonwood, and fir. The cabins are constructed of native wood, each with a stone fireplace, private bath, and handmade furniture. Family-style meals, with an emphasis on fresh, healthy foods, are served in the main lodge.

The ranch combines a traditional dude-ranch atmosphere with an in-depth natural history program: Guests can enjoy horseback rides, naturalist-led hikes, wildlife-photography outings, and numerous other activities. Several special sessions are conducted as well, including "Montana Grizzly Bears," "Mammal Tracking," and "Dinosaur Digging."

Ornery Kid Russell

The name "Russell" is every bit as celebrated in and around Great Falls as are the names Lewis and Clark. Charles Marion Russell, born in St. Louis in 1864, was sixteen when he set out for the Montana plains to sample the free life of a range cowboy. His parents thought the boy would quickly get the itch out of his pants and return home. Little did they know, though, that when young Charlie lit out for Montana, he was going home: Russell fell in love with Big Sky Country, and he lived out his life there.

After cowboying for a decade in places like the Pigs Eye Basin in the Judith River country, in 1892 Russell moved to Great Falls, set up a studio, and commenced producing paintings and other works of art. Most depicted the open-range, cattle-growing period of Montana's history, and he quickly became known as "America's cowboy artist." Russell made the landscapes south, west, and east of Great Falls familiar to people throughout the world; among his favorite backdrops were the territory surrounding the Missouri River, Square Butte, the Big Snowy Mountains, and the town of Utica. Charlie Russell became very successful and incredibly popular—almost synonymous with wild Montana—because of his uncanny ability to re-create on canvas the things he'd seen and experienced, his down-to-earth and good-humored nature, and his wife, Nancy, who possessed the acumen for promotion and business matters that Russell himself apparently lacked.

Charlie Russell was a celebrity, no doubt about it, but he was the sort of celebrity that seems all too uncommon today: a modest one. Just before departing this earth for that wide-open, unfenced prairie in the sky, he wrote: "To have talent is no credit to its owner; any man that can make a living doing what he likes is lucky, and I'm that. Any time I cash in now, I win."

A terrific, forty-page brochure, *C. M. Russell Auto Tour,* illustrated with color photos of Russell's paintings, is available to lead motorists through the heart of the country "Ornery Kid Russell" grew to love during his early years in Montana. To request a copy, call Russell Country at (800) 527-5348.

From June through early Sept, guests are restricted to weeklong stays running Sunday to Sunday and costing $1,875 per adult, $1,500 for children thirteen to seventeen, and $1,300 for kids six to twelve (free for those under six). The rate includes the cabin, all meals, horseback riding, participation in the natural history program, and the use of all ranch facilities. During the shoulder seasons (May, late Sept, and Oct), the ranch offers less expensive weekly packages and special group and daily rates. All proceeds help to support the Nature Conservancy's good works in Montana. For reservations (a must) or more information, call 466-2158 or visit www.nature.org and search for "Pine Butte Swamp."

En route from Choteau to Great Falls, immediately after turning east onto

Highway 200 from US 89 (15 miles southeast of Fairfield), you'll spot what is arguably Montana's most beautiful barn. The *J. C. Adams Stone Barn* isn't open to the public, but still the public can't miss seeing and being impressed by it. (Adams, incidentally, often served as a model for Charlie Russell.)

Community dances and other events once were common on the hardwood floor of the barn's second story. Stock grower J. C. Adams built the 120-foot-by-40-foot structure in the early 1880s to serve as headquarters for his endeavor—selling livestock and goods to those traveling the Mullan Trail. The barn's sandstone blocks came from a nearby quarry, and Swedish stonecutters fashioned its unusual architectural details. The structure was added to the National Register of Historic Places in 1979.

montanatrivia

In spring, beginning in mid-March, between 100,000 and 200,000 snow geese congregate to create a white blanket covering the Freezeout Lake Wildlife Management Area near Fairfield.

Great Falls, Montana's third largest city (Billings is number one and Missoula number two), was named for the Great Falls of the Missouri River, source of great trepidation for the Lewis and Clark expedition. Meriwether Lewis wrote, "The river was one continued sene of rappids and cascades. . . . The river appears here to have woarn a channel in the process of time through a solid rock."

The party spent several days mapping their long portage route around the falls (now inundated by hydroelectric works) and then several weeks more traversing it. The route they eventually followed has been designated a National Historic Landmark and can be traced today by obtaining information from the *Lewis and Clark National Historic Trail Interpretive Center* (727-8733), located in Great Falls at 4201 Giant Springs Rd. A host of Lewis and Clark–themed activities and publications are available for travelers in Montana at the interpretive center or through Travel Montana (call 800-847-4868 or visit their information-packed Web site at http://lewisandclark.state.mt.us).

MAJOR ATTRACTIONS WORTH SEEING

C. M. Russell Museum Complex
Great Falls

Lewis and Clark National Historic Trail Interpretive Center
Great Falls

montanatrivia

Mike Mansfield was born in Brooklyn, New York, in 1903, the son of Irish immigrants. He experienced a turbulent youth after his mother died when he was seven and he was sent to live with relatives in Great Falls, Montana. It all turned out quite well, however: Mansfield went on to serve Montana in the U.S. House of Representatives and the U.S. Senate, and subsequently serve the country as the U.S. ambassador to Japan from 1977 to 1988. He died in 2001 at age 98.

On June 18, 1805, Lewis's cohort, William Clark, wrote of another area feature, in his inimitable spelling style, "We proceeded up on the river a little more than a mile to the largest fountain or spring I ever saw, and no doubt if it is not the largest in America known. . . . The water boils up from under the rocks near the edge of the river and falls imediately into the river 8 feet, and keeps its colour for ½ a mile emencely clear and of a bluish cast."

Today, picnickers, hikers, and anglers enjoy the day-use state park at *Giant Springs,* located not far from the Montana Department of Fish, Wildlife and Parks' Visitor Center. The center holds outstanding displays on the rich bird and animal life of the region, including one of the most terrifying grizzly bear mounts you'd ever care to see.

As Clark suspected, Giant Springs is among the largest freshwater springs in the country, and 156 million gallons of water per day bubble from it. As if for contrast, the unimaginably clear waters of the spring's pool feed the Roe River, the shortest river in the world, according to *The Guinness Book of World Records.*

This is one of the best urban birding areas in the Northwest, with bald eagles, loons, and other winged critters common in the winter, and more than one hundred species, including white pelicans, prairie falcons, and pheasants, present in the summer. Kids will enjoy feeding the ten-pound rainbow trout that swim about in the outdoor pond.

Giant Springs Heritage State Park is located 3 miles east of US 87 on River Drive, between Black Eagle Dam and Rainbow Dam. In summer the visitor center is open from 8 a.m. to 5 p.m., Mon through Fri. Call Montana Fish, Wildlife and Parks at 454-5840 for more information.

So vital was the role the explorers played in the discovery and settlement of this region that Great Falls celebrates an annual *Lewis and Clark Festival* in late June. The festival includes river tours, guided visits to expedition sites, buffalo-hump barbecues, running races, and performances of *Proceeding On,* a play based on the party's journals. For information on the festival, call 452-5661 or visit www.lewisandclarkia.com.

While in the Great Falls area, don't miss paying a visit to **First Peoples Buffalo Jump State Park** (formerly known as **Ulm Pishkun State Park**). Excavations during the summer of 1992 resulted in new findings at this, one of the largest buffalo jumps in the United States. By following the short trail leading below the cliffs, you'll spot bison bone fragments, some with obvious butcher marks, scattered about the ground where countless bison died. Over the span of more than six hundred years, Native Americans stampeded bison over the edge the mile-long cliff here. Today, from the top of the jump, you can enjoy a spectacular panorama encompassing the Rocky Mountain Front, the valley of the Missouri River, and the distant buttes and grasslands characteristic of the Great Plains environment.

montanatrivia

Both Oscar Cooke, the late proprietor of the now-defunct Oscar's Dreamland outside Billings, and Carl Mehmke, owner of the Mehmke Steam Museum east of Great Falls, have been inducted into the Hall of Fame of the Early Day Gas Engine and Tractor Association.

To get to the park and its visitor center, go 10 miles south of Great Falls on I-15 to the Ulm exit, and then go 4 miles northwest Ulm-Vaughn Road. The park, maintained by the Montana Department of Fish, Wildlife and Parks, is open daily 8 a.m. to 6 p.m. Apr 1 through Sept 30. The rest of the year the park and visitor center are open 10 a.m. to 4 p.m. Wed through Sat and noon to 4 p.m. on Sun (closed Mon and Tues). For more information call 866-2217.

Hidden in the Smith River country, 55 miles south of Great Falls, is the **Heaven on Earth Ranch,** a working cattle ranch where Old West fans can

Re-cycling Canal Paths

As I discovered quite by accident one autumn day several years ago, irrigation canal paths running across the prairies east of the Rocky Mountain Front offer great riding opportunities to those with mountain bicycles in tow. One such path parallels the Sun River Slope Canal; it begins on the southwestern shore of Pishkun Reservoir, found approximately 18 miles southwest of Choteau on county roads. The path encounters US 287 after twisting for some 12 miles to the southeast, amid rolling hills but at a steady, nearly imperceptible gradient.

Another path follows the Pishkun Canal, leading westerly from the west side of the same reservoir into Sun River Canyon, ending not far from a pleasant Lewis and Clark National Forest campground. These little-used canal paths lead through areas visited by very few people, and the views earned from them are absolutely stunning.

come to enjoy wagon rides, cookouts, target shooting . . . and golf, on what just may be the most isolated and underutilized nine-hole, par-three course in the country. Riverside cabins are also available to rent; call 866-3316 or visit www.deepcreekoutfitters.com to learn more.

Military and airplane buffs will fall all over themselves at the **Malmstrom Air Force Base Museum and Air Park.** Called Great Falls Army Air Base when established during the months following the Japanese attack on Pearl Harbor, the base was renamed in 1955 to honor Col. Einar Axel Malmstrom, a World War II hero who died nearby in a training accident.

montanatrivia

The feature at the heart of the new Tower Rock State Park, a 400-foot-high igneous rock formation, was named by Meriwether Lewis on July 16, 1805. The 140-acre park sits alongside the Missouri River between the town of Craig and the Pelican Point fishing access site.

The museum highlights the roles played by the base in the Cuban Missile Crisis, the Vietnam War, and the Gulf War. Included among the many flying machines displayed in the air park are an F-84F Thunderstreak fighter bomber, a Minuteman intercontinental ballistic missile, a UH-1F Iroquois helicopter (the "Huey" of Vietnam fame), and a 1,200-mile-per-hour Voo Doo air-defense fighter.

Malmstrom Air Force Base Museum and Air Park, funded by donations and staffed by volunteers (not by the Air Force and your tax dollars, as they're quick to point out), is located at the east end of Second Avenue North in Great Falls. The air park is open during daylight hours, and the museum weekdays from 10 a.m. to 4 p.m. For information call 731-2705 or visit www.malmstrom .af.mil. (Nonmilitary visitors should begin by checking in at the visitor center located at the base's Second Avenue North gate.)

Fans of the lower-tech machinery that prevailed before humans took to the skies can also be accommodated in the area, at the **Mehmke Steam Museum.** Here, at a working farm set back from the highway in a protected draw, awaits one of the country's largest privately owned collections of operable steam-driven equipment. The museum is located 10 miles east of Great Falls on US 89 and is open year-round during daylight hours, weather permitting. Call 452-6571 for more information.

After witnessing how farmers did their duties early in the century, head for the **MSU Central Agricultural Research Center,** where you can learn about modern techniques employed by the northern plains farmer. For decades the research center's goal has been to serve central Montana's farmers and ranchers by helping them produce and market their products in more profitable ways.

The center consists of several buildings, including a laboratory, a seed-cleaning plant, and a shop, and also works a diversified, 640-acre dry-land farm. The approximately 480 acres of tilled land are divided into thousands of tiny plots, no bigger than 3 feet by 20 feet. Among other purposes, these are used to test the relative performances of different seed varieties of wheat, barley, oats, and oil-producing crops, such as sunflowers.

The Central Agricultural Research Center has achieved a long list of accomplishments since its establishment in 1907, achievements largely responsible for the success of central Montana's dry-land farming industry. To learn more about past successes and ones in the works, you can visit the facility weekdays from 8 a.m. to 4:30 p.m. It's located 2 miles west of Moccasin on US 87. For information on annual visitors' field days, call 423-5421 or visit http://ag.montana.edu/carc.

At the junction of US 89 and US 191, swing into **Eddie's Corner** (374-2471) for a great home-style breakfast, lunch, dinner . . . or midnight snack. In fact, you needn't worry at all about what time it is or what day it is, because the diner has never closed—not for five minutes, not even for a holiday, snowstorm, or owner's vacation—since hanging out the shingle in 1951. Talk about lunch-evity!

In **Harlowton,** stop at Fischer Park and tour the **E-57B Electric Train Engine.** The Chicago, Milwaukee, St. Paul & Pacific Railroad, better known as the Milwaukee Road, in 1917 completed the longest stretch of electrified railroad in the United States, spanning the distance between Harlowton and Avery, Idaho. The railroad saved a great deal of money along this line simply by taking advantage of gravity: On long mountain descents, electric motors became generators, driven by the train's momentum. Energy that otherwise would have been wasted was converted into electricity in a clever "regenerative braking system." On descents the engines could store about half the energy needed for getting up hills of equal length and grade.

montanatrivia

The development of the hardy Yogo winter wheat, together with the 1920s perfection of furrow drilling—both advancements taking place at the Central Agricultural Research Center in Moccasin—resulted in Montana's wheat belt moving northward some 300 miles.

Still seen west of Harlowton are some of the utility poles that formerly carried electricity from the huge brick transformer stations positioned every 30 miles between Harlowton and Avery. One such station still stands on Highway 294 west of Martinsdale (and another near the Nimrod Tunnels, 30 miles east of Missoula).

Harlowton was a primary hub for the Milwaukee Road. Here, in round-houses, eastbound trains swapped electric engines for steam engines, and westbound trains did the opposite. The three-story, century-old **Graves Hotel,** one of the flagship hotels along the Milwaukee Road line, has obviously seen better days, but fans of lavish architecture should drop by to have a look. Like several other buildings in town, the hotel was constructed of massive sandstone blocks quarried from a nearby bluff.

Around forty Hutterite colonies, claiming a total of some 4,000 residents, are scattered throughout the northern plains of Montana. Many, like the **Martinsdale Colony** (572-3329), located just outside **Martinsdale,** sell meat and produce to the general public. They've also gotten into the business of having wind turbines erected on their land in recent years.

Here, as elsewhere, telltale rows of neatly kept buildings—and an obviously successful farming operation—inform those passing by that this is a Hutterite colony. **Hutterites** live spartan, communal lifestyles based on the tenets of a sixteenth-century religious sect that emerged in Austria. Their predecessors escaped to North America in 1874 after living in Europe and Russia for more than three centuries. Hutterites, who speak a dialect of German, cannot own their own homes or cars and are not supposed to watch television or listen to radio; they dress in homemade clothes of Old World style and are paid no money for their work, nor do they earn vacations.

Why, then, does their culture flourish? Perhaps it's because in their society harmony prevails; murder, mental illness, and divorce are said to be almost nonexistent. Hutterite families enjoy a closeness all but lost in twenty-first-century American culture, and the number of colonies in Montana continues to grow. (Another several hundred colonies, with a total of approximately 30,000 residents, are located in the adjacent northern states and Canadian provinces.) If you'd like to explore their culture further, visit www.hutterites.org. Also, there's an outstanding book titled Hutterites of Montana, written and photographed by Laura Wilson.

Also in the Martinsdale area: the **Charles M. Bair Family Museum.** Open to the general public since 1996, the museum showcases the splendid home and stunning array of belongings of one of the state's foremost pioneer

Best of the Byways

In April 1996 the American Recreation Coalition honored two Russell Country scenic drives by including them among just six "Best of the Byways." The **Kings Hill Scenic Byway,** a 71-mile stretch of US 89 passing through the Little Belt Mountains, links White Sulphur Springs with the town of Belt to the north. Highlights along the way include rugged ranchlands, steep-sided limestone canyons, a short side trip to Sluice Boxes State Park, and the Showdown Ski Area. The Great Falls cross-country ski club also grooms Nordic trails in the area.

The **Trail of the Great Bear,** the other honoree, is a 2,100-mile, international tourism corridor linking Yellowstone, Glacier-Waterton, Banff, and Jasper National Parks. A substantial portion of the trail runs through Russell Country, as well as through other tourism regions of Montana.

families. It wasn't until he had tried his hand at several careers that Charles M. Bair became a rich man. He arrived in Montana in 1883 as a conductor on the Northern Pacific Railroad, then entered the ranching business in 1893; finally, a few years later, he struck it rich in the goldfields of Alaska. During the ensuing years he invested in numerous interests, becoming the owner of one of the world's largest sheep herds in the process, running as many as 300,000 head of sheep at a time.

After moving permanently in 1934 to the ranch that they'd owned for two decades, the Bair family began adding to the existing ranch house until it totaled twenty-six rooms. The daughters, Alberta and Marguerite, who became renowned Montana philanthropists and patrons of the arts (you may have happened across the Alberta Bair Theater in Billings), filled the house with paintings and antiques acquired during their numerous trips to Europe. The resultant mix of Old World art, Old West art, and memorabilia—the family was friends with, among other notables, Charlie Russell, Will Rogers, and Chief Plenty Coups—constitutes one of the West's most valuable and unforgettable family collections. It was the wish of the daughters that the home be retained as a museum for the people of the state they loved, and now it is. (Alberta, the last of the family, died in 1993.) The museum is open daily from 10 a.m. to 5 p.m. Memorial Day through Labor Day. During the rest of May and Sept, it's open Wed through Sun from 10 a.m. to 5 p.m.; closed the rest of the year. For more information call 572-3314 or visit www.bairfamilymuseum.org.

North of the settlement of **Lennep,** which is a few miles southwest of Martinsdale on Highway 294, along a bumpy back road known as the Lennep Route, you'll find the **Bonanza Creek Country Guest Ranch.** Here David and June Voldseth and their kids—the fourth and fifth generations of the family on the ranch—work hard to ensure that a stay will be among their guests' most cherished memories, and a maximum of sixteen at a time enjoy the personal attention and beautiful countryside, where they're within view of half a dozen mighty Montana ranges, including the Crazy Mountains and the Castle Range. Working the cows on horseback (these folks aren't just playing cowboys and cowgirls; their cow herd numbers around 1,500), pedaling the back roads and trails on the ranch's mountain bikes, fishing, swimming, hayrides, and four-wheel-drive tours in the surrounding mountains are among the activities that'll keep you hopping. Lodging is in western cabins, and the wholesome food is reputed to be "the best home-cooking this side of the Crazies." A six-night stay goes for $1,600 per adult and $1,100 per child ages eight to twelve. For information, reservations, and precise directions, call (800) 476-6045 or visit www.bonanzacreekcountry.com.

montanatrivia

Many of the Old Country names of towns along the Hi–Line—Glasgow, Malta, Zurich, Havre, Inverness, and others—were picked not by pioneer sodbusters, but by a Great Northern Railway employee in St. Paul, Minnesota. The railroad hoped that seeing these names on the map would attract Europeans to the high plains as visitors and residents.

In *White Sulphur Springs, The Castle,* home to the Meagher County Museum, sits high on a hill like . . . well, like a castle. The mansion was completed in 1892, for rancher-businessman B. R. Sherman, from granite blocks that were hand cut in the Castle Mountains, then hauled to town by oxen. Inside you'll find a varied collection of artifacts from area ghost towns and elsewhere in the county. The rich tones of the dark oak and cherrywood used in the woodwork lend the interior an air of dignity. The Castle, located at Fourth Avenue and Jefferson Street, is open to visitors daily, 10 a.m. to 6 p.m., from May 15 to Sept 15. Admission is $3 for adults and $2 for children and seniors. For information on tours call 547-2250.

A fitting place, indeed, to crown your backcountry journey through the Big Sky State.

Places to Stay in Russell Country

LEWISTOWN

Historic Calvert Hotel
216 7th Ave. South
(406) 535-5411
Moderate

Lewistown Super 8
102 Wendell Ave.
(406) 538-2581
Moderate

Mountain View Motel
1422 W. Main St.
(406) 535-3457
Moderate

Pheasant Tales Bed & Bistro
1511 Timberline Rd.
(406) 538-2124
Expensive

Yogo Inn of Lewistown
211 E. Main St.
(406) 535–8721
Moderate

FORT BENTON

Fort Motel
1809 St. Charles St.
(406) 622-3312
Moderate

Grand Union Hotel
1 Grand Union Sq.
(406) 622-1882
Expensive

Pioneer Lodge
1700 Front St.
(406) 622-5441
Moderate

HAVRE

AmericInn of Havre
2520 US 2 West
(800) 396-5007
Moderate

Best Western Great Best Northern Inn
1345 1st St.
(406) 265-4200
Moderate

Havre Super 8
1901 US 2 West
(406) 265-1411
Moderate

Townhouse Inn
629 1st St. West
(406) 265-6711
Moderate

CHOTEAU

Big Sky Motel
209 S. Main Ave.
(406) 466-5318
Moderate

Pine Butte Guest Ranch
close to Pine Butte Swamp Preserve
(406) 466-2158
Expensive

Stage Stop Inn
1005 N. Main Ave.
(888) 466-5900
Moderate

GREAT FALLS

Best Western Heritage Inn
1700 Fox Farm Rd.
(406) 761-1900
Expensive

Collins Mansion Bed & Breakfast
1003 2nd Ave. Northwest
(406) 452-4444
Expensive

Comfort Inn
1120 9th St. South
(406) 454-2727
Moderate

Holiday Inn Great Falls
400 10th Ave. South
(800) 257-1998
Moderate

Russell Country Inn
(house rental)
2516 4th Ave. North
(406) 761-7125
Moderate

WHITE SULPHUR SPRINGS

Montana Mountain Lodge
1780 US 89 North
(406) 547-3773
Expensive

Spa Hot Springs Motel
202 West Main St.
(406) 547-3366
Moderate

Places to Eat in Russell Country

LEWISTOWN

Bon Ton Soda Fountain
312 W. Main St.
(406) 535-9650
Moderate

Main Street Bistro
122 W. Main St.
(406) 538-3666
Moderate

Mint Bar & Grill
113 4th Ave. South
(406) 535-9925
Moderate

Yogo Restaurant
211 E. Main St.
(406) 535–8721
Moderate

HAVRE

Andy's
658 First St. West
(406) 265-9963
Moderate

Canton Chinese Restaurant
439 1st St. West
(406) 265-6666
Moderate

4-B's
604 1st St. West
(406) 265-9721
Inexpensive

Wolfer's Diner
126 3rd Ave.
(406) 265-2111
Inexpensive

FORT BENTON

The Banque Club
1318 Front St.
(406) 622-5272
Moderate

Union Grille
1 Grand Union Sq.
(406) 622-1882
Expensive

CHOTEAU

Circle N
925 N. Main Ave.
(406) 466-5531
Inexpensive

Elk Country Grill
925 N. Main Ave.
(406) 466-3311
Moderate

John Henry's Restaurant
215 N. Main Ave.
(406) 466-5642
Moderate

GREAT FALLS

Bert & Ernie's
301 1st Ave. South
(406) 453-0601
Moderate

The Breaks Ale House & Grill
202 2nd Ave. South
(406) 453-5980
Moderate

Chinatown
1709 Alder Dr.
(406) 454-2388
Moderate

Tracy's 24-Hour Family Restaurant
127 Central Ave.
(406) 453-6108
Inexpensive

WHITE SULPHUR SPRINGS

Montana Roadhouse
904 3rd Ave. Southwest
(406) 547-3638
Moderate

Stage Line Pizza
210 E. Main St.
(406) 547-3505
Moderate

Index

Travel Like a Pro

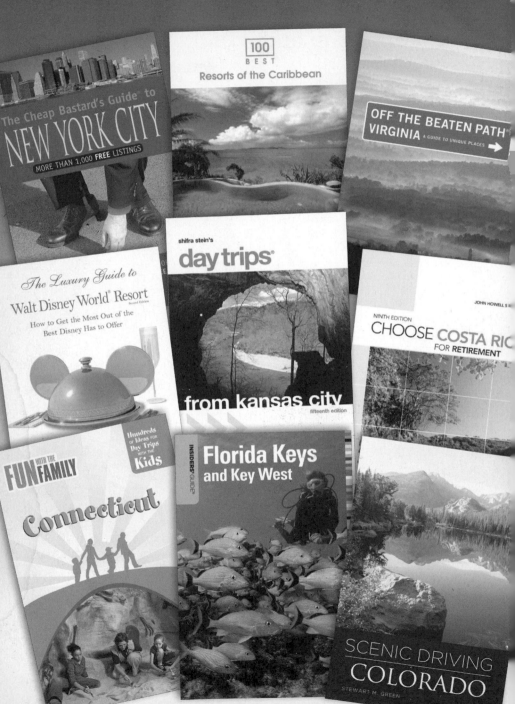